Great British Bikes

Edited by Ian Ward and Laurie Caddell

With a Foreword by Bob Currie

LITTLE, BROWN AND COMPANY

A LITTLE, BROWN BOOK

First published by Orbis Publishing Limited 1984
This edition published by Little, Brown in 1999

The publishers would like to thank the following
for supplying illustrations: Allsport, C. Bailey, B.
Betti, Blandford Press, Boschetti, T.D.Collins, P.
Dobson, M. Erdon, J. Greening. R. Harper,
J. Heese, D. Jackson, Keig Collection, J. Lloyd,
A. Morland, Le Moto, Motor Cycle, I. Mutton,
N. Nicholls, N.M.M., Olyslager, Publifoto,
Radio Times, Hulton Picture Library, Rimmer,
I. Rhodes, Saga, The Science Museum,
R.Sheldrake, E.Thompson, V. Tossi, P. Vincent,
C.H. Wood, F. Zagari

Contributors: Cyril Ayton, Jeff Clew, Bob Currie,
Ivor Mutton, L.J.K Setright, Eric Thompson

ISBN 0-316-84762-3

A CIP catalogue for this book is available from the
British Library

Little, Brown and Company (UK)
Brettenham House
Lancaster Place
London WC2E 7EN

Printed and bound in Czech Republic
60065

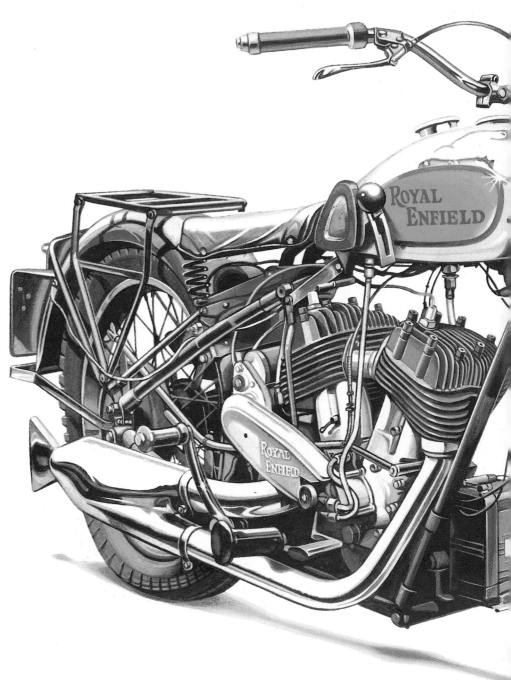

Contents

Introduction

Pick up a yellowing copy of either of the two weekly motor cycle journals that flourished in Britain in the decade immediately following World War II, and somewhere or other there is sure to be a BSA advertisement proclaiming this to be 'The Most Popular Motor Cycle in the World'. Publicity man's licence? No, just a bald statement of fact: in those heady days of peace the BSA was indeed the world's most popular motor cycle.

Nor was BSA alone, for Triumph at this period were supplying (or so it seemed) half the police forces of the globe with their excellent vertical-twin patrol machines, while Norton – and to a lesser extent Velocette (world 350cc road-racing champions in 1949) and AJS – still dominated the Grand Prix circuits.

It must be said, however, that the motor cycle world at that time was a much smaller place than it is today, and even at the very height of its fame the British industry taken as a whole enjoyed an output only a fraction of that of just one of Japan's present-day giants. Even America was a dormant market, for in pre-war days pleasure motor cycling was virtually dead, and two-wheelers were used mainly by the law-enforcement agencies. But it was beginning to awake, as servicemen returned from Europe (where, as like as not, they would have seen motor cycles of a livelier and lighter breed than their own native dinosaurs) with money in their pockets and an urge to be up and doing.

To some extent it was Triumph top man Edward Turner, in person, who opened up the potentially huge American motor cycle market, by introducing British 'iron' to the sunny West Coast – fortunately so, because this was a time of 'export or die' for our industry, operating under the handicap of a home steel shortage which allowed a manufacturer a supply of the precious metal only if he could produce justification in the form of firm overseas orders.

We, too, had our returning servicemen eager for the freedom of a motor cycle after the frustrations of six years of war; except that the frustrations were very far from over. Allocations of machines to the home market were so restricted that there were waiting lists at every dealer's and, even when the promised model did arrive, the chances were that it was incomplete in some respect. For instance, on my own release from Army service I blued my ex-service gratuity money on a 350cc 3T Triumph, my very first brand-new bike; it came through, in time, but minus the tank-top panel light, for Triumph were still awaiting supplies of these from Joseph Lucas. The panel light turned up some weeks later, in a postal

delivery. It should be remembered, too, that petrol rationing was to remain in force for some while yet (and the petrol itself was still the anonymous 73-octane 'Pool').

There were some famous makes which failed to re-appear with the return of peace, with Rudge perhaps the most-mourned of the war-time casualties. And where were Brough Superior, or New Imperial or Coventry-Eagle? Where were OK-Supreme, or Calthorpe, or Wolf or Montgomery?

The reasons for demise were many and various. Brough Superior, the 'Rolls-Royce of Motor Cycles' in pre-war times, had switched during the war years to the manufacture of precision parts for the aircraft industry (including, ironically enough, sub-contract work for Rolls-Royce themselves) and, although there had been 'teaser' advertisements in the motor cycle press in the closing stages of hostilities promising that the flat-four Dream would return, it never happened. New Imperial, acquired by BSA-Triumph in 1939 when the death of the firm's founder left them in financial difficulties, nearly *did* come back – but one Edward Turner-designed 350cc vertical twin prototype (which still exists) was as far as the would-be comeback went. And Coventry-Eagle, which had relied on a bread-and-butter range of unusual pressed-steel-frame machines, were scuppered when the German blitz bombing of Coventry wrecked the expensive press tools.

Still, there were new manufacturers to take the place of the old, like DMW, Greeves and Ambassador, while some of the older names re-emerged with exciting new models – Vincent-HRD, with majestic vee-twins claimed with perfect justification to be the fastest standard roadsters in the world; Douglas, with transverse flat-twins which made use of the intriguing new principle of torsion-bar suspension; Sunbeam, with a sleek in-line overhead-camshaft twin featuring shaft final drive, and, from virtually every major maker, new vertical twins which followed the fashion set by the Triumphs of the late 1930s.

The euphoria wore off, however, and by the late 1950s the British motor cycling boom was already fading. The signs could be seen in many a town, as one motor cycle dealer after another moved the bikes into one corner of his operation and transferred his allegiance to selling cars.

Don't let them kid you that the home motor cycle industry was killed off by the coming of the Japanese, for that just wasn't so. The truth was the the British bike was already on the floor, and the main cause of that was the improving economy of the country. Traditionally the

Norton Commando 850

motor cycle had been looked upon as a utility object – up-market models such as the Ariel Square Four or Vincent Rapide were but a small part of the total output – and with more money to spend, the family man who might have gone for a trundling sidecar outfit opted instead for a small car. At the same time, the image of motor cycling suffered severely at the hands of the 'black leather boys', the 'By-pass Caff' ton-up brigade who may have looked like heroes in their own eyes, but were loathed by society as a whole.

So when, at last, the Japanese did arrive they had to revive the whole motor cycling scene and make it respectable ('You meet the nicest people on a Honda', remember?) before their unusually styled, but unusually

well-equipped models could gain acceptance. In time, too, the motor cycle would largely lose its workaday image and become something quite different – a leisure tool. The great pity is that, by then, there was virtually no home industry left, to share the enjoyment of this new market.

In the pages which follow, the histories of Britain's major makes are traced in great detail – the models, the personalities, the fortunes and the misfortunes. For anyone with petrol in his veins, and a leaning towards two-wheelers, it is fascination unlimited.

Bob Currie, Birmingham 1984

AJS

Albert John Stevens was one of five brothers. The others called him Jack, and three of them were sufficiently sympathetic to his interests to assist him in building a petrol engine as early as 1897. The necessary skills came as easily to them as the interest, for this was in the Black Country, where father Stevens was one of those many midland smiths who had raised their vocation from farrier to engineer during the spirited Victorian unfolding of the industrial revolution. It was probably curiosity rather than cupidity that inspired the youngsters for, although at that time the motor cycle was already a dozen

years old in principle, another half-dozen years were to pass before the Stevens brothers were set up as engine manufacturers, supplying their wares to manufacturers of powered bicycles and tricycles in their Wolverhampton locality. The most notable of these customers (using success rather than merit as a criterion) was the Wearwell Motor Carriage Company Limited – also proprietors of the Wolf and Wolfruna trademarks – who survived until 1939. In those early days, they favoured the Stevens engines, which were mounted high up in their bicycle

Top and above: the 1901 Wearwell-Stevens, probably 125cc, used an A. J. Stevens engine and was the forerunner of the AJS. The machine was built at Retreat Street, Wolverhampton

Right: 1928, 350cc, overhead-cam model K7 was the forerunner of famous 7R. This was the first production ohc machine and when new it cost £62 with electric lighting £5 extra

frames between the steering head and the pedalling gear.

As the decade progressed, it became apparent to Jack, as to many others, that there was good business in motor-cycle manufacture. It must also have been evident to him that making the entire vehicle was better business than just making engines for others: there was already a marked tendency for backyard assemblers by the dozen to set themselves up in business as motor-cycle manufacturers, buying most of the necessary bits and in particular exploiting the reputations and the commercial frailties of the proprietary-engine manufacturers. Jack wanted to produce his own machine, and he wanted it all to be his own. The policy was eventually to create troubles for riders of certain AJS racing machines, but that was forty years on. . . .

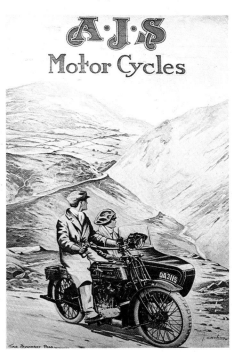

It was 1909 when Jack's scheme got under way with the formation of A. J. Stevens & Co Ltd, at an address in Retreat Street, Wolverhampton. Jack and his brothers were committed riders as well as manufacturers, and in the best traditions the boss made frequent appearances in long-distance trials while developing his machines. The fruits of this endeavour came on the market in 1911 as a choice of lightweights, conventional enough in layout but graced with a particularly neat little single-cylinder engine driving the rear wheel through a two-stage chain which was punctuated by a two-speed countershaft gearbox. This latter transmission was evidence of reasonably forward thinking, for multi-speed devices were few and far between in those days: it was only in that very year that the adoption of the daunting Mountain Circuit for the Tourist Trophy races in the Isle of Man drew everybody's

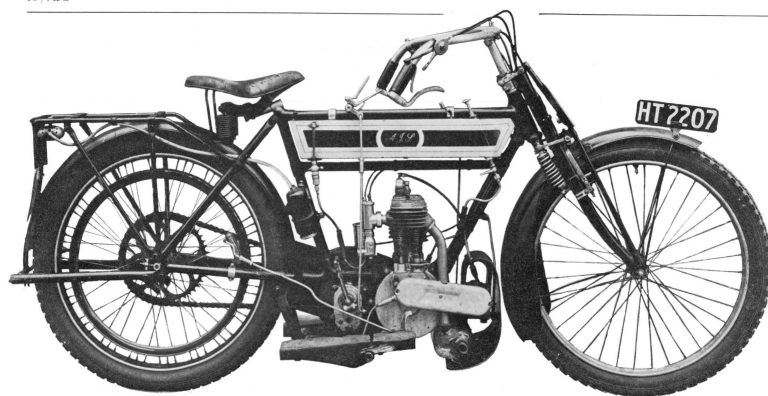

attention to the need for some form of variable-ratio transmission, with such urgency as was responsible for (among other things) the astonishingly rapid gestation of the Rudge Multi.

In due course, the AJS, as the new brand was known, extended its sporting ambitions to embrace the TT and a life-long association with top-flight racing. In that first year, however, it was perhaps more significant that, while other firms hedged their marketing bets with cycles of all sizes, AJS concentrated on light-weights.

Their own engine had a bore of 70mm and a stroke of 76, giving a capacity of 292cc, which was then a less curious figure than it now seems, corresponding to $2\frac{1}{2}$ horsepower on the old rating system that was to persist among motor cyclists in Britain for the next twenty years. According to this rule of some curiously erratic thumb, a 500cc engine was classed as a $3\frac{1}{2}$ horsepower (Stevens supplied a $3\frac{1}{4}$, as well as a $2\frac{1}{2}$, to Wearwell), the 350 was $2\frac{3}{4}$ horsepower, and would seem to be established as the classic AJS size, while a 250cc engine was reckoned to be a $2\frac{1}{4}$ horsepower job. In France, however, there was a class of racing for motor cycles with engines displacing one third of a litre, which did not quite correspond to anything and, although the AJS engine came fairly near it, Gallic influence upon Wolverhampton was more evident in 1912 when the frame design of the AJS was altered. French riders had been modifying the top tubes of their 333 racers, sloping them downwards in alignment with the seat stays to the rear hub so as to permit a lower saddle height, and thus reduce frontal area; and

this became a fashion in production motor cycles, emerging in 1910 and growing rapidly stronger so that, within a couple of years, AJS were one of many firms to adopt it. Of more lasting significance was the announcement in that same year of a big V-twin engine, of 800cc displacement and having mechanically operated valves, accompanied by such refinements as a three-speed gearbox and kick-starter in a substantial motor cycle intended for sidecar work.

Two years later, this still young company won a reputation that was to become practically immortal, by featuring in one of the most important TT races

Top: one of the first AJS machines, built in 1909

Above: the AJS workshops in 1924

in history. Amongst other things it was of historical importance because, as a result of a fatal crash to the third place man at the end of the race, it led to the adoption of the chequered flag which has brought a conclusion to all motor and motor-cycle races ever since; but it was also interesting on technical grounds. So far, twin-cylinder engines had always dominated the TT results: no single-cylinder machine had ever won a race, none had ever held a lap record. Nobody thought that a single could last the distance at a competitive speed and, when the 1914 Junior TT started, nobody saw any reason to change this view. There was a terrific scrap for the lead, fought between the twin-cylindered teams of Douglas and Royal Enfield, while the leading single was an AJS 350 lying in sixth place. Once again, it had an interesting transmission, with a two-speed primary chain drive (similar to the type pioneered by Phelon & Moore and parallelled by Scott) leading to a two-

speed counter-shaft gearbox, and enabling permutations of the drive line to be made offering four different ratios. Nevertheless, sixth place was no better than meritorious – until Walker on the leading Enfield suffered a puncture and the Douglas team suffered various mechanical disasters as a result of trying to keep up with him. Suddenly, AJS were in command: Eric Williams won from his team-mate Cyril Williams, no relation. What with one-lunger machines coming first and second in the Senior race as well, it was all the evidence people needed to warm to the mechanically simple single-cylinder engine. Certainly, it was all that AJS needed to make them famous and popular, so popular that they had to reorganise themselves to move into new premises in Penn Road, Wolverhampton; and thereafter they never looked back. However, the trouble is that disaster can overtake without warning . . .

For a while, AJS, like so many of their rivals, carried on as though unaware of the disaster that had plunged millions of people into the bloodiest war in Christendom. Not until November 1916 did the Ministry of Munitions order the end of production of civilian vehicles for the remainder of the war. When it was all over, the thunder of the captains and the shouting, AJS popped up as lively and as interesting as ever. In 1920, there was a brand-new Junior model for the TT, an 80mph machine with a 350cc engine proving that what Jack Stevens wore back-to-front under his riding goggles was his thinking cap. The generality of

Below: the 1914 'Luxury Sports', a special torpedo sidecar fitted to the 6hp, three-speed, 698cc AJS twin model D

overhead-valve motor-cycle engines carried their poppets vertical and parallel, but the last and best of the Grand Prix racing cars in the pre-war era – inspired by the Peugeots of Henry, the Hispano-Suiza designs of Birkigt, and the Fiat groundwork of Cavalli – had their valves inclined in opposition in cross-flow heads whose combustion chambers, where the valves numbered but two per cylinder, were hemispherical in shape. Two valves seemed to Stevens to be enough for the little AJS cylinder, even if Peugeot had used four and J. A. Prestwich had achieved promising results with three in their pre-war racing twins; and so the new 350 had its pushrod-operated overhead valves inclined at a wide angle in a hemispherical head. Perhaps because he had been aware that the Peugeot racing engines had been singularly inflexible and demanded very close gearbox ratios, or perhaps because a proliferation of gears had become a successful AJS design gambit, Jack made the new machine a six-speeder, by combining a two-speed primary drive with a three-speed gearbox.

For one reason or other, the handsome little machine, finished in glossy black with gold lining and lettering, had the legs of everything else in the Junior TT, Eric Williams lapping the Island at an average of 51mph. The winning speed should have been comparable, but was not: the AJS team riders threw discipline and responsibility to the winds, and fought a furious private battle that eventually crippled all their machines. Only one, Cyril Williams, was left who could finish; but they had been miles ahead of the field and, although he had to push his bike the last $3\frac{1}{4}$ miles (mostly downhill, so it was not as bad as it sounds), he crossed the finishing line nine minutes ahead of the next man. On the other hand, his average speed was only 40.74mph, nearly 5 less than Eric Williams' 1914 average. It looked bad, but next year the tarnish was polished off the AJS reputation in the most spectacular way: the 349cc single won not only the Junior TT but also the Senior, giving away 150cc to its rivals. The 1922 results were less remarkable, the AJS merely winning the Junior event; but this made four such victories in a row, and the latest AJS was distinguished by new internal-expanding brakes. The production model of the following year also carried these as part of a race-developed specification that made it one of the most distinguished thoroughbreds among sporting roadsters, a connoisseur's motor cycle that passed into the language of fame as 'the big-port Ajay'. Although the exhaust pipe had a bore that would not have disgraced a sousaphone, it was the inlet port that was big, the value of this being emphasised in 1924 when the latest works racer sported the novelty of an inlet valve larger than its opposite number in the exhaust port, and made the most of it to establish a record lap of nearly 65mph in the Junior race. This was actually faster than the new Senior lap record set by Freddie Dixon on the Douglas; but that may have been due, not to the traditional AJS speed, but to the legendary dash of the factory's new rider Jimmy Simpson.

Simpson was to become famous for being the fastest rider in most races, and for hardly ever winning. Having been the first to lap the TT course at over 60mph on the AJS in 1924, and being destined in due course to be the first to lap at over

80 (on a Norton in the 1931 Senior), it was fitting that he should also have been the first to do a 70mph lap: this he accomplished in 1926 on a new 500cc ohv AJS. It was in the best Stevens tradition, virtually an enlarged version of the 350 but, although it was the big-port ohv singles that attracted all the limelight, the firm was doing very well with its less glamorous products as well, which ranged from the big side-valve V-twin of 800cc capacity, through side-valve singles of 500 and 350ccs, down to a sprinkling of 250 models. There were also some abortive half-litre V-twins mounted transversely (that is with their crank-shafts longitudinal) in the style later to be endorsed by Brough Superior and Guzzi. Even more intriguing was a design for an in-line four-cylinder engine, a 500cc device whose air-cooling evidently took no regard of the cooling difficulties experienced in similar machines from others such as FN and Henderson.

These curiosities did not disclose any

Above: the 1922 B1 three-speed standard sporting model. It had a 2¾hp, 349cc engine, with an Amac carburettor and a Lucas magneto. The cost new was £85

faltering of the hand at the drawing board. In 1927, there appeared a new 350 that would be recognised as a direct ancestor of the last 'real' AJS more than a quarter of a century later. Its charac-teristic feature, as lineally significant as a Hapsburg lip, was an overhead camshaft driven by a long chain enclosed in a cast-ing on the right-hand side of the engine. A Weller tensioner took up the chain slack, and a transverse camshaft gave the AJS single a new lease of life. Simpson could finish no higher than third in the Junior TT, but he won the Swiss, Belgian and European Grands Prix. The only reason why this demonstrably successful new development did not take the entire motor-cycling world by storm was that its denizens were all potty with pleasure over the performance of a new Norton that also had an overhead camshaft, also went very fast, but had the advantage of another 150cc to make it sound even more formidable, and a TT win in the appropriate class to make it seem rather less fallible.

Like Norton, AJS made their new overhead-camshaft model a catalogued item for 1928, casting a glory that might be reflected to advantage from their new side-valve 250 which cost a mere £40 – an interesting comparison with the 47 guineas price tag on the 1914 model, the 2¾ horsepower AJS from which it was still clearly derived.

A year later, the entire range was redesigned. Already, conventional short

studs holding the cylinder down at its base had replaced the traditional long ones clamping it with an inverted stirrup over the head; but now the engines were given dry-sump lubrication, pushrods and rockers were enclosed, and some of the singles were given the newly fashionable twin-port exhausts that fed a pair of prettily symmetrical pipes. Saddle tanks crowned new frames, concealing straight top tubes and exposing centre-spring front forks. Less obvious was the expansion of the 800cc V-twin to 996; but it was obvious that things were changing, for the traditional black and gold finish had

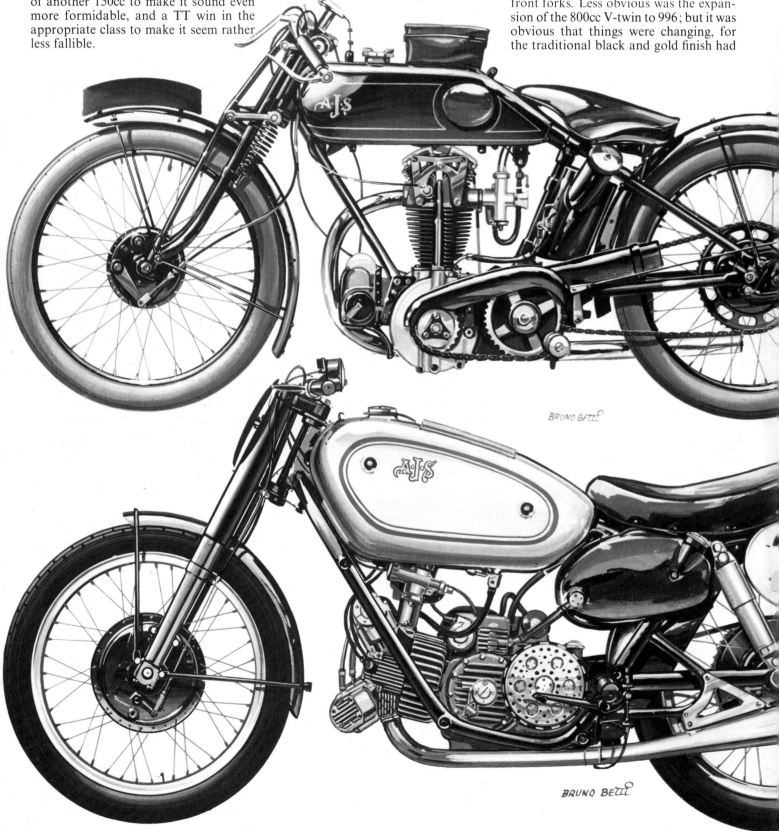

Above: the famous 350cc ohc 7R 'Boy Racer' of the immediate post-war era; it was most successful in the hands of private entrants

Above: the 349cc AJS 'Big Port' of 1923. This famous single-cylinder machine, whose valves were located in-head, produced some 20bhp

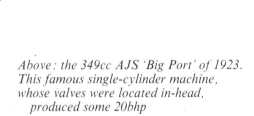

Left: dubbed the Porcupine on account of the cooling fins all around the parallel-twin engine, this 500cc AJS developed only 40bhp and proved disappointing

been corrupted by purple panels.

Perhaps the hand was faltering – or was it the judgment? It could have been greed, or it could have been a simple misunderstanding of the market's needs, or it could have been a reasonable desire for diversification that was responsible, but in the late years of the 1920s AJS tried to do too many things too quickly. They were a big firm now, and their ambitions were running away with them. In 1927, they had started making commercial vehicles; at about the same time they broke into the radio business; and in 1930 they embarked on the manufacture of a light car. This four-door saloon, powered by a one-litre side-valve engine made by Coventry Climax, bore very little resemblance to the Clyno 9 that AJS were accused of copying, and neither did the cheaper open two-seater version. They were both doomed, and so were the new motor cycles. Only a year after the extensive changes of 1929, the middleweight singles were reconstructed with fashionable sloping cylinders. There was also a range of lightweights pared down below the new 224lb taxation limit, and these contained vertical cylinders, including the two-port pushrod 350. The AJS that won the lightweight TT of 1930 also had an upright cylinder, but it was crowned by that overhead camshaft that no longer appeared in the catalogue. And then? Then it was 1931, the year of the slump, the end of an era and the end of AJS or at least of A. J. Stevens Limited.

The car was taken over by Willys-Overland-Crossley, surviving for only another year; and all the factory equipment was bought by the Stevens brothers' old rivals, the Collier brothers, for their Matchless factory in south-east London. They bought not only the machinery but also the name, and they made it meaningless by embarking on a cynical programme of badge engineering that reached its nadir in the years following 1949, when the production AJS was

merely a Matchless with a different badge on the tank and a nice black and gold colour scheme. By that time, the firm was known as Associated Motor Cycles, having bought and re-sold Sunbeam, and going on to accumulate the reputations of James, Francis-Barnett and even Norton.

There remain three stories that the Matchless history cannot tell, three lines of racing machinery that will always be known by the AJS name, although only one of them really deserved it. The R7 and 7R single-cylinder 'boy racers' really were in the AJS tradition, whereas the Porcupine twin was conceived as a Cockney copy of the Gilera four, and the AJS V-four was simply a disaster.

It was in 1938 that the four-cylinder 500 made its racing debut, with one pair of cylinders sloping forward and the other back in an effort to bring to bear sufficient sheer power to rival the foreigners that were beginning to dominate Grand Prix racing. It had a sprung rear wheel, which was new to AJS but by then was essential to any high-performance motor cycle. All it achieved was some chronic overheating, so Matt Wright designed a water-cooled version that might be more successful in absorbing and dissipating the heat generated by the chain-driven supercharger set low in front of the engine. It too encountered cooling troubles when it made its first public appearance at Brooklands in May 1939, and Wright's fond reliance on thermosyphon circulation had to be sacrificed to an external water pump. There was enough external clutter on the contraption already, what with four exhaust pipes, two magnetos, three exposed chains, and a tangle of plumbing. By the time it sent to the Isle of Man for the TT, it had accumulated a little more racing experience, but it was still uncompetitive; it was the heaviest machine in the race, 99lb heavier than the 306lb BMW that was the lightest of the 500s and was to emerge the winner. With its prodigal thirst and fuel tankage to match, the V4 AJS was a great deal heavier still at the starting line; after stopping several times for fuel and water, the two examples that started were eleventh and thirteenth over the finishing line. Only in the Ulster GP did the V4 accomplish anything to its credit, in completing the first 100mph lap of the Clady circuit; but completing the race was beyond its accomplishment.

Not such a bad motor cycle, but an unluckier one, was the Porcupine. Its name was a reference to the spiky 'fins' for optimal air-cooling of the forward-facing cylinder heads of its engine, a parallel-twin 500 whose cylinders were set horizontally so as to keep the weight low. Once again it was a supercharger that was expected to make heat dissipation a major problem: the machine was designed during the war years in anticipation of a return to racing with motor cycles essentially similar to the formidable blown Gilera of the late 1930s. Building the Porcupine took but little time as soon as the war was over, and it was only after the 'bike was complete that the FIM – in a ruling that was probably designed to protect Norton and penalise the continentals – banned supercharging. AMC never recovered from the shock sufficiently to undertake an intelligent redesign, but insisted on muddling along with the original one, blower cradle and all. Even the cams were unchanged, so it was hardly surprising that the engine never gave the power of which it should have been capable. The only positive step was a revised cylinder head that gave a more suitable combination of compression ratio and combustion-chamber shape for unforced aspiration. Handling problems were also rife, but the factory's refusal to use proprietary dampers rather than their own made at least some of those problems insoluble. Seven years dogged development was not enough to solve some of the others, despite a revamped engine with cylinders sloping at 45° (to present more cooling air to the exhaust ports), conventionally finned heads, and a fuel system involving floatless weir-type carburettors and some hilarious starting-line antics to get everything properly primed. By 1954, the Porcupine had evolved to become the E93 and developed 54bhp at the crankshaft at 7500rpm; it was a lot better than the footling 40 of 1947, but it was less than the Italian fours were producing at the rear wheel.

While the E93 kept AJS fans fairly consistently disappointed, their allegiance to the brand was sustained by the reputation of the 350 single that was the traditional AJS racing speciality. Directly descended from the chain-driven overhead-cam engine of the 1927 racer was the R7, which by 1938 had a light-alloy barrel and head with hairpin valve springs. Better still, it had a fairly advanced chassis featuring big light-alloy brakes and an interesting spring-heel frame that looked like a plunger-sprung affair after the fashion of Norton's 'garden gate' frame but in fact incorporated a trailing fork of multi-tube girder design. These features paved the way (in principles, but not in detail) for the recoded 7R when the 'bike was revived in 1949. Here was a handsome, even a beautiful, machine that was to win a lot of races, win a lot of friends and win a place in immortality with its affectionate *soubriquet* 'Boy Racer'.

The Junior 'Ajay' was still a single with chain-driven overhead cam and trailing-fork rear suspension. Otherwise it was all new, with an elegant duplex cradle frame and WD-proven (!) Teledraulic front

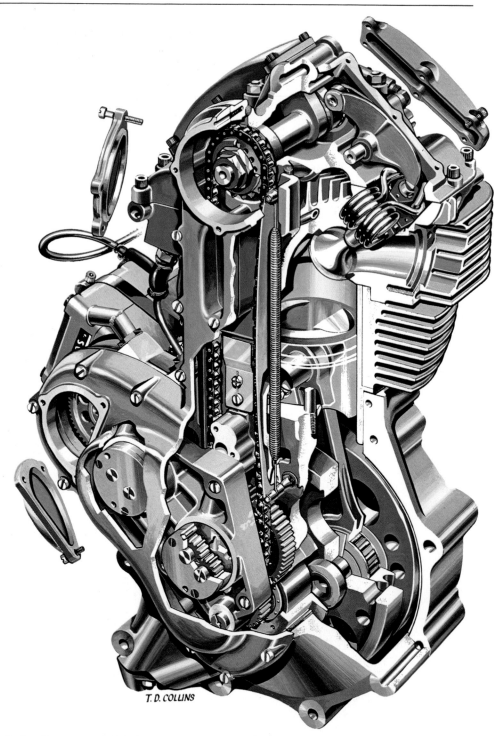

T. D. COLLINS

forks. It was a well behaved and lively roadracer that remained steadily in the picture until 1961, dominating the Junior class in domestic events as thoroughly as the Manx Norton ruled the Senior. In the mid 1950s, some fascinating engine development was carried out by Jack Williams, during which he proved among other things that gas-flowing was not a panacea: the port shapes that gave the greatest gas flow were not associated with the greatest power, and by lining the bench model with blotting paper and feeding ink to the carburettor Williams was able to show that fuel distribution was the more critical factor. He could have done even more had he been allowed to, for he got better results from an experimental three-

Above: a cutaway illustration of the single-overhead-cam engine of the AJS 7R

valved version of the engine; but the AMC bosses enforced stifling economies in the racing development shop, and the 7R gradually faded from the limelight. Its greatest achievement was actually before Williams' time: in 1952, the late Bob McIntyre not only won the Junior Manx GP on his 7R, but also took 'second place in the Senior on the same machine.

Strangely, AJS survived its partners in the AMC conglomerate, regaining its independence in 1974. Based in Andover, the company was producing 250 and 350cc off-road two-strokes – powered by its own engine.

Ariel

There are (or rather, there were until Japanese technicians proved otherwise) two major snags to designing a four-cylinder motor cycle. Set the engine in line with the frame, and the wheelbase tends to be inordinately lengthy. Mount it crosswise, and there are width and transmission problems.

However, a young London engineer named Edward Turner had a bright idea. Why not arrange the cylinders two-by-two in a square – two vertical twins, in effect, one behind the other. That way, the unit could be particularly compact, and installation in a frame would be no problem at all.

Turner was not entirely an unknown and, in the small machine shop at the rear of his Dulwich premises, he was already building and marketing a single-cylinder 350cc overhead-camshaft machine of his own. Now, with the germ of his 'Square Four' idea sketched on the back of a Wild Woodbine cigarette packet, he went to try his luck with the midland motor-cycle industry.

One factory after another turned it down but, at last, Edward Turner found a man willing to take a chance. He was Jack Sangster, head of the Ariel works at Selly Oak (a southern suburb of Birmingham), and he provided Turner with a separate office, wherein to work out the design in detail, and an assistant; the assistant was a youngster named Herbert Hopwood who, in the course of time, was to become a top-line motor-cycle designer in his own right.

The machine that emerged from the monasterial seclusion of Turner's office was revolutionary. Of 500cc and with a chain-driven overhead camshaft, it was a double-twin in which the crankshafts were coupled by gears. The drive to the gearbox was taken from the left-hand end of the rear crankshaft, which meant that the left-hand rear cylinder employed a

full crank; the other three cylinders had overhung cranks.

So light was the prototype unit that it could be fitted for test purposes into the frame of the standard 250cc Ariel single. It could, moreover, be started merely by sitting on the saddle and paddling off. However, before the machine made its public début as the sensation of London's 1930 Olympia Show, the manufacturers felt it judicious to use a rather more substantial frame, in fact the same frame that

was already in production for their 500cc sloper single.

So, the immortal Ariel Square Four made its bow, a machine which, over the years, was to earn world-wide respect. Before the last of the line was built, almost thirty years later, it was to grow in size (eventually to 1000cc) and change to pushrod valve operation; in that time it was to become a motor-cycling legend.

Ariel's own name can be traced back to the invention of the wheel! Although, to be more precise, back to the invention and joint patenting by James Starley and William Hillman of the tensioned wire-spoke wheel in 1870. Far lighter than anything that had been seen before, the tensioned wheel enabled Starley and Hillman to produce Britain's first all-metal, relatively lightweight, penny-farthing bicycle. The name they gave it, Ariel, was that of the Spirit of the Air. The Ariel cycle achieved considerable popularity, both on the road and in the cycle-racing stadia of the time, and the manufacturers, Starley Brothers, of Coventry, even devised and built a ladies' penny-farthing on which the rider sat side-saddle and turned the front wheel through a system of levers and links.

In 1896, James Starley amalgamated his firm with that of the Westwood Manufacturing Company, of Birmingham and, with £130,000 capital, the new Starley and Westwood company (producing, among other things, cycle rims and tyres) became one of the cornerstones of the Components Ltd empire. This, in the course of time, was to grow into a huge factory complex at Selly Oak.

Ariel's first venture into powered transport came in 1898, when a few quadricycles were built. These were virtually four-wheeled bicycles, with a De Dion engine mounted behind the rear axle and driving it through gearing. A year later, a more satisfactory vehicle had evolved; this was a tricycle, based on the De Dion design but with the engine now carried ahead of the rear axle and within the wheelbase. As can be imagined, this gave better roadholding than did the De Dion idea of carrying the engine right at the back.

Around 1902, the first Ariel motor cycles, as such, made their appearance. Powered by Kerry engines, and with magneto ignition and a float-type carburettor, they were slightly more advanced in conception than the products of their competitors, and it was not really a surprise that an Ariel should have been chosen by the Auto Cycle Club to take part in the preliminary trials from which a team would be selected to represent Britain in the 1905 International Cup Races. The rider was J. S. Campbell, and the Ariel (a 6hp model) put up the best performance of the trials by averaging over 41mph.

By this time, control of the Ariel works had passed into the hands of Charles Sangster, and it was he who designed and patented a lightweight two-stroke (to be known as the Ariel-ette) which incorporated such advanced features as a three-speed gearbox with clutch and kick-starter; unhappily, however, the outbreak of World War I made the Arielette to be stillborn.

Back in 1910, Ariel (and Swift of Coventry, with which Ariels had been associated since the late 1890s) had introduced a solidly built 4hp model with a side-valve engine of White and Poppe design. In this (the valves were so widely separated), it was said, an owner, after adjusting the inlet tappet, had a five-minute walk before he could attend to the exhaust! An exaggeration, of course, but that good old engine was to serve Ariel, with very little modification, right through to 1925. And, although the company's wartime motor-cycle contribution was very much less than that of Douglas or Triumph, a batch of the Ariel 'four-horse' models saw Army service in Mesopotamia.

The truth was that Sangster's interests at the time lay more with car production than with motor cycles, and so the two-wheelers (basically the old White & Poppe-engined 4hp, plus a big V-twin with Abingdon King Dick or Swiss-built MAG engines) took second billing. There was a certain amount of updating – pressed-steel fork blades, patented by William Starley, were offered in 1920 but found little acceptance among the buying public – but, in general, Ariel were lagging behind motor-cycle trends.

It was at this stage that Jack Sangster, son of Charles, took a hand. He had designed a flat-twin, air-cooled car of which the design and manufacture had been taken up by the Rover company.

Now, for Ariel, he evolved a light car to be known as the Ariel Nine. But also, he had the foresight to tempt away from the JAP company a motor-cycle designer of immense talent. This was Valentine Page, whose previous work had included the overhead-camshaft engine with which Bert Le Vack had broken a number of Brooklands records.

With a clean sheet of paper, Val Page set to work. The result was a pair of entirely new models (500cc overhead valve and 557cc side valve which, unveiled at the 1926 Olympia Show for the following season, had the buying public reaching for their wallets. There was nothing unconventional in the engine design – although they were certainly sound, the 557cc side-valve surviving, with only slight modification from time to time, through to the 1950s as the Model VB.

Below: an example of a 1913 Ariel, which used the famous 4hp, side-valve, single-cylinder engine

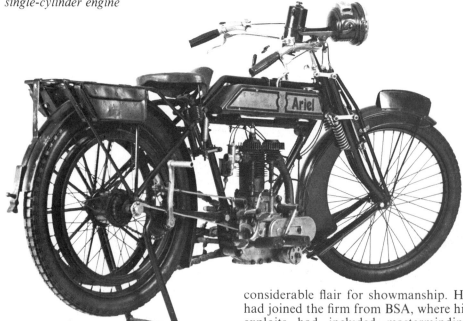

What caught the public fancy, however, was the styling, with a new lower riding position, shortened wheelbase and smart, saddle-type fuel tank. The saddle tank as such was not new (it had been used by Quadrant, Dot, Alldays and others since 1919), but its shape was, and so briskly did the new Ariels sell that, within two more years, every other motor-cycle maker in the country had switched to tanks of generally similar outline.

The Ariel factory never did support racing to any extent, although private owners hit the headlines from time to time. Best known of the Ariel exponents of the 1920s and 1930s were Ben Bickell (who crashed his Ariel fatally in the 1936 Ulster Grand Prix) and Lawrie Hartley – whose tuning ability was such that he

tweaked one of the 557cc side-valves to 96mph (on alcohol). Hartley-tuned overhead-valve Ariels were particularly well known on the grass-tracks of the south, with Jock West as the foremost rider. In the midlands, Charlie Bowers was the local equivalent of Lawrie Hartley, and Dick Tolley took the Jock West role.

In the late 1920s, the nippy little 250cc Colt was added to the Ariel stable, and Val Page's 500cc overhead-valve engine was developed into the Red Hunter (a name first used in the Ariel catalogue in 1932). And, while Edward Turner, in his hideaway drawing office, was evolving the Square Four, another part of the Selly Oak complex saw Val Page at work on a group of inclined-engine models – so inclined as to be almost 'flat singles' – among which was an eight-valve ohv.

Another name in the Ariel history should be mentioned, to complete the team. This was Harry Perrey, who was not only one of Britain's best-known trials riders but, also, a salesman with a considerable flair for showmanship. He had joined the firm from BSA, where his exploits had included masterminding (and taking part in) a mass assault by motor cycles on Snowdon, the highest mountain in Wales. Harry's best-publicised stunt for the Ariel company was the crossing of the English Channel on a 500cc ohv single machine mounted on floats. The building of the craft was a saga in itself but, suffice to say, suitable floats were eventually constructed by the same Thames boatbuilder who fashioned the successful Oxford eight for the University Boat Race. The machine was quite standard, except that an extra sprocket was added to the rear hub, with a chain driving downward to a gearbox from which the propshaft protruded; to give clearance for this second chain, a narrower-than-standard rear tyre was fitted.

To give the propeller sufficient bite in the water, Harry Perrey took a pillion passenger (Ted Thacker, another well known trials man). The Ariel 'Flotor Cycle' made the double crossing without incident, and was then sent around the continent on exhibition. It was in Danzig when World War II erupted, and nothing has been heard of it since.

With the coming of the Square Four for the 1931 season. Brooklands habitué Somerville Sikes evolved a supercharged version, in which a vane-type blower (driven by chain and producing 15lb

Below left: a 1914 racing Ariel, which used direct-belt drive

Below right: a 1918 4.99hp touring machine

Bottom: the 1899 Ariel tricycle was a much better proposition than its four-wheeled predecessor

boost) was interposed between the carburettor and engine. Claimed output of the blown model was 40bhp, but the original Square Four had an inherent fault in that there was insufficient space between the top of the cylinder head and the underside of the cambox and, with a poor flow of air over the head, distortion was a problem.

Sikes entered the supercharged machine for the 1931 Senior TT, but it was still incomplete when practice began, and not until the morning of race day was he able to wheel out the blown job. Inevitably, he retired, with a blown cylinder-head joint.

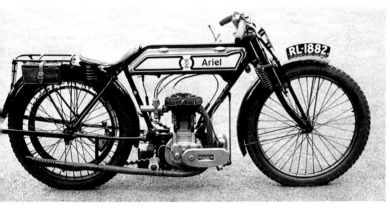

The same troubles beset Ben Bickell, with the supercharged Square Four he had built in 1933 with the 'Motor Cycle Cup' in mind. This trophy was being offered, by the weekly journal, for the first British machine to pack 100 miles into an hour on British soil which, with the shortage of suitable venues, meant Brooklands. Helped by his brother, Joe, Ben Bickell chose a 600cc version of the Square Four, reducing the bores to bring the engine into the 500cc class – the 500cc model had been dropped from the Ariel range by this time – and added a Powerplus supercharger.

Bickell's machine was certainly fast enough to take the cup, and was well able to lap Brooklands at over 100mph (on one occasion it clocked a 111.42mph lap) but, time after time, blown cylinder-head gaskets brought their record attempts to a halt. Before any solution to the problem could be found, Ginger Wood took the 'Motor Cycle Cup' with a V-twin New Imperial, and the whole purpose of the exercise disappeared. Ironically, that very morning Ben Bickell had got the Ariel cracking around the Brooklands bowl at a consistent 100mph. But that, as they say, is show biz!

Back in the sales office, Harry Perrey felt it time for another publicity splurge, and he thought up a comprehensive scheme whereby seven different models would be selected from the range and put through seven different tests with the figure seven running through each as a motif. This was the celebrated 'seven sevens' test, the most ambitious section

of which included an attempt, by the 500cc Square Four, to cover 700 miles in 700 minutes.

In fact, that last test did not quite come off as planned, a piston 'picking up' after the first 300 miles. However, a restart was made and this time the 700 miles were reeled off in 668 minutes, to average 62.58mph. For light relief, Ariels next picked seven schoolboys and, to demonstrate the ease of starting of the four, asked them to kick-start it seven times each. Six of the lads did it without trouble; the seventh, and smallest, failed.

Although the 'seven sevens' demonstration brought the coveted Maudes Trophy to Selly Oak, the factory was heading for disaster, as the shock waves of world depression spread across Britain. The slump hit Ariels in 1932, and the factory doors closed.

At that point, Jack Sangster threw in his personal fortune and, concentrating Ariel production into one part of the factory complex, sold off the remaining property to acquire working capital. Under the new style of Ariel Motors (JS) Ltd – the 'JS' recognised Sangster's personal involvement – the company

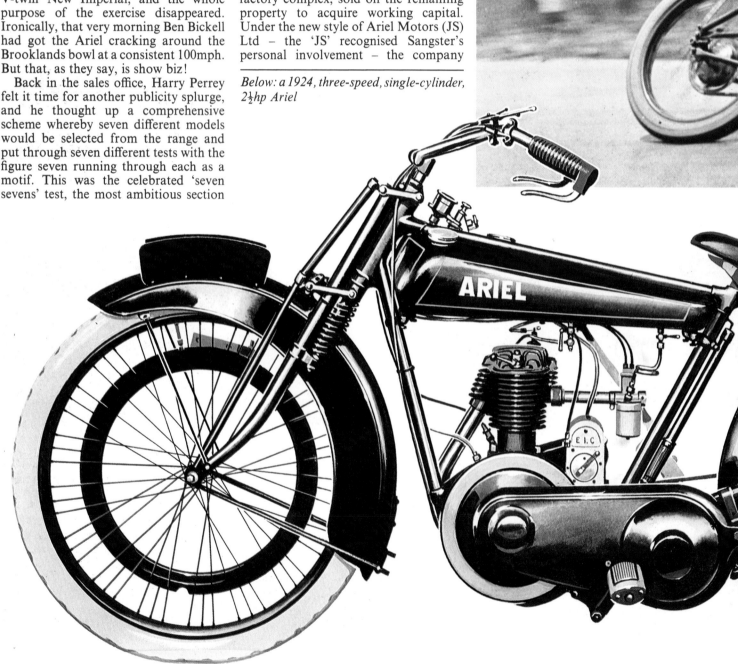

Below: a 1924, three-speed, single-cylinder, 2½hp Ariel

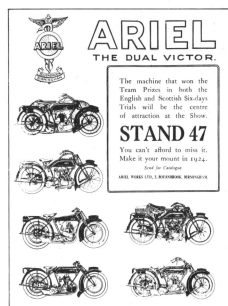

began again, with a reduced workforce and a slimmed-down programme of models in production.

Among those who had left were Val Page and Harry Perrey. Both had found other employment at the Triumph works, where Val evolved a new range of engines including the first 650cc Triumph Twin – which Harry publicised in typical fashion. After yet another move, this time to BSA, where he designed the famous M20 and Gold Star, Val Page was to return to Ariel – but that is getting ahead of the story.

Edward Turner had an eye for beauty

Above: a 1928, 500cc, ohv, twin-port, modified road bike in competition

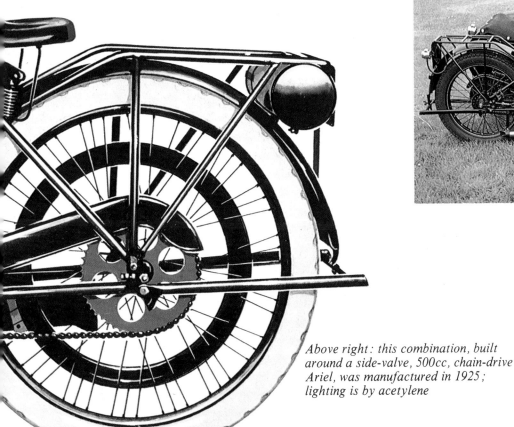

Above right: this combination, built around a side-valve, 500cc, chain-drive Ariel, was manufactured in 1925; lighting is by acetylene

of line (as he was to prove later when, at Triumph, he took the Val Page range of singles and, giving them a cosmetic treatment, turned them into the eye-catching Tigers), and he helped Ariel along the road to recovery by prettying-up Page's single-cylinder models. With a gorgeously contoured tank, decorated with chromium-plating, a tank-top instrument panel, and a bright-red finish, he turned them into the Red Hunter range.

The Square Four, meanwhile, was

undergoing a top-to-toe redesign. No longer was it overhead-camshaft, and the new version, launched for 1937, featured pushrod valve operation. The overhung cranks had given way to full crankshafts, and these were now coupled by gearing on the left-hand side, instead of in the middle. Two sizes of engine were on offer – 600cc and 1000cc – and the bigger of these had a power output of 38bhp at 5500rpm. 'Ten to a hundred in top gear' was the selling slogan, and that is exactly what it would do.

Assistant designer Frank Anstey added, for 1939, an unusual rear springing system which, although basically of plunger type, incorporated pivoted links so that the rear wheel spindle moved through an arc, maintaining constant chain tension. The sprung heel was available (at option) on the Red Hunters and also on the Square Four. It worked very well, too, except that with the passage of time, wear developed in the link pins.

Much of Ariel's war-time work was on military projects other than motor cycles, but production did continue of an Army mount, the 350cc Model W/NG. This was based on the 1939 Red Hunter, although the frame had improved ground clearance, and owed much to the machines produced for Britain's ISDT team.

Understandably, the 350cc single (back in its red and chrome finish) was the first to be announced by Ariel when peace returned but, before long, the 1000cc Square Four, too, was back in production; the 600cc version had been dropped, in the interest of regaining maximum production quickly.

Val Page was once more in control of the Ariel drawing office, and soon from his board there came a neat 500cc vertical twin, enabling Ariels to advertise that they had 'the world's only range of singles, twins and fours'. Behind the scenes, financial control had passed into the hands of the BSA Group, but there was, as yet, no outward sign of this and, under the directorship and general management of one-time TT rider, Ken Whistance, the Selly Oak brigade trod their own path to glory.

Telescopic front forks, with hydraulic damping, was now adopted, and the Square Four engine went on a diet, shedding 33lb by the substitution of a light-alloy cylinder block and head. For 1954, it was again subjected to a revamp, and emerged as the famous Mark II 'four piper' with two separate exhaust pipes at each side, sprouting from beautifully finned and polished manifolds. Compression ratio had been raised to 7.2 to 1 (mainly because better-quality petrol was now available) and power output was up to 42bhp at 5800rpm.

The Mark II represented the ultimate flowering of the Square Four because, although the Red Hunters, and the 500

and 650cc vertical twins, were given the fashionable pivoted-fork rear springing in the course of time, the Four retained to the end of its production life the plunger-and-link sprung heel.

That end came in 1958. Good although it was, the Square Four by that time needed drastic redesign if it was to hold its own in world markets, and the cost of such an undertaking would be too high in the light of estimated future sales.

Indeed, four-strokes as a whole were temporarily on their way out, the factory having staked everything on a completely new two-stroke twin from Val Page. This had a revolutionary frame construction in which the power unit was suspended from the underside of a pressed-steel box member extending from steering head to rear-suspension top mountings.

The fuel tank, a simple two-piece pressing, was lodged within the hollow beam, and access to it was gained by raising the side-hinged seat. A dummy 'tank' pressing covered the main beam and offered, through a lockable lid on the top face, space for carrying parcels.

Other features included total enclosure of the engine behind detachable panels at each side, built-in dashboard and leg-shields, and a trailing-link front fork of which the side members were formed from welded-up pressings. Flashing direction indicators, a parking lamp, an eight-day clock and a rear bumper bar were among the comprehensive accessories on offer. This, then, was the 250cc Ariel Leader, a machine so far in advance of contemporary design as to be almost out of sight. For its production, the Ariel works invested heavily in press-tools, casting dies and jigs, but, although

Opposite page top: the Ariel Red Hunter, a 250cc machine built in 1936

Centre left: a 1931 example of the 497cc Square Four motor cycle

Centre right: also seen in the 1950s is the busy competition department

Bottom: Sammy Miller and his famous trials machine, which weighed in at just on 240lb. Sammy is seen at Beaulieu on 15 August 1971

This page: the stripped version of the Leader was the Arrow, although it used the same twin-cylinder two-stroke power unit

the public enthused mightily over the new Ariel Leader, they were reluctant to lay down their cash. Well, the Ariel people had an answer to that. By stripping off the legshields, dashboard and side panels, and fitting a simpler type of top pressing, they produced the Ariel Arrow; and this time it did catch the public by the purse-strings. There was, too, a sports counterpart, attractively finished in gold and white and with whitewall tyres as a finishing touch.

It was soon discovered that the Ariel twin two-stroke engine would accept a modest degree of tune, and Mike O'Rourke, whose Arrow was tuned and prepared by Hermann Meier, scored several successes on mainland circuits and took the machine to seventh place in the 1960 Lightweight TT. Another exponent of the Ariel Arrow in race trim was Peter Inchley, while Ernie Earles became even more ambitious and installed two Arrow engines, sparked by electronic ignition, in a sidecar chassis. The Earles Arrow Four was tried out by

Bill Boddice but, although it was potent, the power band was too narrow for success in sidecar racing.

Although the Ariel factory itself eschewed road racing, they did take an interest in the scrambles and trials side of motor-cycle sport, the trials team at various times including Don Evans, Gordon Blakeway – and a young Ulsterman who was destined to become a living legend of the trials world. His name was Sammy Miller and, if he chose, he could have been a world champion road racer; instead, he opted out of the racing circus and, instead, devoted his time to paring a 500cc Ariel trials model (GOV 132) down to the lightest weight possible.

Now exhibited in the National Motor Museum at Beaulieu, GOV 132 eventually got down to about 240lb, with the aid of such non-standard components as titanium wheel spindles. However, it was not so much the machine which won whole sideboard-loads of silverware, but Sammy himself, as he was to show when, later, he joined the two-stroke revolution and rode a 250cc Bultaco.

Miller's sojourn with the Ariel company lasted long after the four-strokes were, officially, dead and buried, because his trials successes kept the name before the public eye, and that was what mattered. Sammy did prepare an Ariel Arrow for use in the International Six Days Trial, however (it was not an unqualified success), and, later, rode it

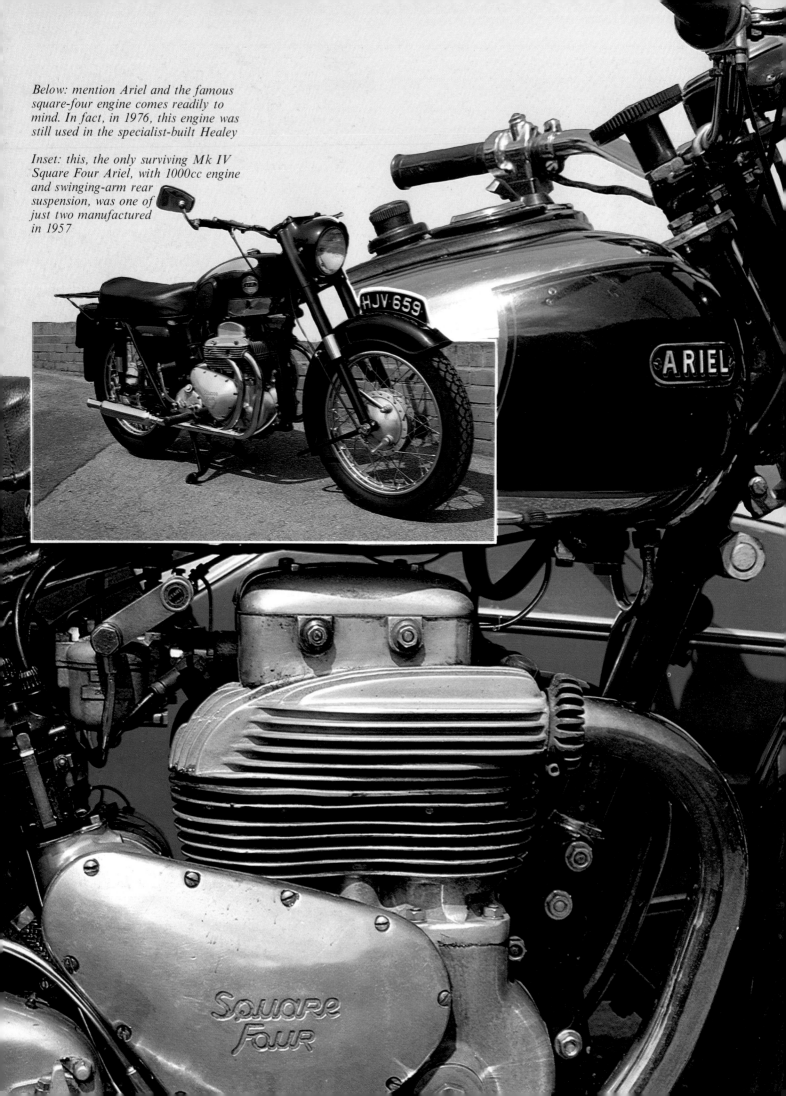

Below: mention Ariel and the famous square-four engine comes readily to mind. In fact, in 1976, this engine was still used in the specialist-built Healey

Inset: this, the only surviving Mk IV Square Four Ariel, with 1000cc engine and swinging-arm rear suspension, was one of just two manufactured in 1957

Above left: the prototype straight-four shaft-drive Ariel, which may have saved the company had it reached production

Above right: the last 'Ariel' was this Three, built by BSA and dogged by virtually impossible handling

almost to the top of Ben Nevis before being stopped by deep snowdrifts.

With the coming of the 1960s, so the BSA Group began to run into financial difficulties, and a decision was taken to close the Selly Oak works and transfer Ariel production to vacant space within the huge BSA plant at Small Heath.

One of the last of Val Page's projects at Selly Oak had been a new ultra-lightweight, the 50cc Pixie which employed a pressed-steel-beam frame on the same general lines as that of the Arrow. Initially there was, too, an Ariel power unit with a camshaft driven by toothed rubber belt but, meanwhile, BSA technicians were working on a similar but larger 75cc lightweight, the Beagle, with an engine which was, in effect, a miniature version of the Triumph Tiger Cub unit. Obviously, it made sense to rationalise production by using basically the same engine for both BSA and Ariel models; but, alas, it was the Val Page design which lost out and, instead, the Pixie reached the market with a 50cc edition of the Beagle power unit.

With the production line safely installed at Small Heath, the 250cc Ariel Arrow was soon back in dealers' showrooms and, now, it was joined by a 200cc Arrow, aimed at filling a corner of the British market where a two-hundred attracted lower insurance rates than did a two-fifty. However, the Arrow was essentially a British-market machine with a very low export performance; the Americans, especially, disliked the pressed-steel construction. True, the BSA experimental department did tinker with a prototype (they were thinking of calling

it the Red Hunter, incidentally) which housed an Arrow power unit in a duplex tubular loop frame but, for some reason, the idea was dropped.

With demand for the Arrow sinking lower and lower, production was brought to an end in 1966. And that, it seemed, was the finish of the Ariel marque.

Not quite, though. Small Heath had been developing a most peculiar 50cc tricycle, of which the fore section of the frame could be banked through bends as though it were a two-wheeler. The original design had been by George Wallis, who had produced the low, hub-centre-steered Wallis machines of the mid 1920s, but BSA had cheapened it for production, using narrow, pressed-steel wheels and a Dutch-made Anker engine. The ultimate insult, in the eyes of many thousands of Ariel devotees, was the name given to this monstrosity by BSA.

It was, they said, the Ariel Three – but it was a long, long way removed from the Ariel Four of hallowed memory, and there were few to shed a tear when, almost inevitably, the tricycle moped failed to attract custom. No, this time the Ariel motor-cycle company was dead.

Yet there had been one design which, had events turned out otherwise, might have saved both Ariel and the Selly Oak factory. This was to have been Val Page's swan-song, and he stayed on in

the drawing office until after retirement age, just to see it through the paper stage.

Again it was a four-cylinder, but of very different conception to Turner's Square Four. Of 600cc, it was an in-line design, with integral four-speed gear box, electric starting, and shaft final drive. Metal cowling shrouded the cylinder block, and permitted a rear-mounted fan to draw cooling air across the unit.

The straight four was mounted in an Ariel Leader frame, complete with side panels, in such a way that the cylinder block lay on its side, plugs pointing to the left. A detachable sump offered immediate access to the crankshaft and bearings, should that have proved necessary; one prototype was built.

In fact, the bike was a by-product of a scheme hatched out, largely by Ken Whistance, for a lightweight, four-cylinder engine to drive an Army generating plant. Had the plot worked, development and tooling-up charges for the 600cc could have been booked to the military unit, leaving the surplus engines – for motor-cycle use, of course – as a bonus.

The coup very nearly came to pass, too. A couple of prototype portable generators were built and despatched for Army evaluation. They gained official approval and, it seemed, there remained just the contract to be signed. But then the blow fell, the government of the day announcing a massive cut-back in military expenditure. Tooling-up for 600cc production, as a motor-cycle unit only, would have been too costly.

And so the straight-four died and, with it, went Selly Oak's last hope of independent survival.

Brough

Above and left: the Brough Superior SS80, a side-valve model of 1923, which was capable of 80mph and could be purchased for £150

The story of Brough motor cycles is told with the lives of Father William and Son George. Unlike the 'father William' of Lewis Carroll's 'Wonderland', William Edward Brough was born with a brain, and an engineer's brain at that. Born in 1861, Mr Brough Senior arrived in a world where industry was in the middle of a revolution, and he grew up in time to see the birth of motorised transport. Work in the colliery did not occupy William Brough's thoughts 24 hours a day, however, and he started

This Ariel Red Hunter, owned by Norman Webb, was the winner of many Concours competitions

and completed the building of his own motor car in the last decade of the nineteenth century.

By 1899, when the car was ready to be driven on the highways of Britain, Brough's second son George was old enough to appreciate his father's achievement and enjoy the fruits of that labour. The motor car and then the motor tricycle, both built by his father using De Dion engines, no doubt encouraged young George's interest in the construction and development of motor vehicles. George was only twelve years of age when William Brough was able to put his first motor bicycle on the road in 1902, and only sixteen when he partnered his older brother William in the ACC End to End (John O'Groats to Lands End) trial. The word 'trial' was appropriate for George's ordeal as he endeavoured to propel the heavy machine the length of Britain mainly with the aid of what was euphemistically called 'lpa' (light pedal assistance). Brother William was more fortunate in his machine, also naturally a Brough and, whilst George toiled merely to finish, William won a gold medal in the event. Far from dampening George's interest in motor cycles, this experience merely served to harden his resolution and perhaps to make him more critical of the standard of motor cycle being created by his father. It may well have been this experience which sowed the first seeds of doubt in his mind about the quality of the Brough motor cycle. If it was, it did not deter him from going into partnership with his father, although he may have believed he could put all his ideas into their mutual product. The partnership was successful for a while but, as with so many 'father and son' business, problems arose when ideas did not coincide and, by mutual agreement, they parted company. '"You are old Father William", the young man said' and although the words of Lewis Carroll were not used, the sentiment was present.

George Brough had new and ambitious ideas which he wished to see put into production, and he found that this was not possible whilst remaining in partnership with his father. His father, for his part, having made the Brough motor cycle, wanted no confusion as to which marque was which. It would be nice to think that the ready wit of George responded to the paternal insistence that there should be no ambiguity with the declaration that his (George's) new models were to be luxurious, revolutionary and in every way superior to William's product, and that he would therefore use the name Brough 'Superior'. In fact, history, in the tangible and very human form of C. E. (Titch) Allen, discloses that it was a name suggested by a drinking pal of George and that William greeted the proposal, when it reached his ears,

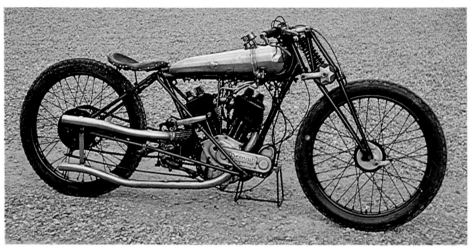

Below: George Brough's 1000cc racing Superior, affectionately known as 'Old Bill' and very successful in sprints and hill-climbs

with less than enthusiasm, commenting that presumably this made his product the 'Brough Inferior'!

The new venture started in 1919, although it would be true to say that preliminary steps had been taken to create the new ideal motor cycle when still at the old firm. George opened premises in Nottingham where he remained until 1935. Whilst William had favoured flat-twin engines, George immediately favoured the V twin and it will be seen that the majority of his models were powered by this arrangement.

One of the earliest announcements was made in the motor-cycle press that Mr George Brough was 'producing a new motor cycle which would not be exhibited at the forthcoming show at Olympia in November/December, 1920'. For the creator of what was to be termed the 'Rolls-Royce of motor cycles', this was obviously a fitting and proper announcement to make; no doubt it saved disappointment on the part of paying customers at the Show who went just to see the Brough Superior. The announcement went on to inform the eager public that machines would be available early in the new year (1921).

The public were indeed eager as, without a price being mentioned, many ordered the new motor cycle and even placed deposits to ensure they received the goods. At this time, there was little competition offered by British manufacturers to the Americans in the big twin-cylinder-machine market for solo riding and, therefore, the Brough Superior was a welcome newcomer. The first Brough Superior, both solo and with sidecar attached, was road tested and reported on 20 January 1921. The tester rode the machine powered by a specially designed 986cc overhead-valve JAP engine with Sturmey Archer three-speed gearbox, Brampton Biflex Forks, Enfield Cush

hub and that, unlike most of its contemporaries, was already fitted with number plates, horn, acetylene lamps and generator. The all-in retail price was £175.

The tester commented that handling was excellent, both solo and with sidecar, that it had a superb top gear performance (solo 8 to 80mph) and that the appearance and finish of the machine was excellent. The 'appearance and finish' of the Brough Superiors were undoubtedly excellent due to the heavy nickel plating, which was incorporated to prevent rust as well

as to enhance the appearance. The oval bulbous plated tank, which was a standard feature of the Brough Superior, also attracted attention and was soon readily identifiable and all but synonomous with the marque.

George Brough managed to exhibit at Olympia in 1921, but for the 'de luxe' motor cycle it was a slightly degrading experience, as the Brough Superior stand was next to the stand of the Economic lightweight: the Rolls-Royce was effectively parked next to the Ford Popular! However, George Brough overcame what might have been an unsavoury environment. The press were able to report that he was starting out offering a super luxurious speedman's overhead-valve big twin and a side-valve version as well; a further addition was offered with the 5/6MAG engine. Saddle tanks were used of course and some models were fitted with Montgomery leaf spring front forks. The price of the side-valve model (the immortal SS80) was £150 for the solo version and £180 when fitted with sidecar.

Even as early as 1922, the Brough Superior was recognised as a special make and referred to as the 'Rolls-Royce of motor cycles'. Rolls-Royce cars have always been justly acclaimed not only for their intrinsic quality, but also for their quiet and smooth performance. It is this latter aspect, also a feature of the Brough Superior, which no doubt encouraged the Rolls-Royce analogy. Brough Superior cut out much of the usual noise created by poppet valves and tappets and, with a good silencing system, created the impression of a quiet giant.

It would be wrong to progress too deeply into the Brough Superior story

Below: the SS80 of 1924 was fitted with a side-valve JAP engine which was pressure lubricated. The machine used internal expanding brakes front and rear, and featured a twist-grip throttle and electric lighting.

Below centre: the Alpine Grand Sports of 1925 was fitted with a 984cc ohv Jap engine

Bottom: this is Noel Pope's Brough Superior powered by an 8/80 JAP engine, at the Bonneville Salt Flats, Utah, 1949. A 150mph crash terminated the occasion, happily without injury to the rider

without mentioning the stalwart back-room figure of Ike Webb. Webb joined George Brough at the outset in 1919, and remained a loyal and able ally throughout the production life of the marque. He was the man for all seasons, the jack of all trades, the works manager tackling all tasks necessary for the preparation of a machine up to the time of sale and, on the occasions when a machine was returned for service or repair, the one who ensured that the work was carried out to the highest standard as decreed for the quality prevailing at this factory. George Brough and Ike Webb (creating on the basis of these designs) made a pretty formidable team. George also rode his own machines to great affect, winning gold medals in the Lands End Trial and other events in the early 1920s and, no doubt, reflecting as he rode on his more arduous and less successful first trial many years before. Together with his skill in trials he had an aptitude for racing, winning his first ever race at Brooklands. Thereafter, he thrashed the opposition off the track in speed trials and hill-climbs winning over fifty events in 1922 and 1923 on George's most successful machine which was fondly nicknamed *Old Bill*, and which still runs well and is maintained in excellent order.

The public were first given an opportunity to purchase the SS80 side-valve model in 1923 for the not inconsiderable price of £150. However, it was capable of 80mph. Apart from the fact that this was an interesting and unusual selling device, it does emphasise that Brough Superior were not interested in mass production or mass sale, but preferred to sell one high-quality, high-speed touring motor cycle rather than ten ordinary cheaper machines. During the year, George suffered an accident which meant that the 1924 models displayed in the 1923 Motor Cycle Show revealed only one new model. There were, of course, refinements on the existing models. The new model had a redesigned frame and a 'four cam' JAP engine fitted as standard with mechanical lubrication; it also featured internal expanding brakes front and rear, twist grip control and electric lighting.

The SS100, with the new design 50° Twin ohv engine, was introduced at the Olympia Show in November 1924, for the 1925 season. This model was considered by many to be the best-looking model ever produced by the firm, excelling even their previous outstanding exhibits. This SS100 tag was accompanied by the guarantee that it had exceeded 100mph on the track. The design was based on the record-braking machine developed at Brooklands by Bert le Vack, and featured a sturdy duplex cradle frame to which were fitted the new 'Castle' forks, similar in principle to the Harley-Davidson design;

its price was £175. The SS100 was accordingly adapted and an alternative was named the Alpine Grand Sports, a really superb-looking mount, but the accent again changed away from the speed feature, towards, dare it be said of the luxury motor cycle, economy. A 750cc side-valve model was prepared for 1927 which was, according to tests, able to average eighty miles to the gallon. However, with petrol at 1/7½d (under eight new pence) a gallon in 1927, the modern motor cyclists may wonder why

it was necessary to feature the economic angle. At this time, the first of the four-cylinder Broughs was introduced at the show, a 1000cc with a side-valve inclined engine. Whilst it served as a 'Show Stopper', though, no more was heard of it, perhaps the price quoted of £250 acted as a deterrent. Mind you, it was an outstanding exhibit, being housed in a handsome glass case! The 'Castle' forks, with their shock absorbing qualities, were designed by George Brough and Harold 'Oily' Karslake, and were fitted to all models, giving good steering and fine road holding.

The overhead 680cc twin-cylinder model was also offered at this show and this was followed a few years later by a veritable baby: a 500cc overhead-valve twin-cylinder bike; it never found favour, however.

In 1932, a machine designed for sidecar use had an 800cc Austin water-cooled four-cylinder engine with the unusual feature of having twin rear wheels and shaft drive. As the gearbox had a reverse gear, being a car unit, it was an unusual sight to see a sidecar outfit on occasion being driven backwards! Even larger and more powerful models were to come in the next couple of years, and another engine manufacturer, Matchless, supplied engines for fitting to some bikes.

As stated earlier, when William Brough died, George returned home to continue manufacture where he had learnt his first lessons in motor-cycle design and construction and where he first had dreams of his ideal machine. It was there, too, that George endeavoured to realise his ambition to create the 'Dream' which had a 997cc flat-four engine in unit with the gearbox, transversely fitted to the frame and, as would be expected, similar to the previous four, shaft drive transmission was employed. A special spring frame had been designed and the superb finish which was associated with this maker, indicated a potential winner, which alas was not to be, despite including all features which George had considered ideal: like most dreams, it did not come true. Shown at Earls Court in 1938, it unfortunately never went into production and indeed production of all Brough Superiors ceased by 1940.

Celebrated riders of Brough Superiors included such racing stars as Bert le Vack, Eric Fernihough and E. C. E. Baragwanath, as well as the redoubtable Freddie Dixon. Many others scored racing successes both solo and with sidecars.

As one would expect in the hands of such experts, Brough held many records for both long and short distances. The maximum-speed record was first held by Brough Superior in 1924, piloted by Bert le Vack at 113mph. In 1929, the same rider recorded 129mph at Arpajon, again a world record, but Henne on a BMW then raised the speed to 134mph in 1936. In an attempt to regain this coveted crown, Eric Fernihough recorded the incredible speed of 175mph one way only in 1937, suffering a mechanical breakdown which prevented a run in the opposite direction, which is necessary for these records. At his second attempt,

Below left: an SS80 de Luxe of 1928 fitted with an attractive Watsonian launch-style sidecar. The engine is a 980cc JAP unit, powerful enough to make this a very pleasing combination

Below: the side-valve, 1096cc, 11/60 Brough Superior of 1933 was usually fitted with a sidecar and could cruise easily at 75 mph and still return an economical 60mpg

he was successful, recording 169.786mph average and, for good measure, he secured the sidecar record at 137.109mph. His final attack a year later caused his death at a venue near Budapest, having achieved over 180mph in one direction, the return resulting in the fatal crash due, it was suggested, to the streamlining which was of such design that lifting was suspected, causing steering to be 'light' with front-wheel lift. An all-time record which is held and cannot be beaten is the Brooklands lap record for both solo and sidecar machines at 124 and 106mph respectively, the rider being Noel Pope.

It should be recorded that two attempts to regain 'The World's' fastest record using Brough Superiors, were attempted after the war, both unsuccessful.

Bob Berry adopted a 'prone' position on the machine, lying flat on the tank with his legs stretched back, to minimise wind resistance; he used Pendile Sands for the attempt.

A more ambitious venture was undertaken by Noel Pope who prepared a fully streamlined machine and installed a much modified 8/80 JAP engine which he took to Bonneville Salt Flats but a crash prevented the attempt fortunately without serious injury to Pope.

A notable enthusiast was Colonel T. E. Lawrence, who was a personal friend of George, and he rode Brough Superiors for over a decade, calling in at the

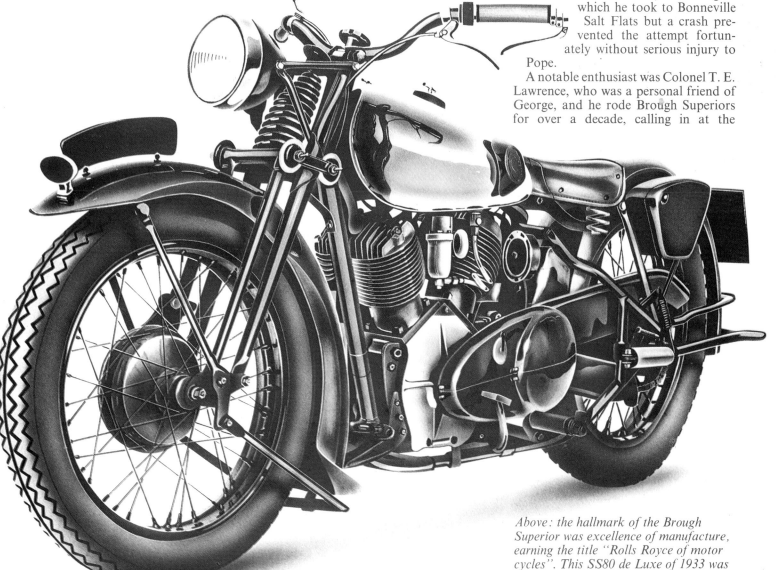

Above: the hallmark of the Brough Superior was excellence of manufacture, earning the title "Rolls Royce of motor cycles". This SS80 de Luxe of 1933 was fitted with a 980cc, four-cam JAP engine

Above: the SS100 of 1939 was one of the last machines the company produced

Left: an SS100 'Pendine' model, guaranteed by the makers to exceed 110mph

Below left: this 1939 SS80 is fitted with a Brough Superior Cruiser sidecar, which would have added some £40 to the purchase price of the machine

Nottingham works whenever he wished to discuss the specification of new machines. He owned several, two of which are known still to be in existence. Lawrence of Arabia was a dedicated motor cyclist and enjoyed his riding to the fullest extent, so it is tragic to record that he met his death whilst astride a Brough.

It is interesting to note some police forces in the 1930s adopted Broughs as their standard patrol machines, which no doubt alarmed wrong doers if they attempted to get away, since it would be unlikely that the culprit would be also mounted on a 100mph machine!

Brough Superior were dreams and rare too: only about three thousand machines were produced to the highest standard in quality set at all times. From 1940, the factory continued as precision engineers, but no more Brough Superiors were made. The remaining machines are jealously cared for by their owners who recognise their worth.

BSA

There is one overwhelming snag to setting up an armaments factory, as the Birmingham Small Arms Company were to find time and time again. Once the shooting stops, so do the government contracts. Forges and lathes stand idle, and the workforce has to be laid off.

To take just one instance: in 1876 the situation was so desperate that BSA sent in a tender to the War Office for 30,000 Martini rifles on a cost-price only basis, at no profit whatever to themselves, just to keep the Small Heath works occupied. When that order was finished, two years later, there was no alternative but to close the factory down completely for over twelve months.

In the beginning, BSA had started as a kind of gun trades union when, in 1854, at the time of the Crimean War, fourteen Birmingham gunsmiths grouped themselves under the banner of the Birmingham Small Arms Trade Association.

It was this body which, in 1861, took the momentous decision to form a public company, with a nominal capital of £50,000 in £25 shares. It would be named the Birmingham Small Arms Company, and its avowed object was 'to make guns by machinery'.

'By machinery', that was the vital clause, because to this point guns had been made individually, with hand-filed mechanisms. Times were changing, however, and the advantage of producing rifles of which the parts would be interchangeable was becoming clearer.

A suitable site was found, on a 25-acre patch adjoining the Great Western Railway at Small Heath, to the east of Birmingham, and there a fortress-like works, in the form of a hollow square, was erected. In part, at least, it was to serve BSA to the very end.

It was the bicycle boom of the late 1880s and 1890s which proved to be the salvation of the firm. Admittedly, a few Otto bicycles and tricycles were built in their entirety at Small Heath during this period, but it was small-time stuff. Meanwhile, the bank was getting restive, the £25 shares were being quoted on the Stock Exchange at not much above £1 each, and the directors were trying (in vain) to sell the under-utilised Small Heath plant to the government.

To a large extent, the remedy was the outcome of a walk through the works by one George Illston, a cycling enthusiast who happened to be a friend of a BSA director. Pausing to look at a special-purpose machine for spinning shell cases, he suggested that it could be adapted for the production of bicycle hubs.

It was a brilliant idea and, from then on, the factory began to produce a steady stream of bicycle components – not only hubs, but frame lugs from the foundries, pedals and chainwheels from the forging

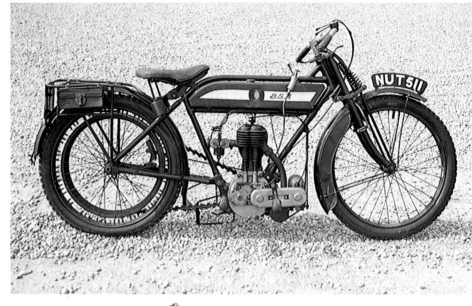

shop, and freewheels and other intricate parts from the workshops that had been making firing mechanisms.

In time, there were frame lugs and fittings for motor cycle use, too, and, from around 1903, machines built up from BSA parts and powered by proprietary engines such as the Belgian-made Minerva, began to be seen on the roads. However, BSA themselves seemed reluctant to go the whole way and it was not until the 1910 season that a genuine BSA motor cycle was seen, designed and constructed entirely at Small Heath, and

Top: a 1913 TT BSA, without the pedals featured on standard models; this machine features belt drive

Centre: a 1925 2.49hp BSA 'Round Tank'

Above: another 1925 BSA; this is an ohv 3.49hp machine

with the green and cream tank colours that were to become so familiar in the decades ahead.

Not that there was anything revolutionary about the new BSA. It was a perfectly straightforward 499cc side-valve single, with direct belt drive to the rear wheel and equipped with auxiliary pedalling gear; its price was £50. However, it was very well made and, for its day, was capable of quite a respectable performance ('By no means a potterer', commented *Motor Cycle*, in a contemporary road test). Anyway, the respectability of the BSA name was guarantee enough for most folk.

Soon, the 499cc model was joined by a 557cc of similar design, and the two models were to remain the backbone of BSA motor cycle production for several years to come. Indeed, one batch was to

because, in order to produce such a vast quantity of material, expansion was necessary, and a big new four-storey workshop was erected alongside Armoury Road. This was known as the '1915 Building' and from it in later years BSA motor cycles by the many thousand were to emerge.

With the declaration of peace came a resumption of motor cycle manufacture, by this time under the control of a new company, BSA Cycles Ltd, subsidiary to the main Birmingham Small Arms firm. The 557cc model was back, now with a gearbox, and offered in a choice of all-chain or chain-cum-belt transmission. The 499cc single, too, was available, but as a 'TT Model' only. That was rather ironic because, although the BSA company had attacked the Senior TT in 1913, entering six bikes, all but one had packed

moved from the world of the sidecar tourist. This was nothing less than an all-out bid for Senior TT honours – by weight of numbers, as in 1913, if needs be. Eventually, the work was to occupy eighteen months and to absorb a reputed £10,000 in development costs. However, the machine, unveiled shortly before practice for the 1921 TT series was due to start, was a BSA like none that had been seen before.

The most obvious departure from previous practice was the choice of an inclined engine housed in a duplex frame, the engine position contributing to a very low and sleek overall appearance. The cylinder itself was well finned, but cylinder-head finning was rather sparse. Valves were disposed vertically, and the rocker arms were not pivoted on conventional spindles, but were held by valve-

find its way to the Western Front in World War I, but that was little more than incidental because, with the return of war conditions, Small Heath was far too occupied with its traditional business to spare much time for motor cycle manufacture.

In the four war-time years, no fewer than a million and a half Lee-Enfield rifles poured out of the plant, together with Lewis guns, folding bicycles for the Army, aircraft components, shells and other assorted items of military hardware. Mention of this is indeed relevant

up in the race (the exception finished seventh); basically, the machines were standard roadsters, some of single-speed design and others with a two-speed rear hub gear.

A further introduction for 1919 was a 770cc vee-twin, with the cylinders disposed at the customary 50°. Essentially, this was a machine for the family sidecar man and, accordingly, BSA offered a matching sidecar made in their own workshops.

Behind the scenes, however, the factory had embarked on a project very far re-

Above: this BSA V-twin combination was manufactured in 1921 and was a perfect choice for the family man

spring pressure against knife edges made from case-hardened tool steel.

In the experimental stage, the very advanced feature of a four-valve, light-alloy cylinder head had been tried out, but this idea was dropped in favour of a more orthodox cast-iron, two-valve head. Nevertheless, a decision was made to use aluminium slipper-type pistons, each carrying a single ring. At the front of the cylinder was a one-into-two exhaust manifold, leading to a pipe at each side of the model.

From the oil tank clipped to the frame saddle tube, two independent oiling systems were served. There was a mechanical pump housed in the timing chest and feeding the cylinder walls but, in addition, the crankcase bearings were supplied by a pedal-operated pump. On the right of his machine, therefore, the rider had two pedals to play with – a conventional pedal for the oil pump, and a heel pedal for the dummy-vee-rim rear brake. A knowledge of how to play the organ must have been an advantage!

Preliminary tests at Brooklands showed that the BSAs had a suitably rapid turn of speed and, with riders of the calibre of Gus Kuhn, Howard Riddell and Tom Simister signed up to ride them, designers Pearsall and Heather must have felt that they were in with a pretty good chance. Yet, so much for high hopes. The race turned out to be an utter disaster and, by the end of the second lap, all six machines stood silent at the roadside. Aluminium, alas, was well called 'trouble metal' at this period, and melted pistons accounted for most of the retirements; on a couple of the others, the case hardening of the knife-edge rockers had broken up.

Tails between their legs, the BSA party returned from the Isle of Man, flung the racers into a dark corner (one has survived, incidentally, and is currently in a Birmingham collection) and swore off road racing for ever.

However, one flop does not make a bankruptcy and, although Birmingham Small Arms as a whole was still living dangerously (in the 21 years between the two wars, they were to pay dividends on only eight occasions), the motor cycle side was going quite nicely. For one thing, they had acquired from Daimler, a brilliant designer by the name of Harold Briggs, and his first offering was a very sporty little 350cc ohv machine with duralumin pushrods, straight rockers and a 75mph potential. By 1925, the engine was turning out 16bhp at 5200rpm.

Moreover, Harry Poole, down at the BSA branch works at Redditch, had come up with a real winner in the shape of a little 250cc side-valve two-speeder. Telegram boys scuttled around city streets on it, and, in long, navy-blue raincoats, gas and water-board officials used it on their rounds; second hand, it was the universal machine for learners. Late in life, minus mudguards and any other

Right: the BSA Sloper of 1928. This 493cc machine was so called because of its distinctive forward-sloping cylinder and was the first BSA to feature a modern-style fuel tank

The BSA company had certainly not done with flops, and yet another happened along in 1928. It was the factory's first essay at building a two-stroke machine, and was a unit-construction 175cc two-speeder in a pin-jointed frame. Perhaps fortunately, it lasted for little more than a single season.

No matter, for by that time BSA had another best-seller on their hands. Again from the drawing board of Harold Briggs (who, tragically, was later to commit suicide following an unlucky love affair) this bike was the 493cc overhead-valve Sloper, which carried its oil in a forward extension of the crankcase. In one form or another, and including a 350cc version and both ohv and side-valve variants, the

Above: a 250cc BSA on the front cover of the 1934 BSA Motor Cycling Annual

Above right: an advertisement in the Motor Cycle magazine of 1930 for the 250cc model, featuring the new handlebar-mounted instrument panel

removable items, it was scrambled into the ground of many a farmer's field by eager schoolboys. In short, it was the Bantam, or Honda 90, of its period – and everybody called it the 'Round Tank'. For three years, the Model B (its catalogue designation) was to remain in production, and in that time 35,000 of them were built.

The Motor Vehicles (Construction and Use) Act insisted that a motor cycle should be equipped with 'two independent brakes', but the act forgot to mention that they should be on two independent wheels. So, BSA fitted the 'Round Tank' with hand and foot brakes, both working on the rear wheel and, although the police brought a test case or two, this was shown to be quite legal.

Anyway, the 'Round Tank' was to adopt a brake on each wheel as time went on. A three-speed gearbox replaced the two-speed job and even the famous cylindrical fuel tank had to give way to a

wedge unit. In the course of time, the little side-valve bike was to evolve into the workaday Model C10.

Before we say goodbye to the 'Round Tank', however, one of its exploits is worth recalling. It happened back in May 1924 when two of them, in company with a couple of the 350cc sports mounts, took part in a mass BSA climb of Snowdon. The riders included Harold Briggs himself, trials ace Harry Perrey, George McLean and sales chief George Savage. McLean's two-fifty, travelling alongside the mountain railway track, made it to the summit in the remarkable time of 30 mins 55 secs.

Sloper was to remain in the BSA catalogue unit well into the 1930s. Reputedly, the handling was a little short of perfect, but nobody worried too much about that. Besides, for the sportier-minded customer, the company were soon able to offer something nice in the form of the Blue Star range. Like the Slopers, these carried their oil in the crankcase, but the engines were disposed vertically. Actually, they were semi-tuned versions of the standard upright-engine BSA roadsters, available in 250, 350 and 500cc varieties, and were derived from the competitions machine on which Bert Perrigo had scored so well. Indeed, Bert was in the happy position of receiving a halfpenny royalty on each Blue Star sold!

At about the same time, a neat little 500cc overhead-valve V-twin machine came into the range (750 and 1000cc models followed) and this was adopted by the British Army and several police forces for official service. The early 1930s were, however, also a time of economic depression and, to meet the demand for a low-cost lightweight, the Model X came on the scene, a very attractive little 150cc overhead-valve machine with a surprisingly manly performance. As late as the 1950s, a few of the lightweights, sleeved to 125cc, were still keeping their tails up in the scrambles world.

After the Blue Stars came the Empire Stars, and the range began to take on a modern image, with foot-change gear-boxes, chromium plated fuel tanks and dry-sump lubrication systems. In passing, however, mention should be made of an eyebrow-raising model which appeared on the BSA stand at the 1933 Olympia Show. The engine was conventional enough, but the transmission included a miniature Daimler fluid flywheel, and the gearbox was a Wilson preselector design. Possibly, it was just a design exercise, or an attention-getter for, although the fluid-flywheel machine was included in the 1934 BSA brochure, it was never put into production.

Back to the Empire Star, though. Previously with Ariel and Triumph, Val Page had joined the Small Heath design staff, and BSA's M-range were from his drawing board (the fact that there was a distinct family likeness between Page-designed BSA models and their counterparts from Ariel and Triumph is beside the point!). One of the new 'M' models was the 500cc side-valve M20, which became the standard sidecar hauler for the AA road patrols, and was soon to achieve even greater immortality in the hands of the British Army.

On 30 June 1937, habitués of Brooklands had a double surprise, because on to the starting grid of a British Motor Cycle Racing Club event came a works-prepared 500cc Empire Star BSA: surprise number one. Surprise number two was the rider, the great Wal Handley, who had retired from road racing just about a season before.

Running on an alcohol mixture, the Handley BSA had little difficulty in disposing of the opposition, winning the race at 102.27mph and putting in a fastest lap at 107.57mph. Now, the BMCRC had the charming custom of awarding a little gold-star lapel badge to any rider who topped 100mph during one of their meetings and, accordingly, Wal Handley was granted his.

The background to the story was that BSA were aiming to introduce a brand new 500cc sports model for 1938 (the Val Page-designed M24) with light-alloy cylinder barrel and head. Ostensibly, this was evolved from the Handley racer – which in fact had a cast-iron head and barrel – and the Brooklands exploit provided the ready made name, Gold Star.

Above left: a group of New Zealand soldiers from the Signals Division receive instruction at Aldershot on the 1940 BSA model, which was used by dispatch riders during World War II

Left: a BSA Empire Star of 1936. The 'Star' nomenclature evolved from star decals stuck on certain Sloper series bikes fitted with special cams and high-compression pistons

War came again and the BSA factory shelved motor cycle manufacture except for the M20. In all, 126,334 M20 side-valve machines were to be supplied to the British and allied armies between 1939 and 1946, but concentration on a single model permitted the factory to diversify into other military needs. Mainly, it was a matter of 'back to gun-making', His-pano, Sten, Browning, and Oerlikon machine guns by the thousand being just part of the output. In addition, Small

Heath supplied ten million shell fuses, 750,000 anti-aircraft shells and, for parachute troops, the inevitable folding bicycle!

However, the works did not come through unscathed and, in one frightful night, a large section of the 1915 building was destroyed by German bombs, killing 53 workers on the night shift. Two nights later, the BSA works were again hit, and this time three-quarters of the original 1863 premises were flattened. In the two raids, BSA had lost 1600 machine tools, which was more than had been destroyed in the entire blitz on Coventry.

Yet that which was lost was replaced in time and BSA carried on. Every war must end at some time and when BSA again faced peace in 1946 it was with a motor-cycle range based largely on the 1939 programme. The M20 was there now in civilian dress, as were the 250s with both side valve and ohv; there, too, was the sturdy 350cc B31. After the initial production batch had left the factory, girder front forks were given the 'heave-ho' and, instead, the fashionable telescopic type of fork was standardised.

All this was predictable and the first post-war surprise, in January of 1946, was the announcement of a new competitions model, based on the B31 and master minded by Bert Perrigo. This was the Model B32, with greater ground clearance than its road-going counterpart, plus a high-level exhaust and chromium-plated mudguards.

The motor cycle press had already noted the application, by BSA, for patents covering a vertical twin, and this was eventually revealed as the 500cc Model A7, the first example of which was put on display at the Paris Show. However, the A7 was not as good as it might have been (for one thing, it suffered from 'running on', or self ignition), and the original model was withdrawn after Bert Hopwood joined the staff, by way of Nortons, where he had designed the Dominator twin. Bert's major contribution was the superlative 650cc Model A10 twin, known and loved by thousands as the Golden Flash and, in turn, the Golden Flash served to generate a new and better 500cc A7, plus a sports 500 listed as the Star Twin.

In what must rank as the most inspired Maudes Trophy attempt of all time, BSA entered three standard Star Twins in the gruelling International Six Days Trial of 1952, held that year in Austria. The machines were selected by an ACU representative from a batch coming off the assembly line and, before the trial, they were given a 1000-mile 'running-in' test, under ACU observation, from

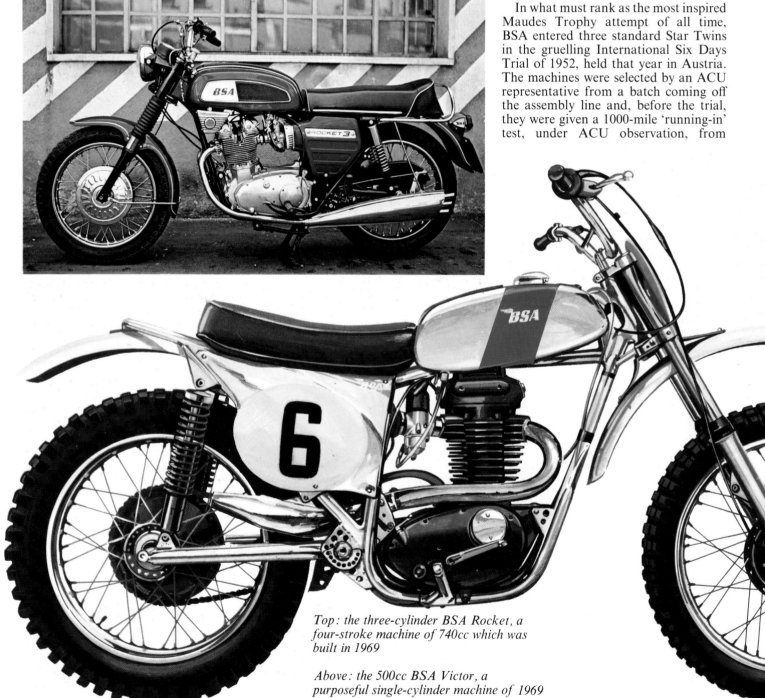

Top: the three-cylinder BSA Rocket, a four-stroke machine of 740cc which was built in 1969

Above: the 500cc BSA Victor, a purposeful single-cylinder machine of 1969

Above: Jeff Smith was the World Champion Motocross rider in 1964/65, riding a 500cc BSA Victor

175cc D14/4, over half a million Bantams were made before the machine was killed off in 1970.

Bantam power units were a product of the Redditch branch factory (where, also, the post-war Sunbeam in-line twins were manufactured), but assembly was carried out at Armoury Road, alongside an ever-growing stream of four-stroke machinery.

'The Most Popular Motor Cycle In The World', declared BSA advertising, and it certainly seemed that way. Thousands went for export to the British Commonwealth, to Europe and to the new and seemingly limitless market of the USA, where the joy of motor cycling had but recently been rediscovered. Indeed, so great did the American trade become, that a subsidiary, BSA Inc, of New Jersey, had to be set up to handle it.

The competitions B32 led to a 500cc version, the B34, and in the hands of men like John Draper, Bill Nicholson, Arthur Lampkin, John Burton and Brian Martin (who was eventually to take over from Bert Perrigo as competitions-shop manager), BSA machines carried all before them in trials and scrambles.

At first in 350cc form only, but later joined by a 500 model, the Gold Star came back, as an even more highly tuned edition of the B32 sportster. The springboard had been the introduction for 1949, of the ACU Clubmans TT, a race over the full Isle of Man course for amateur riders on standard production motor cycles.

Over thirty BSAs entered for the first event, and it was hardly surprising that one of these, ridden by Harold Clarke, gained the new trophy at a race speed of 75.18mph (incidentally, on 73 octane 'pool' petrol and with a compression ratio of only 7.5 to 1).

By September of 1949, the 500cc Gold Star had come on the scene, although its debut was not on a race circuit, but at the International Six Days Trial, held this time in mid Wales. Goldies, one of them included in Britain's Trophy team, collected eleven gold medals.

So far, the Gold Star utilised plunger-type rear springing, but the ISDT was again the platform, in 1950, for the introduction of full swinging-arm rear suspension. Very rapidly, Gold Stars achieved total domination of the Clubmans TT races (in 1955, for example, 33 riders, of the total entry of 37 in the Junior event, were mounted on them). However, in so doing, it sowed the seeds of its own demise. The Goldie was just that little bit *too* good at its job, and the object of production-machine racing – to improve the breed of sporting roadsters in general, not those of one particular make – was defeated.

As the 1960s rolled on, so BSA began to go into decline. The last Gold Star was

Birmingham to Austria by way of Holland, Belgium, France and Switzerland.

The riders were Fred Rist, Norman Vanhouse and Brian Martin, and all three were to obtain ISDT gold medals (plus a team award, because they represented the Birmingham MCC also). After the trial, the test continued, until 4900 miles had been covered, with not a scrap of bother on any of the models.

Another landmark, in 1948, was the production of the first 125cc BSA Bantam two-stroke motor cycle. In truth, the design had a DKW origin, and came to BSA as war reparations, but it was to make a very valuable contribution to BSA output. From the 125cc D1, through the 150cc Bantam Major, to the final

made in 1962, the factory declaring that they were no longer economic to produce. Instead, the competitions department began to develop the little 250cc C15 roadster for trials and scrambles use; successfully, too. It expanded to a three-fifty, to a four-forty and, finally, to the Victor five-hundred. Light and handle-able, it was good enough to bring Jeff Smith two World Motocross Champion-ship titles; but in motocross, as in trials, the day of the four-stroke was fading, and not even the use of an exotic all-titanium frame could restore past glory.

One disaster, it seemed, followed an-other. A venture into the scooter field, with a 250cc twin and a 175cc Bantam-

In an effort to keep afloat, BSA started selling off assets, including the semi-automated assembly line but recently installed in the four-storey 1915 building, and reputed to be the most modern to be found outside Japan. They were still building at least one machine in world-wide demand, the three-cylinder 750cc Rocket Three, but it was not enough.

The sands were now fast running out for BSA. The research and development department at Umberslade Hall closed down. In mid 1973, dealings in BSA shares on the London Stock Exchange were halted. Soon after this, the firm's assets passed into the hands of Dennis Poore's Norton-Villiers group.

based two-stroke machine, was less successful than had been hoped for. The 90cc Dandy step-through was a good idea that had also failed. The 75cc Beagle had far too many teething troubles and then there was the catastrophic 50cc Ariel Three moped tricycle – Ariel by name, but a BSA product. Perhaps the 350cc Fury parallel twin could have staved off the coming end, but it was des-tined never to reach the production line.

Under the new banner of Norton-Villiers-Triumph, the proposal was that production of Triumphs at Meriden and Nortons at Wolverhampton should be transferred to the Small Heath works. That never did come to pass, partly for political reasons and, although motor cycle production did indeed restart at Small Heath, the machines were not BSAs, but Triumph Tridents: the marque was dead, and buried.

Top: one of Mike Hailwood's last major bike races was on a BSA Rocket three-cylinder machine at Daytona in 1971; he is seen here with team-mate Jim Rice

Above: one of the most famous names in the BSA story is Gold Star, a title which first appeared in 1938 and finally died in 1962. This is a 500cc model of 1954, with swinging arm rear suspension

Douglas

Jas Stewart in full flight on his 2¾hp Douglas approaches the bottom of Bray Hill in the 1912 Junior TT Trophy Race at the Isle of Man

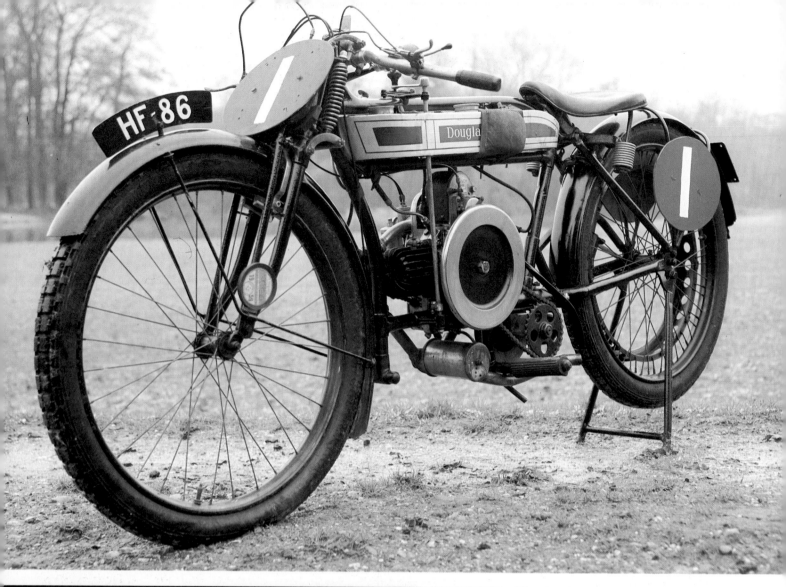

Lots of motor cycles have won TT races, lots of manufacturers dabbled with cars as well as motor cycles (or vice versa), lots of post-war survivors built scooters alongside their traditional motor cycle lines, a few built aero-engines, while several bought Villiers engines in spite of their ability to produce their own units. None of these characteristics alone would enable you to say without risk of error that the company in question must be X. However, if you ask which manufacturer did all of these and more, the field narrows to one: Douglas.

The Douglas companies, over more than fifty years, built cars, tractors, scooters, motor cycles, industrial engines, dirt-track racers, TT winners, industrial trucks, bits of aircraft, complete aero engines (their own, not a 'shadow factory' replica), electric floats, draincovers and even a great big wheel with the driver sitting inside.

Such diversity, and the engineering innovation it implies, would suggest a capacity for survival. With hindsight and a knowledge of the post-war British motor cycle industry they also suggest the ingredients of failure. It is no shame to have failed in the company of the fifty-plus other firms which made motor cycles in Britain after World War II and have

ing operations. The original Douglas interests were in foundry work and the move to light engineering of any kind was a significant step. The Barter design which eventually went into production was a 350cc flat twin, which powered the first ever Douglas, but sales for 1907 and 1908 totalled less than a hundred. 1909 was better and in 1910 the second big design precedent paid off. The machine had previously been single speed, belt driven. The 1910 model had a two speed gearbox, which *Ixion* compared to the back gear of a lathe. Customers and dealers responded, in spite of the defects of the rest of the machine, which was prone to inlet pipe icing, poor distribution of mixture between the two distant cylinders, unique belt slip, wet front plug and poor top-end performance, ascribed with good reason to the retention of automatic inlet valves (this did not stop Eli Clark taking the End to End record in a still remarkable 39hrs 40mins on one of the single geared machines in July 1910).

1911 was the first year the TT Mountain Circuit was used, and two of the four Douglas entries finished, in seventh and twelfth places, while the Six Days Trial team tied for the Team Prize. A bigger prototype twin was announced with a capacity of over 600cc and the basic model at last acquired mechanically operated inlet valves. There were further tuning experiments and, as the 1912 TT races drew near, a four-speed prototype emerged. There were six Douglas riders, five on two-speed machines, and three of these five took first, second and fourth places in the wet Junior. Harry Bashall won at 39.65mph and Teddy Kickham, who finished second, achieved fastest lap at 41.76mph. 1913 gave the company second place again in the Junior and saw an experimental ohv 350 racing model later in the year followed by a 500cc road machine and the latter permitted two Senior TT entries in 1914; neither finished, however.

The new three-speed gearbox which was undergoing tests gave Douglas the Six Days Trial Team Prize, with the basic 350cc ($2\frac{3}{4}$hp) models. All this competition success and the general ease of handling and relative reliability of the standard machines were instrumental in getting Douglas a war-time contract for

now stopped doing so; Douglas, however, did better. The reason we have to say 'Douglas companies' is that there were five companies from 1907 to 1957, plus the Barter company from which the original engine design sprang. Some, although not all, of these corporate changes were the result of commercial failures.

TT success, world records, Ministry contracts and press affection do not guarantee survival. Douglas had all of these but, like so many motor and motor cycle companies, it may have been blessed from time to time with managements whose affection for motor cycling and the product exceeded and overshadowed their business abilities.

In spite of the failures, Douglas bikes had considerable success and made a large contribution to the history of motor cycling, and they were known for their almost unfailing adherence to the flat-twin configuration and their Bristol roots. It is ironic that the flat twin which

to so many enthusiasts is the one hallmark of Douglas was actually inherited from Barter. The early history is slightly patchy but there is ample evidence that J. J. Barter produced between 1902 and 1904 a singularly unusual single-cylinder motor cycle which, with the final drive taken from the camshaft, failed to attract popular support; few were sold and Barter turned his attention to a new engine design. The result was a horizontally opposed twin which he called the *Fée* (French for Fairy), and Light Motors Ltd was formed in 1905 to take over the design. The name was soon changed to Fairy and the first production engine was of 200cc. It was largely an assembly job, with some components being bought in from the nearby Douglas Foundry. Before the company failed in 1907, they had also produced a 300cc twin and a prototype of over 800cc.

When Light Motors failed, Barter joined Douglas Bros of Kingswood to establish their motor cycle manufactur-

Opposite page top: a 350cc Douglas twin of 1914, from John Griffiths Collection at Stanford Hall

Opposite page bottom: despondent J.T. Bashell astride his Douglas, having come to grief at Ballacraine Corner, 1913 TT

Above: the front hall of the 500cc flat-twin 1928 speedway engine, again from Stanford Hall

WD machines, of which around 25,000 were made, including the new (600cc) 4hp model intended for sidecar use. These two existed largely on reconditioned ex-WD machines. All of these were side valve, of course, and development work started on new ohv designs which led to racing machines for 1920 and road models for 1921. The 1920 and 1921 TT results were uninspiring but the pre-war models still held over a dozen British and World records, and Tudor Thompson added eighteen more in 1920–21. By the end of 1922, five Douglas riders held over 100mph and Cyril Pullin had been timed on a 500 at over 'the ton' at Brooklands.

Mechanically, the new designs were becoming more modern. With a shorter wheelbase, low engine position, gearbox near the rear cylinder, low overall weight, overhead valves, twin lower frame tubes forming an engine cradle and all-chain

drive, the relatively light machines had considerable potential. They gained a seventh place in the 1922 Senior TT and, by this time, Pullin, Freddie Dixon and Rex Judd were all taking an interest in Douglas.

The model range now included a 500ohv, 733ohv, 350sv (the old WD model, with two speeds and no clutch) and 595sv. At the beginning of the last decade under the old management, the signs were rosy, apart from the size of the model range. There is some possibility that the availability of the foundry tempted them into a multiplicity of models which a firm buying-in its major engine components would have avoided. Nevertheless, it was a fabulous decade: racing and design triumphs, royal patronage and brilliant men all added lustre to the 1921–31 period.

A look at the design changes in the

1920s is instructive. Expediency dictated the addition of chain final drive to the obsolescent WD model, plus three-speed gearbox, clutch and kick starter. On the racing front, the RA model (named after its Research Association brakes) was being developed in 346, 494 and 596cc derivatives. Tom Sheard won the 1923 Senior on an RA in foul weather, and Freddie Dixon collected the Sidecar TT with the infamous banking sidecar.

Above: S. L. Bailey loses control of his 2¾hp Douglas, negotiating Hairpin Corner in the Senior TT at the Isle of Man, 1912

Right: all in a day's work, a policeman, assisted by young boy, moves Douglas to clear a way for traffic in the 1913 TT

Far right: a 1925 CW 348cc of 2¾hp

The production RA models (346 and 596cc) were introduced at the 1923 Show and a detuned racing model 500cc RA/25 appeared at the 1924 Show but sold poorly. Cyril Pullin was by now working on the new EW series with a completely new engine design and numerous detail improvements. The 348cc side-valve prototypes performed well, one of them clocking 72mph at Brooklands in touring trim. Len Parker won the 1925 Sidecar race, with a non-banking sidecar, locked rigid by choice, before the production EW models appeared at the Show. Still very light, at under 200lb for road tax reasons, it had reliability problems, just as today's fatuous tax regulations force Reliant to build flimsy three wheelers when commonsense would suggest an extra wheel and some extra pounds.

Ironically, the EW's success in 'Reliability Trials' helped to offset the poor image being earned on the road, while the works gradually sorted out the problems. Nothing dramatic happened in 1926 except the first successes in dirt-track racing 'down under' and the 1927 models at the Show, including two 600cc EW variants and three 350cc bikes, plus a prototype supercharged 350cc which went no further. The EW series continued to improve and the 1928 models included a new 350cc ohv Sports model, derived from but not too close to the EW.

By 1929, Freddie Dixon had developed the S5 and S6 models with an impressive range of new ideas or new applications, including dry-sump lubrication. 1930 also brought a new Dixon-influenced model, the 350cc A31.

Looking back, apart from the racing and dirt-track machines, Douglas had seven distinct model ranges during the 1921–31 period. Even if we allow for the fact that model changes in the motor cycle field were cheaper and simpler then, we are still talking about seven

engines with a multiplicity of capacity permutations. By the end of 1931, yet another range, the ohv K32 and M32, appeared and the Douglas interests gave way to outside investors. Douglas Motors (1932) Ltd came into being and also in that year Cyril Pullin rejoined. The year marked the quarter of a century of Douglas motor cycles, the withdrawal of Willie Douglas, the last (Pullin/Atkins-designed) Senior TT model for a long time and developing sales problems; within a year, the company had folded again. With hindsight, it is possible to suggest that the family might have done better to stick to foundry work, but people are not made that way.

Very tidily, Douglas as a motor cycle manufacturer lasted another twenty five years, but the second half had neither the successes nor the stature of the first.

The 1933 models included a design step that has tempted many British manufacturers from time to time, a lightweight with a Villiers engine. This example of motor cycle 'Meccano' also had an Albion three-speed box, steel side panels and leg shields. The other venture on the drawing board (and only on the drawing board) was a 250cc transverse twin. By late 1933, old William Douglas had dragged William Douglas (Bristol) Ltd, phoenix-like from the ashes of the 1932 company. Remarkably, the new company continued the two-stroke. Less remarkably, they dropped the unreliable 150cc Villiers in favour of a new Douglas design. The Show range, with a 250sv, 350sv, 500sv, 600sv, 750sv, 500ohv, 600ohv and even the Army 350sv on display, may have looked superb but sales were slow. 1934 brought a new

500cc sv with alloy barrels, alloy head and cast-iron liners, the valve seats being in a unique iron fillet interposed between head and barrel. It sounds something of an engineering nightmare but it worked. This model was called the 5Y2 or Blue Chief. The revived company was by now facing further writing on the wall but yet another new model appeared, following detail improvements on the older ranges, using the iron/alloy engine transversely across the frame with shaft drive, and it is believed that the transmission was partially Morris! There were numerous new design features scattered around the machine and it sold for the then massive price of £72.10s. Like all ideal machines, it spelt the death knell of the company, sold probably less than a hundred units and received public interest but no sympathy. The latest company collapsed and the Douglas family seemed to be out of motor cycles again. The motoring and aero pioneer Gordon England controlled the British Aircraft Company, which promptly bought the remains and let Pride and Clarke dispose of everything in stock and everything that could be assembled from the remnants.

Although it is impossible to say accurately what is in any businessman's mind when he makes an acquisition decision it seems likely that BAC wanted the assets and labour force to manufacture other things, like aero engines. Perhaps the war did not come soon enough, perhaps the contracts they anticipated did not materialise. Whatever the reasons, the Bristol Meccano line was at it again in 1937, under the new company 'Aero Engines Ltd'. The side-valve 350, 500 and 600 models were revived and late in 1937 another 150cc two-stroke single appeared, with an improved 600cc engine; William Douglas and his son John both died before this.

Once again, a war boosted the Douglas sales revenue and the site was fully active again, producing bits of aircraft, light industrial trucks, generators, industrial engines and components for other products. Some motor cycle manufacturers at this stage would have given up the ghost and, come to think of it, several did. However, in spite of the new name, changed management and troubles of war, a certain amount of illicit thought had been going on at Hanham Road and in late 1945 a really revolutionary transverse 350cc twin was announced. In design terms, it stands comparison with things produced in the fifties and sixties. True to form, the company changed its spots again and, in early 1946 Douglas (Kingswood) Ltd became the new name.

The new machine was to run through the last decade of Douglas with some distinction and its design was a credit to the company at a time when some competitors were making do with WD or pre-war designs. Douglas had dabbled with spring frames before, without much success, but this time they got it right. Rear suspension was by torsion bar, carried inside the lower frame tubes, while front suspension was also by torsion bar, with the bars inside the front fork tubes. The front wheel was free to move up and down within a fairly short travel on leading links whose vertical movements were translated, via bell crank, into a circular rotation of the torsion bars. The war-time industrial engines, for generators, preceded and inspired the new 'square' transverse engine which, unlike the Endeavour, reverted to chain final drive, although the primary drive was able to go, car fashion, from crank to clutch to mainshaft. The whole machine was known as the T35.

Space prevents mention of all the design exercises and prototypes that did not reach production over the years but one other post-war design (which went to prototype stage) deserves mention before we follow the 350 to its fame and fate. This was a rigid transverse 600sv twin built with Government contracts in mind. Light weight (under 3cwt), a

Right: a close-up side view of the intriguing banana-styled 350cc engine of the 1954 Douglas Dragonfly

Above: the unusual shaft-drive configuration of the 1934 Douglas Endeavour. The Endeavour featured a 494cc side-valve engine

big tractable engine and sensible gearing gave a low maximum speed (around 70mph) but a superb fuel consumption, at around 90mpg overall. The figure is worth comparing with many later big twins which fail to achieve this even on today's better petrols; this was the DV60.

It is ironic to note that the Mk III Sports model which was evolved from the T35 had a maximum speed somewhat under 80mph, but was still the fastest available production 350 machine on the UK market. Compare this with the genuine 72mph achieved at Brooklands in 1925 by the EW 350sv prototype. All through the Douglas story we are reminded of the massive changes which took place in motor cycling in short periods and the relative stagnation over one or more decades which followed each great leap forward. This is a convenient point to observe that, although the wars taught us a certain amount about making motor cycles more reliable, their irrelevance as fighting machines relegated engine and suspension development to the post war period. Aero engines, guns, airframes and fighting vessels get accelerated development in wartime, but bikes do not. In consequence, the major developments in motor cycling came in the early 1920s, consolidated from 1928 to 1939 and in the 1950s (in the UK) before England fell by the wayside.

Douglas, by the way, did not get into the fifties without a spot of bother. A receiver was appointed in late 1948, and the company freewheeled into the second half of the twentieth century still under his hand. Yet another company, Douglas (Sales and Service) Ltd was formed to do the things that the receiver was by law inhibited from doing – like exhibiting at the Motor cycle Show. To its credit, that latest name still exists, having survived longer than any since the original firm at the foundry.

There was less than a decade to go for the real motor cycle side, but interesting things were still happening. The concentration on one basic engine and machine makes it easier to chronicle the closing years than it was to review the multimodel chaos of the between-war periods. There were of course derivatives of the basic road machine. The 80 Plus of 1949 and beyond, together with its faster kin the 90 Plus, looked good at the '49 Show, as did the new Vespa. The 90 Plus pushed out a healthy 28bhp and was backed by a rigid framed competition model which did moderately well in subsequent Trials events. The Silverstone 'Junior Clubman's' event was more memorable as

Douglas won for the first time in many years on a race track. In much the same manner that earlier Douglases had woffled round the Island, while faster machines were falling apart or falling over, a Douglas allegedly capable of 10,000rpm and ridden by D. Chapman was first. The 90 Plus entrants were somewhere behind this Mk III model, as were the ohc Nortons, Gold Stars and ohc Velocettes. Later results altered this order of priority and, although the 'Plus' models were catalogued for some years, they never again achieved victory in anything noteworthy. Fourth place in the 1950 Junior Clubman's TT was the next best.

Improvements on the theme kept Douglas sensible until the 1952 announcement of a 500cc prototype. Freddie Dixon's improvements to the racing models were significant but failed to keep pace with the more sophisticated opposition. The prototype failed to reach production but partially inspired the 1954 introduction of the Dragonfly. Dragonflys were quite common around suburban streets and its engine was not all that different from the earlier post-war designs but the rest of it was much changed. The rear was swinging forks and combined spring/damper units. At the front, Reynolds-Earles forks with similar units on long leading links were employed. The weight went up again to over 365lb and the result was a machine no faster than the Mk V it replaced

(slower in some tests) which, at just over 70mph maximum, reminds us yet again of the successful formula of the early light, simple EW side valve. During this period, the manufacture of Vespa scooters, first UK produced in early 1951, was taking precedence. Two years later, Westinghouse bought up the shares and, in 1957, manufacture of Vespas and Douglas motor cycles ceased. Once again, Pride and Clarke picked the bones and were able to dispose of the remaining motor cycle stocks, although the assembly of KD Vespas continued. Big business had struck again.

Douglas had three great phases: the early light TT winners that gave them their primitive successes and World War I production; the second phase in which volume sales of basic 350cc side-valvers and some RA ohv models, plus the dirt-track machines, supported all the racing, oddball models and comic design exercises; and the third post-war phase in which they had a machine which was unusual enough and right enough to survive the troubles of the rest of the industry. Perhaps if the post-war world had found motor cycles more acceptable socially or morally, the Princes of today would have followed Prince Albert and his brother Prince Henry on Douglases rather than in cars. Perhaps, perhaps and, yet again, perhaps. . . .

a 1951 example of the Douglas 90+, a 350cc racing machine

Excelsior

Of all the would be significant 'clever' names coined for motor cycles, for example, Triumph, Ambassador, Panther, Sunbeam and Ariel, Excelsior must be the best and, at the same time, quite the worst! *Excelsior* – 'loftier; more elevated; higher . . . to exceed or go beyond; to surpass'. That is fine, but what motor cyclist, more typically the 'man in the street' than any mere pedestrian, is going to muse on Latin derivations and applaud the wit and sophisticated judgment of a factory in faraway Birmingham? If he does pause to think of the matter, it may in some circumstances give him little comfort, and indeed bring him to the edge of madness. Who, for instance, alive to the claims implicit in a title like Triumph or Excelsior would be immune to an aggravated frenzy while struggling on a cold, wet night to repair a punctured wheel rendered almost immovable by inept or 'could-not-care-less' design? It would be better in such a situation to be dealing with bland AJS or plain and straightforward Cotton. In fact, the 'clever' name very soon becomes just another name, no better, no worse than the eponymous Cotton or Honda or Norton.

Below: trendy young ladies on motor cycles, it seems, are not such a modern innovation as may have been imagined. This intrepid female liberationist is demonstrating the attractions of a 1921 Excelsior, complete with acetylene lamps at front and rear

Still, after saying that, one can appreciate the pleasure it must have given Messrs Bayliss, Thomas and Slaughter when they – or perhaps it was some outsider, a lad with literary leanings working a lathe in B, T and S's bicycle works in Coventry – came up with 'Excelsior' as the name for their latest machine. R. R. Holliday, who years ago wrote in the weekly *Motor Cycling* about the early days of the firm, imagined the conference to find a title . . .

'The Pinnacle of Perfection', suggests Bayliss, stressing the second word.

'The Summit of Achievement', counters Thomas, doing likewise.

'Ex-cel-sior!' carols the lyrical Slaughter.

What is certain is that the 'Excelsior' trademark, incorporating a mountaineer waving a banner, after Longfellow, was used on the bicycles produced at the Bayliss, Thomas factory in 1874. Bayliss, Thomas and Co – the two principals had earlier worked in the same motor firm in Coventry – continued to turn out bicycles in the 1870s and '80s and were almost certainly the first English firm to do so on any scale. In the 1890s, the new motoring enthusiasm began to percolate into England from the Continent, from France mainly, and in 1896 a 1¼hp Minerva engine (single-cylinder, air-cooled) was brought over from Belgium and fitted into a Bayliss, Thomas bicycle. Minerva engines, with the French De Dion and Werner, were to come into England in ever-increasing numbers over the next decade, to be fitted into a bewildering variety of frames marketed under names once familiar in the motor cycle industry but long since defunct. To Excelsior, however, goes the credit for selling the first motor cycle in Britain.

The Minerva had a surface carburettor and hot-tube ignition and drive to the rear wheel by twisted rawhide belt, with most of the control levers mounted on the petrol tank. There was nothing very distinguished about the Bayliss-Thomas-Minerva, but it was marketed in a more enterprising way than most of its contemporaries. The directors of the company were quick to catch on to the publicity value of advertising, of 'stunts' and sporting successes.

In the same year (1896) the first Excelsior motor bicycle was built, and was shown at the Crystal Palace exhibition, with free rides for all who conquered their fears of the noisy and shaky device; this was the beginning of regular appearances at the annual Crystal Palace Motor Show. In 1902, the Excelsior was advertised with MMC engines (derived from the De Dion) in two main forms – standard, with 24in frame and 28in wheels, and as a Cob, 'suitable for riders of short stature', when the wheels were down to 24in. The improvements listed in 1902 were numerous and none too easy to comprehend . . . such as the anti-vibratory socket, the automatic oil lubricator, the patent rim pulley attachment and the exhaust-valve lift. This last item replaced the once general Continental compression tap and was a far simpler way of stopping the engine (and of reducing the compression, when pedalling the machine to start the engine). Advertisements for the company at the Motor Show always stressed 'Free trials on application to our stand'.

Ixion, one of the most influential columnists of the day and for long afterwards in the motor-cycling weekly *The Motor Cycle*, chose an MMC-engined Bayliss-Thomas-Excelsior for his personal transport and wrote of his ownership with infectious enthusiasm. 'Ixion' was the pen name of a clergyman and with hindsight (for few readers would have been aware of his identity) we should, no doubt, take his writings as models of veracity untainted by any hint of commercialism. However, the possibly unworthy thought occurs that the shrewd directors of B, T and Co might have seen the benefits to be gained from making one of their products available to a gentleman of the press on advantageous terms. The practice is not uncommon these days; it would be ingenuous to think it did not occur seventy years ago.

Then, there were the sporting activities, mainly conducted by one Harry Martin at the principal tracks in the country. There is a picture of him in the Holliday article, at speed on the Canning Town track, one hand dropped to juggle with the air lever of the surface carburettor. No doubt it was Martin's complants, among others, about this crude device, which needed frequent handling to balance the ever fluctuating petrol/air mixture, that helped to introduce the spray carburettor, recognisably the modern instrument, to the English motor cycle.

In 1903, Harry Martin, who was with Excelsior more than a half century later (although not at that later date as a sporting rider) was the first motor cyclist to break the mile-a-minute barrier, covering the distance at the Dublin Phoenix Park speed trials in 59.8 seconds.

So, Excelsior progressed, and the Bayliss, Thomas part of the title was dropped in 1910 when the company became the Excelsior Motor Co, Ltd, although for many years after that 'Bayliss, Thomas' was used when there could be confusion with the American Excelsior marque. On the Continent, in fact, the English Excelsior was known almost invariably as a Bayliss, Thomas, even into the 1930s.

Engines were developed and, at Excelsiors, to a prodigious size. In 1914, the firm was using MMC engines of 4½hp

Above: J. S. Worters seated on a 246cc Excelsior JAP in front of the Vickers sheds at Brooklands during the 1926 BMCRC Cup meeting. He won the 250 scratch race at an average speed of 74.89mph

(650cc) and even 5.6hp (850cc), in single-cylinder form, with the cylinders as tall as the front-down tube of the frame. This was at a time when other makers going in for big engines were devoted to the V-twin; Excelsior's involvement with the V-twin appears to have been limited to a Blackburne model, in 1916. A footnote to the history of the mammoth singles: two of them were salvaged from the cellars of the Birmingham works in the 1950s for an appearance in the annual Brighton Run and were later sold to Vintage Motor Cycle Club stalwart Tony Twycross who lovingly restored them to original condition and regularly rides them on VMCC occasions.

A year or so after World War I, Bayliss, Thomas sold their Excelsior business to R. Walker and Sons of Birmingham. The Walkers (Reginald the father, who died in 1950, and his son Eric) made marine instruments but had a good reputation for their motor cycle components which they supplied to many of the midlands firms. When they took over Excelsior the decision was made to move from Coventry to Birmingham – to Tyseley where the firm was to remain until its dissolution as a motor cycle manufacturer more than forty years later. R. R. Holliday records that the Bayliss, Thomas motor car of the early 1920s was the design of Eric Walker and named thus, rather than Excelsior, presumably to avoid confusion with the two-wheelers.

The new directors believed in the value of racing, both to improve the breed and as a means of bringing the product to the notice of the buying public. From 1923, they regularly supported the Isle of Man TT races, in the 250 (Lightweight) and 350 (Junior) categories, using engines of JAP and Blackburne manufacture. The peak in those early days was Crabtree's 1929 Lightweight win at a record speed of 63.87mph on a JAP-engined model. Quick to exploit the commercial advantages of this outstanding performance, the Walkers rushed out a TT Replica of the Crabtree machine, the legendary B14, with a price tag of £78 (for reference, the ordinary Excelsior 250 of that year was priced at £40).

The 250 Excelsior in the 1920s, in whatever form, was part of a comprehensive range from 100 to 1000cc. As the years went by, the money supply tightened, unemployment soared, and the phenomenon known as The Depression gripped the western world. Many motor cycle firms crashed – although not so much 'crashing' as limping quietly into oblivion – and Excelsior, too, was at risk for much of the early 1930s. Their response to their potential customers' shortage of money was to concentrate on small bikes, two-strokes mainly, with engines from the Villiers firm, to cut costs, and retail prices. At one time in the

Above: Excelsior were staunch supporters of the Isle of Man TT races and scored many successes on the island. Syd Gleave is seen here on his way to victory in the 1933 Lightweight race. His average speed was 71.59mph

1930s, they sold what was almost certainly the cheapest motor cycle on the market – a lightweight – at under £20.

Excelsior did not withdraw from racing, which was to be the stock response of British motor cycle firms suffering similar privations thirty years on, but, instead, they actually spent money on a new design for the factory racers. Obviously, the management reasons 'if we and all our competitors have access to virtually identical engines from JAP and Blackburne it is going to be a matter of luck, and perhaps who has the best rider, getting another TT win'. They conferred with Blackburnes, and the result was the aptly named Mechanical Marvel Excelsior, with four radial valves actuated by pairs of pushrods. It was a hopelessly complicated design, and so costly that only half a dozen were built, but, in 1933, it proved unbeatable, with Walter Handley leading in the Lightweight race on one of the models, and then having to let Syd Gleave on another 'MM' pass to win. Handley later retired, but it was a remarkable debut for the new design. Unlike 1929, however, there was no prospect of the Walkers cashing in on their TT success by marketing a production version of the Mechanical Marvel. It would have been too expensive – to make or sell – too difficult for a private owner to maintain in tune and it was doubtful, in any case, whether it would have been particularly

successful in production form or anything but a headache to the firm. Something simpler was needed and it made its appearance in the 1935 TT. The 250cc Manxman, a single-cylinder design with two valves and an overhead camshaft driven from a vertical shaft, inordinately massive crankshaft assembly and a pleasing, purposeful appearance in the ohc Velocette/Norton idiom, never won a TT race but gave a great many riders thousands of trouble-free racing miles. It was sold up to the outbreak of World War II and in its later years was available in 350 and 500cc form, although never in those capacities achieving the success it enjoyed as a 250.

In 1936, the Manxman appeared, in very limited numbers, as a four-valver. Motor cycle historian C. E. 'Titch' Allen has written of how H. G. Tyrell-Smith, lately recruited to Excelsior from the rival Rudge concern, early in that year had to go to Blackburnes at Bookham to pick up castings and jigs for the four-valve engine. Blackburnes were not free to continue with manufacture of the engine, and Tyrell-Smith had to organise production in a hurry elsewhere, at Beans Industries. The first four-valver was not ready for the Isle of Man TT until partway through the practice period, and then suffered from severe handling problems which, when cured, at least temporarily, allowed him to chase Bob Foster (the Lightweight TT winner on a New Imperial) home to a respectable second place. The four-valve Manxman notched up impressive performances in the 1936 race season, at home and on the Continent and, in 1937, finished second in the Lightweight (when the rider was S. 'Ginger' Wood). In 1938, it was again

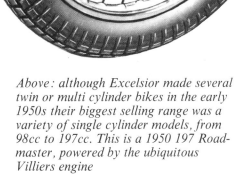

Above: although Excelsior made several twin or multi cylinder bikes in the early 1950s their biggest selling range was a variety of single cylinder models, from 98cc to 197cc. This is a 1950 197 Roadmaster, powered by the ubiquitous Villiers engine

Below: a racing Excelsior Manxman; this is a 249cc machine built in 1937, it has a single cylinder engine with bore and stroke of 67mm × 70.65mm. The engine used four valves operated by a single overhead camshaft and it breathed through two remote needle Amal type carburettors

second, with Wood, and in 1939 third (Tyrrell-Smith), being outpaced by the State-sponsored German DKW and the Benelli from Italy. In the Isle of Man 'amateur' races, the September Manx Grands Prix, the Manxman was a several times Lightweight class winner in the hands of Denis Parkinson. All in all, the Manxman of the middle and late 1930s was the most successful 250 racer produced at home or abroad, and brought further fame and some fortune to Excelsior.

After experimenting with a few off-beat models in the early 1930s – at one stage there was a 250 water-cooled two-stroke on the books – Excelsior settled down to a sensible, middle-of-the-road programme that was about par for a small to medium-size firm with racing pretensions. By 1937, the range of models comprised 125 Universal and Pioneer two-strokes, a 250 Villiers-powered machine, the Manxman in various sizes and the 250 Norseman and 350 Warrior, unremarkable

pushrod ohv singles with some fleeting, probably intended, resemblance to the overhead-camshaft models. Although publicity material never suggested that the engines were other than Excelsior-conceived and built, there seems little doubt that the ohv engines were Blackburne design creations. To round off the list there was the 98cc Excelsior-engined autocycle – a sedate heavyweight bicycle with pedals and engine at the bottom bracket. It was the moped of the late 1930s and early post-war years, intended to perform a similar service for undemanding owners and usually built to rock-bottom specification to permit the lowest possible selling price. The Excelsior autocycle was advertised at nineteen guineas and known as the Auto-byk, an interesting variation in accepted spelling which was to reappear after the war when the autocycle's engine was listed as the Spryt.

During the war, Excelsior produced the Welbike (had the 'y' for 'i' enthusiast been called to fight for home and country?) which was a tiny wheeled scooter that could be folded up for use by troops in parachute drops; it was resurrected after the war as the Brockhouse Corgi, by which time it had put on weight, enough to promote hernia trouble in any but the strongest owner, and was clearly impracticable for mundane civilian usage.

In 1946, the Excelsior programme consisted of the faithful Auto-byk, selling at £32 15s, and the £49 125 Universal. The latter had an ingenious through-the-tank gear shift that offered no conceivable advantage, except novelty value, over the then common foot change or beside-the-tank hand change, and a 'rattle-proof rear mudguard'. Shortly afterwards, a Super Auto-byk, a two-speeder, was announced.

There were plans to re-introduce the Manxman in a revised form as a 250 with the camshaft operated by a chain enclosed within the cylinder and head castings. However, there were lubrication problems, the Manxman did not appear, and no four-stroke Excelsior of any sort was made after the war.

In 1949, in the early post-war period when most of the (few) innovations made by the complacent British motor cycle industry were to be introduced, to tempt the world-wide market that was then Britain's for the asking, Excelsior came out with a 250cc twin-cylinder two-stroke, the Talisman, and advertised it as a unique engine giving undreamed of smoothness and efficiency. In fact, it was not at all bad, with good initial acceleration and reasonable fuel consumption, although top speed at 60mph was far from awesome. It had certain snags, however. Its bolted-up crank could become a little out of joint, with the result that the two pistons would lose their calculated differences and the one-time 250 Talisman owner would be saddled with an under-powered 125. At Excelsior, they were undismayed by reports from owners and pressed on with bigger, not necessarily better, things like the 328cc twin (achieved by opening the 250's bores from 50 to 58mm, while keeping to a 62mm stroke) which produced 18bhp at 5000rpm. This compared with the 250's 12 at similar revs and was found, although the fact was not acknowledged by the makers, to perform rather better in Berkeley three-wheelers

than in the Excelsior S8 motor cycle. It is probable, however, that this was more the result of differing ignition systems (Siba Dynastart for the Berkeley, Wico-Pacy on the two-wheeler) than any mysterious, inherent advantage that might be associated with three wheels. As this multi-cylinder operation of Excelsior is being dealt with, it is convenient to round off the matter by mentioning the 500cc three-cylinder two-stroke introduced at Tyseley around 1962, which was intended for the four-wheeler Berkeley and had a short, reasonably successful life, to 1964.

Twins and threes notwithstanding, the bed rock of Excelsior's programme was the ride-to-work single – the 98cc Consort – with two-speed foot change, primitive front springing (first simple girders, later telescopic) and rigid, or plunger-sprung, rear end. Its tyres were 2.25in section, its brakes a shade under 5in, and it consistently outsold any of the other models (the 125, the 150 or the 197) in the range. Its popularity survived even the introduction of a similar-engined model shrouded in reverbatory panelling (costing an extra £4) and labelled by the Excelsior wordsmith as the Skutabyke.

In 1955, the ageing Eric Walker was still managing director; his two sons, although involved in the business, were not enthusiastic. A slackness in direction and in day to day running was beginning to show. Eric Walker died in the late 1950s, his sons took over and it was soon apparent that the motor cycle side of the business was to be allowed to run down. Any suggestions from the staff to improve the product were disregarded.

Marine engines in air- and water-cooled form, based on the Talisman, were introduced and sold in moderate numbers. Walker Accessories, a factoring side of the family business, was supported with more drive, and there was a good reception for an Excelsior-designed small truck designed for use on the factory floor.

As the 1960s began, a flicker of interest in two-wheelers revived with the then current trend towards scooters, and the 147cc Excelsior Monarch scooter took a bow. However, it was too big, too heavy and too late (like all the British-made scooters of the time) and it had no hope of competing with the all-conquering Vespa and Lambretta, or even with the relatively few, but highly developed, models from Germany.

By 1964, there were only two models listed, the 98 Consort and the 150 Universal, in kit or finished form. The firm, too, was finished. The Walkers, their problems exacerbated by the ailing Berkeley concern which was failing to meet the bills for considerable numbers of Talisman engines ordered and delivered, sold out to Britax, the car-accessory firm. Now the Tyseley works, birthplace of TT winners, turns out seat belts. Excelsior, however, returned as a name in 1977, when Britax's motor cycle division became known as Britax-Excelsior, and revived old memories for many.

Below: standing out from the crowd of JAP and Blackburne powered competitors in the early 30s was the Excelsior Mechanical Marvel
Right: the 350cc, four-valve Manxman engine

Francis-Barnett

Somewhat gloomily, Captain Gordon Ingoldsby Francis of the Army Service Corps surveyed the line of battered despatch-rider Douglas and Triumph machines awaiting repair at his 70th Motor Transport Workshops, behind the British lines at St Omer, France. They were so many damaged frames to be straightened out. Surely, thought he, there must be a simple way to construct a motor cycle?

Gordon kicked some ideas around, then got out a sketch pad, How about building a kind of space frame, entirely from short, dead-straight tubes? Yes, and if the tubes had flattened ends, the whole lot could be bolted together with no need for brazing at all. If any of the frame tubes did suffer damage, repair would be just a matter of whipping out the bent strut and inserting a new one. Think of the saving in time and effort!

The scheme was indeed a brilliant one, and in due course Gordon Francis was to have the opportunity of putting it into practice. But not yet.

Though American born, Gordon was of British parentage. His father was Graham Francis who, with R. H. Lea, ran the well-known Lea-Francis bicycle and motor cycle business. Gordon had himself had a hand in Lea-Francis design and in immediate pre World War I days, he and young Norman Lea had acted as the works trials team, gaining awards in the English and Scottish Six Days Trials and in the Colmore Cup Trial.

He had taken a Lea-Francis with him to France, too, and it was generally understood that when peace returned he would rejoin the old firm. But on a war-time spell of leave he married a certain Miss Barnett, and that changed the entire course of events. The bride's father was Arthur Barnett, a former Singer Director who, in 1912, had set up in business for himself at West Orchard, Coventry, building cycles and motor cycles under the Invicta trademark.

Arthur suggested that the marital Francis-Barnett partnership should be echoed in peacetime by a commercial one and so, late in 1919, the new firm of Francis and Barnett Ltd was registered. It was an amicable agreement all round, with Graham Francis contributing some of the necessary capital and, in return, gaining a seat on the board. The other Directors would be Arthur Barnett, in charge of sales, and Gordon Francis, responsible for design and production.

The question of finding a suitable home for the new company was very soon resolved. Britain's oldest-established motor cycle builders, Bayliss, Thomas (Excelsior) had just been taken over by R. Walker and Sons, manufacturers of the Monarch. Excelsior production was to be transferred to the Monarch works

in Birmingham, leaving the old Excelsior plant in Lower Ford Street, Coventry, vacant. As Excelsior moved out, so Francis-Barnett moved in.

In the course of time, the Fanny-B (the nickname by which it was to become beloved by generations of riders) was to make its reputation in the two-stroke field. However, the first model to bear the new name, announced in March of 1920, was powered by a 292cc (70 × 76mm bore and stroke) side-valve JAP engine, driving through a two-speed Sturmey Archer gearbox, and featuring vee-belt final drive. It only weighed 180lb.

The Francis-Barnett did not supersede the Invicta but, rather, was complementary to it. For the next several years the two makes, nominally independent, would exist side-by-side. In fact, the Francis-Barnett was a rather more luxurious version of the older marque. Frame design was common to both. Even the Francis-Barnett name style was modelled on that of the Invicta, with the same characteristic flourish of underline.

Yet there were a number of individual touches which gave the newcomer that aura of 'class'. The footboards, for instance, incorporated toe-shields. The primary-chain cover was a light-alloy casting, not just a pressed-steel cover. And the price – the ultimate in snobbery – was listed as 84 guineas.

In Motor Cycle a week or two later, the Buyer's Guide included an alternative model, powered by the Mk II 269cc Villiers two-stroke engine, though it was not until 1921 that this machine took its rightful place in the company's brochure. By that time there was also a 350cc side-valve JAP, with three-speed gearbox and all-chain-drive.

Moreover, the inventive Gordon Francis was experimenting with a super-sports job. This one had a 293cc overhead-valve JAP engine, the cylinder of which was remarkably bare of fins in its lower reaches. Surprisingly for a bike of this age, it had a saddle tank. There was an ingenious centre stand, operated by a long hand lever.

In something of a lash-up state, with an exhaust pipe of flexible tubing and lacking a silencer, the machine was road-tested by Motor Cycle. The engine was surprisingly silent and free from valve clatter, remarked the tester. On the other hand, the exhaust was very healthy indeed. 'Perhaps the flexible tubing forming the exhaust may shock the fastidious', he said – one suspects, tongue-in-cheek, 'but, personally, we rather like it!'.

Not that the test counted for much, because the bike was never put into production. The post-war boom, in which the public bought everything that could be made, had disappeared. Money was getting tighter all the while, and the outlook for small-time makers of quality machinery didn't look too bright. The Francis and Barnett team pondered the problem. For the factory to survive, it would have to change direction. A market did still exist, cer-tainly, but now the demand was for low-cost utility models. Low-cost? Gordon Francis remembered his earlier scheme of building a frame from straight, bolted-up tubes, and got down to the job of making proper working drawings.

The first fully-triangulated, pin-jointed frames were seen at the 1923 Olympia Show and to draw attention to the new models from Francis-Barnett, Gordon made as the stand centrepiece, a special, all-nickel-plated bike decked out with legshields and full lighting.

Lights were extra, however, on the three versions of the standard production 150cc model. For £27, the customer got a Villiers-engined two-speeder, with no clutch or kick-start; for £28 10s, the clutch and kick-start were included; for £30 there was a three-speed gearbox.

The bolted-up frame wasn't the only novelty. Like that of the Triumph Junior, the front fork worked in a fore-and-aft plane, but instead of a coil spring there was a big clock-spring affair, the centre of which was filled by a rubber block to provide a primitive type of damping. Moreover, the steering head was pivoted around the steering stem (which was anchored at top and bottom) instead of the more usual arrangement.

For the time being, a conventional brazed-lug frame was retained for the 350cc side-valve, although in the years to come there would be four-strokes in pin-joint frames, too.

'Built Like A Bridge', declared Francis-Barnett advertising, and so that the point should not be missed, they included a drawing of the Forth Railway Bridge. The similarity was quite striking.

Another advertisement said that this was 'The Frame That Could Be Packed Into a Golf Bag'. Why should anyone want to do a thing like that? Ah, now; this was the clever bit. The factory was embarking on a big overseas sales campaign (they were to sell a lot to South Africa, especially), and the entire bike could be taken apart and put, if not into a golf bag, at least into a packing case no taller than the diameter of the wheels. That saved precious shipping space.

Reassembly was little more than child's play. Timed by stop-watch, two works fitters built a complete bike from its component parts in less than 20 minutes.

As a firm, Francis-Barnett were never especially interested in competition work, and the fact that a TT Model was listed

Left: Tommy G. Meeten with a 172cc Isle of Man Francis-Barnett prototype of 1924 vintage. An ultra-lightweight machine, it featured a gearbox mounted in front of the engine and was made specially for Tommy Meeten by Francis-Barnett. The busy scene is, in fact, on the island

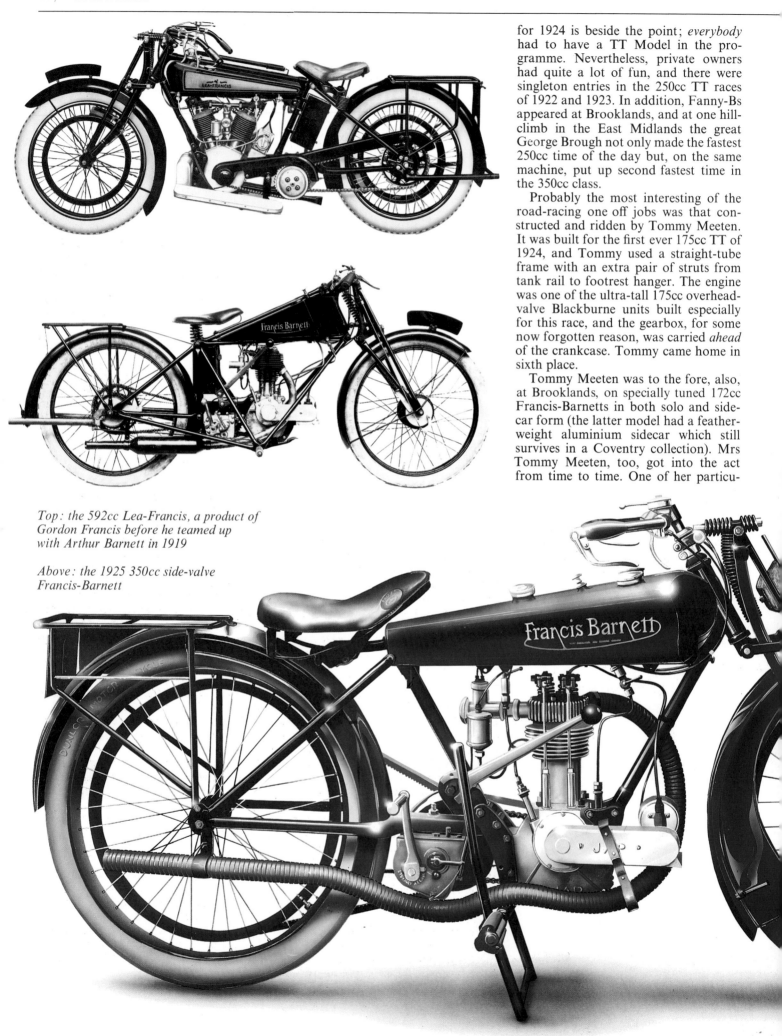

for 1924 is beside the point; *everybody* had to have a TT Model in the programme. Nevertheless, private owners had quite a lot of fun, and there were singleton entries in the 250cc TT races of 1922 and 1923. In addition, Fanny-Bs appeared at Brooklands, and at one hillclimb in the East Midlands the great George Brough not only made the fastest 250cc time of the day but, on the same machine, put up second fastest time in the 350cc class.

Probably the most interesting of the road-racing one off jobs was that constructed and ridden by Tommy Meeten. It was built for the first ever 175cc TT of 1924, and Tommy used a straight-tube frame with an extra pair of struts from tank rail to footrest hanger. The engine was one of the ultra-tall 175cc overhead-valve Blackburne units built especially for this race, and the gearbox, for some now forgotten reason, was carried *ahead* of the crankcase. Tommy came home in sixth place.

Tommy Meeten was to the fore, also, at Brooklands, on specially tuned 172cc Francis-Barnetts in both solo and side-car form (the latter model had a feather-weight aluminium sidecar which still survives in a Coventry collection). Mrs Tommy Meeten, too, got into the act from time to time. One of her particu-

Top: the 592cc Lea-Francis, a product of Gordon Francis before he teamed up with Arthur Barnett in 1919

Above: the 1925 350cc side-valve Francis-Barnett

larly noteworthy exploits was to ride a 150cc Fanny-B, under ACU observation, for an astounding 1007 miles on less than 10s worth of petrol, averaging 196mpg. Francis-Barnett advertising claimed that a walker would have had to have his shoes re-soled twice in that distance, at a probable total cost of 15s. Therefore, it was much cheaper to ride one of their bikes than to walk!

Aiming for the heights, the factory prepared three 172cc Villiers-engined machines for a mass assault on Snowdon by way of the mountain railway track, and on 12 July 1926 the trio of riders (trials exponent John Moxon, Geoffrey Jones of the Villiers company, and Eric Barnett, son of Arthur) were flagged away from Llanberis base station. The climb to the 3600-ft summit took only 22 minutes.

To the Scots, Snowdon is a mere pimple, and so, a year later, Glasgow's Drew McQueen (later to become one of Britain's earliest speedway aces) urged his 172cc model up Ben Nevis, under Scottish ACU observation, in just over two hours.

Moxon, in particular, was making the Francis-Barnett name a respected one in the trials world, and the ACU paid him the compliment of including him and his machine in the 1927 ISDT Trophy team – the first time an under 200cc

Left: the experimental 293cc overhead-valve Francis-Barnett of 1921. A handle operated centre stand, minimal cylinder finning and a saddle tank were the distinguishing aspects of the bike's design. Note, also, the flexible exhaust tubing

model had been chosen to represent England.

On the roadster side, Francis-Barnett caused a stir in 1927 by producing a 344cc model powered by an in-line, two-stroke vertical-twin. The engine was designed and built by Villiers, exclusively for Francis-Barnett in England, though it was supplied, also, to Monet-Goyon, of France. The unit was delightfully smooth, but it did have cooling problems, and relatively few were made; surplus frames were used up by Francis-Barnett in a substitute 250cc single-cylinder model known as the Empire.

During the late 1920s, the company had built up a profitable sideline in the supply of sheet metalwork and steel pressings to the motor trade and, in a way, it was from this side of the business that the next sensation came.

The machine was the never-to-be-forgotten 250cc Cruiser, which first appeared in 1933, and continued in production until 1940. Bill King was the designer, no stylist, but a thoroughly practical engineer with an eye to line. His machine, the Cruiser, was a modestly-powered, all-weather model made for gentlemanly touring.

Main departure from previous practice was a frame built up from an I-beam steel forging combining steering head and front-down member, and a duplex frame-work of channel-section pressings. Very deeply valanced mudguards at front and

Above: the 1933 250cc Cruiser. A touring Francis-Barnett of modest power and thoughtful design, it featured a channel-section duplex frame, pressed-steel front forks and a light-alloy silencer box at the base of the front down-beam

rear, built-in legshields, and smooth-contoured, pressed-steel front fork blades continued the clean-riding theme. But above all, the gearbox and lower part of the engine were encased in detachable pressed-steel bonnets, marrying with a bulbous, cast-light-alloy silencer box at the base of the front-down beam.

On the handlebar was an instrument panel with a lockable ignition switch. An oversize pan saddle assured riding comfort. The entire rear mudguard came away, after detaching four wingnuts, to disclose the wheel. Tyres were 3.25in section.

In the next few years, the Cruiser saw a few subtle changes, such as a bigger fuel tank, a foot-change gearbox, and the choice of a flat-top or deflector-top piston, but in its essentials it remained true to Bill King's original concept – and if you imagine Bill as a desk-bound designer, you would be wrong. He did his own development testing, and it was his picture, in long riding coat, which graced the front of Francis-Barnett catalogues of the time.

After concentrating on two-strokes

only for ten years, Francis-Barnett sprang another surprise in 1935 by announcing the sporty little 250cc overhead-valve Stag, capable of a 70mph performance. Engine of this one was actually a Blackburne, but totally unlike any Blackburnes that had gone before, and designer Harry J. Hatch had produced a model with crossed pushrods enclosed in cast-in cylinder tunnels. It was a textbook example of how to make the best possible use of metals but, unfortunately, it was to be the final design before Blackburnes ceased production.

In 1938 came the unit-construction 125cc Snipe, and the first Francis-Barnett pedal-assisted autocycle, the 98cc Powerbike. With the outbreak of war there were plans to adapt the little Snipe to light-weight military use (as was done with the similarly-powered ML James). But then came that dreadful 1940 night when enemy bombs tore out Coventry's heart.

In the smoky morning light it was seen that the giant Triumph plant lay in ruins; but, also, the neighbouring Francis-Barnett works had been devastated.

Fortunately the presswork subsidiary, based at Clarendon Road, Earlsdon, (in what had been, back in the mists of motor cycle history, the home of the Clarendon) suffered less severely, and Francis-Barnett were able to continue with sub-contract work for the war effort. But not until 1945 were the Lower Ford Street works able to return to motor cycle production, at first with the useful little Powerbike and, later, with the 125cc Merlin.

Arthur Barnett had died in 1936, his son Eric was at the helm, and he was to retain his position of managing director when, in June 1947, the company became a member of the Associated Motor Cycles group, which already owned James. For the first few years, the difference was not very apparent. James

and F-B went their independent ways, but gradually there was minor rationalisation. This was especially evident in the late 1950s, when the Woolwich-based AMC parent concern designed and began to produce a range of two-stroke engines of their own, in 175, 199 and 249cc sizes; later came a 150cc.

Naturally enough, the Villiers company didn't take too kindly to the introduction of the AMC two-stroke units. After all, James and Francis-Barnett were by far the biggest customers for Villiers proprietary engines; awkward customers too, at times, such as when they refused to accept the new inclined-barrel Mk 9E 197cc engine because it would mean redesigning their own frames. So Villiers had to continue with the vertical-barrel Mark 8E, later updating it to 10E, especially for them.

In the Villiers view, it was only poetic justice that the AMC engines should turn out to be only indifferently assembled. In despair, Woolwich stopped the production line and shipped the remaining stocks of parts up to the Villiers works at Wolverhampton, there to be put together properly. Subsequently, the units were labelled 'AMC-Villiers' as a guarantee to potential buyers.

With the coming of the AMC engines, Francis-Barnett revived the old Cruiser name, initially with the 175cc model, which they listed as the Light Cruiser. The early 1960s brought the 249cc single, and this powered a model listed as the Cruiser 80 or (when voluminous rear wheel panels were added) Cruiser 84.

With production rising, a temporary 'Francis-Barnett No 2 Works' was acquired – part of the former Triumph factory – though this had to be vacated when work began on the building of Coventry's new cathedral.

There was even a 'Francis-Barnett No 3 Works', housing the experimental department, up at the Clarendon Pressings factory. On the competitions side, the firm's name was certainly not disgraced. The Spanish Armada had yet to invade the trials and scrambles scene, and for the time being, at any rate, the chunky little 250cc Scrambles 82 and Trials 83 models could hold their own, ridden by experts like Arthur Shutt and Ernie Smith.

But now tragedy intervened. Near Southam, on his way home from work one evening, Eric Barnett found his car misbehaving. He drew to the side of the road and, pennies in hand, was crossing to a phone kiosk to ring for assistance when he was knocked down and killed by a non-stop lorry.

Up at Clarendon Road, Bill King had been constructing the prototype of the futuristic 150cc Fulmer, with its pressed-steel, leading-link front forks and voluminous 'dummy tank' superstructure

which housed a parcels compartment.

The Fulmar proved to be the last motor cycle ever to be built in Coventry (Triumph, at Meriden, were outside the city limits) because the AMC group was running into financial difficulties. In any case, the Lower Ford Street works were due for demolition, to make way for Coventry's new elevated Inner Ring Road. The Clarendon Road works were sold, and the press tools were transferred to vacant space within the James factory at Greet, Birmingham.

Francis-Barnett, too, moved in with James, but in the few seasons remaining all individuality went by the board. In the end, a James was red, a Francis-Barnett was green. All too soon, the troubled waters closed over the AMC combine. Francis-Barnett, like James and Matchless, sank without trace, and many an elderly rider who had served his apprenticeship on a much-loved, pin-joint Fanny-B viewed its going with a special kind of sadness.

Opposite page: Derek Adsett competes in the Jack of Newbury Trial of December 1962, riding a Francis-Barnett

Left: a 1961 Francis-Barnett Cruiser 80. This model used the AMC 249cc single-cylinder engine. A Villiers-powered twin-cylinder version was also available

Below: the Falcon 87, which was manufactured between 1959 and 1966. It was powered by a single-cylinder two-stroke AMC engine of 199cc and from 1962 it had a lower headlamp mounting and adjustable handlebars. A compact and sturdy bike, the Falcon won many friends as a tourer

This page: the Francis-Barnett Cruiser 84 was distinguished from the 80 model by its rear wheel covers. It was powered by a 250cc single-cylinder engine
Opposite: the 380cc, two-stroke single which powered the MkII Greeves Griffon of 1977

Greeves

Buzzing like a demented hornet, the little Atco motor mower stirred the peace of the summer evening as Bert Greeves guided it up and down the lawn of a house at Claines, just outside Worcester. Paralysed from birth and destined to spend his life confined to a wheelchair, Derry Preston-Cobb watched his cousin's activities with a speculative eye. 'Bet you a fiver you can't fit that engine to my chair,' he called. Bert cut the racket of the Villiers two-stroke and spent a moment or two in thought. 'You're on,' he answered. Removing the 98cc Villiers motor from the Atco, he set to work to fabricate attachment brackets and a drive. Maybe the resulting lash-up was not the prettiest vehicle in the world, yet it was the foundation stone of what was to become, in time, Invacar Ltd., Britain's biggest manufacturers of powered invalid carriages.

However, that was later and, at this particular time, Bert Greeves was employed by Heenan and Froude Ltd., the famous Worcester makers of engine test equipment as a draughtsman, but soon Bert and Derry moved south to Surbiton, Surrey. There, in a garage, the first prototype Invacar was made. There, too, around the Blue Lagoon, Derry learned

to become a proficient invalid carriage driver.

By then, World War II was over, and the budding Invacar company had moved, mainly for family reasons, to Westcliff-on-Sea, near Southend. In West Street, they acquired the upper floor of a one-time dairy building, the ground floor of which was already occupied by somebody else. As a factory, it was far from convenient, because to get supplies up, and finished products down, Bert had to cut a hole in the floor, fit a trapdoor, and mount a block-and-tackle above it.

Incapacitated in body he may have been, but Derry Preston-Cobb was a man with a very shrewd business mind and, perhaps fortunately, a tremendous sense of humour. He was determined to play his part in the business from the start – even though it meant that, every morning and evening, he had to be hauled up or lowered, in his wheelchair, through that trapdoor in the floor.

Wartime, of course, had left its quota of limbless ex-servicemen and, as development of the Invacar progressed, so Ministry of Pensions contracts served to boost its production. The temporary premises at Westcliff-on-Sea were vacated, and work was transferred to more

Above: Bert Greeves, the founder of the British Greeves motor cycle company

Below: this prototype production Greeves was introduced in May 1951 and was powered by a 197cc single-cylinder Villiers three-speed engine unit in an all-welded duplex frame

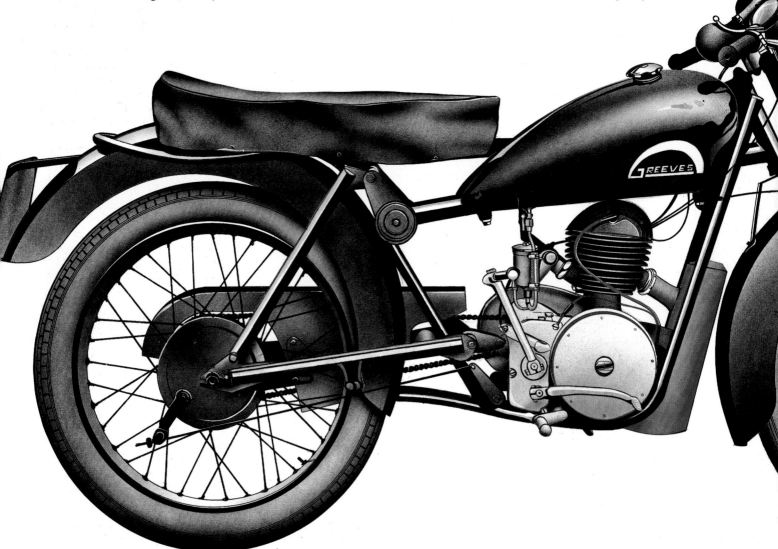

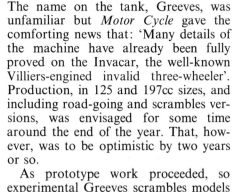

suitable buildings at nearby Church Road, Thundersley.

Thus far, all the work had been in connection with the invalid carriage, had it not? A qualified yes to that, because in pre-war days Bert Greeves had been a keen Norton-owning motor cyclist and, at the back of his mind, there had always been the ambition to become a motor cycle manufacturer in his own right. So, around 1950, a hack Norton equipped with a somewhat peculiar trailing-link front fork employing rubber-in-torsion as the springing medium, began to bump its way across the roughery near the Invacar works. Ostensibly, the bike was merely a test bed for a new type of invalid-carriage suspension but, in fact, it was very much more than that.

News that the Invacar people were contemplating motor cycle manufacture broke early in May 1951, when the weekly press printed a photograph of a most unorthodox lightweight powered by a 197cc Villiers three-speed engine unit. The all-welded frame combined duplex loops with a large-diameter top tube, and there was a crossover arrangement of tubes, at the steering head, rather like that of the newly announced Norton Featherbed.

Rubber bushes in torsion similar to those used on the Invacar, provided the springing medium at both front and rear, and it was claimed that these were un-affected by grit or rain, needed no maintenance and were self-damping. The front trailing-link fork provided six inches of wheel movement, and there were four inches of movement at the rear.

The name on the tank, Greeves, was unfamiliar but *Motor Cycle* gave the comforting news that: 'Many details of the machine have already been fully proved on the Invacar, the well-known Villiers-engined invalid three-wheeler'. Production, in 125 and 197cc sizes, and including road-going and scrambles versions, was envisaged for some time around the end of the year. That, how-ever, was to be optimistic by two years or so.

As prototype work proceeded, so experimental Greeves scrambles models in the hands of Frank Byford, the Inva-car works manager, began to be seen in local events around Essex. In fact, the first product to appear on the market under the Greeves name was a sidecar chassis with (naturally!) rubber-in-torsion springing. Not until September 1953 did the Greeves motor cycle make its official debut, and by then it was a very different-looking animal from the experimental job of two years before. Gone was the ungainly trailing-link front fork, and in its stead was a smart, and much less obtrusive component with, at the base of the stanchions, short leading links pivoting in rubber-in-torsion bushes and controlled by manually operated friction dampers. At the rear, the subframe incorporated similar fric-tion-damped rubber-in-torsion springing for the swinging-arm suspension. Yet, all this was totally eclipsed by the novelty of the cast-light-alloy, I-section beam which served in place of an orthodox front down tube. The beam, in LM6 aluminium-silicon alloy, was cast around the steering head and frame top tube components, and tapered from the steer-ing head to a point ahead of the crank-case. Two massive light-alloy castings cradled the engine-gear unit.

A feature of Greeves machines for many years to come, the light-alloy beam was claimed to have a strength-to-weight ratio far superior to that of a tubular frame member. It was, in fact, a product of the light-alloy foundry which had been added recently to the Invacar factory.

Finished in the same moorland blue as the invalid carriages, the tank carried light-alloy panels bearing a facsimile of Bert Greeves' signature. As originally announced, there were three models, all powered by the 197cc Mark 8E Villiers engine and comprising three-speed and four-speed roadsters, plus a scrambler (which differed from the others in having plain, oil-carrying bronze bushes in the wheel hubs). That year, the complete Greeves line-up for 1954 was displayed at the Earls Court Show in London, by which time a trials machine – again with the Mark 8E Villiers unit – had been added. They had even managed a 'Show surprise' in the form of a roadster twin,

very prettily named Fleetwing, employing a 242cc British Anzani two-stroke engine in which the middle section of the crank-shaft was hollow and served as a rotary valve.

Getting the Invacar operation under way had not been easy, for the immediate post-war years had been times of short-ages of materials and components. It was in this field which Derry Preston-Cobb more than proved his worth. 'He was a jolly character, who could charm the birds from the trees,' recalled a long-serving member of the firm. 'On trips to our Midlands-based suppliers he was able to get promises of delivery, where all previous approaches through normal channels had failed. From being obstruc-tive, people turned to wanting to help.'

By the mid 1950s, most of the earlier frustrations had been overcome and Derry was able to devote his talents to the sales side, while Bert looked after design and production. At first, there was little change, except that a 322cc version of the British Anzani twin (named Fleetmaster) joined the range. However, the conservative British public had yet to be convinced of the merits of the light-alloy beam frame and so, to help boost sales, a cheaper 'standard' edition of the 197 and 242cc roadster models, with an orthodox tubular frame, was designed.

On the competitions side, too, there was a relatively slow start, but things began to perk up after Greeves launched an official factory trials team, comprising Peter Hammond, Jack Simpson and Norman Storer. Technical feed-back from the works team resulted in a re-designed frame in which the rubber-in-torsion rear springing was replaced by conventional Girling spring and damper units. At first for the trials and scrambles machines, but later for the roadsters, too, a new type of front fork was put into production; the layout looked much as before, but the friction dampers of the rubber in torsion bushes had gone, and now slim Girling hydraulic damper units were housed within the increased-dia-meter fork stanchion tubes.

Possibly the most momentous decision ever made by Bert Greeves was to sign, as development engineer and competi-tions manager, Brian Stonebridge. From Cambridge, Brian had started his career as a Matchless works scrambler, later joining the BSA competitions depart-ment. Despite his lanky build, he grew to take a liking for small-capacity machines and while at BSA he turned his attention away from four-strokes and, instead, began to do a David-and-Goliath act with an indecently quick scrambles Bantam.

Joining Greeves around Christmas-time 1956, his first move was to persuade Bert to install an engine test bed – a Heenan and Froude job. Although it

was true that Greeves bought their engines ready made from Villiers, Brian soon showed that a lot more power was to be wrung from the seemingly unpromising material. Nor was it only backroom work. On 7 April 1957, Brian himself startled the motor cycling world by challenging Britain's scrambles stars in a national meeting at the formidable Hawkstone Park circuit. On his little 197cc machine, he not only won the 350cc race handsomely, but finished a storming second in the 500cc event behind Johnny Draper and his works BSA Gold Star. It was this exploit which led Greeves to name their new scrambler, on its introduction, the Hawkstone. In much the same way, a brilliant performance by Jack Simpson in the Scottish Six-Days Trial led to the introduction of the Greeves Scottish trials mount.

Stonebridge was a good picker of future stars, too, and it was on his advice that the Greeves/Invacar factory signed up a young Suffolk lad named Dave Bickers, whom World Motocross Champion Jeff Smith was later to describe as 'A happy-go-lucky youngster, up to the ears in things mechanical from an early age'.

It was Brian who cradled young Dave to stardom, not by ladling out advice by the bucket full, but by example. For the whole of the 1959 summer, Bickers travelled the round of Continental meetings in company with Stonebridge, who left it to the lad to watch closely and profit by the experience. The policy paid off. In those days, the 500cc class had a World Motocross Championship title, but the corresponding 250cc section, although equally arduous and equally entertaining, was still known as the European Championship series. Dave Bickers showed he meant business at the first round of the 1960 250cc championships, held on a hillside course at Payerne, Switzerland; BSA works man Jeff Smith was struggling desperately with a C15 model which, eventually, packed up with ignition failure, and Bickers sailed through to overall victory, with eight championship points in the bag.

That was just the start, and he was to finish the year with the Championship title in the bag. At home, other Greeves successes were coming thick and fast, from riders of the calibre of Ken Sedgley, Don Smith, Bill Gwynne and Mike Jackson.

Cubic capacity of the Hawkstone scrambler had been raised to 246cc, and now it featured a Bert Greeves-designed, Stonebridge-developed, square-finned cylinder barrel on a Villiers Mark 34A crankcase assembly. Perhaps Villiers should have seen the way the wind was blowing, and produced a similar barrel for their production engines, but they appeared to be too set in their ways.

Certainly, Stonebridge tried hard enough to get them to move with the times, but without any effect. For example, the Mark 34A gearbox was no longer man enough for the power the modified engine was turning out. An approach to Villiers having failed, Brian got Greeves to supply him with a small electric oven, and with its aid he used to harden and temper the Villiers gears to his own satisfaction.

Over the 1960/61 winter, the little Thundersley factory revamped the frame

of the scrambles model, and at the Hants Grand National meeting on Good Friday, 1961, Dave Bickers gave the new version its first public outing. A perforated, welded-up, channel-section engine cradle now replaced the earlier cast-light-alloy plates, the rear fork was of tapered box section, and 10lb had been carved from the overall weight. It won, first time out and, when Dave took it across to Payerne, where a 250cc race offered relief to the main bout of the day, the opening round of the 500cc World Motocross Championships, it won again.

The same fabricated-steel engine cradle appeared also on the new machines for the 1961 Scottish Six Days Trial, as did the square-finned barrel. Here, too, there was a good result for Greeves, with Ernie Smith, on a specially built machine, collecting the Best 150cc award, and Don Smith, on a 250cc bike, backing-up by taking the Best Newcomer cup.

Gradually, roadster production was pushed more and more into the background (although not entirely forgotten) as, now, orders for Greeves competitions models came pouring in from the USA

and elsewhere. Production, however, was still related to that of the Invacar, with assembly being switched from one type of vehicle to the other, according to the urgency of the demand. One week, there could be as few as ten Greeves machines leaving the works while, at another time, production could be running as high as fifty a week.

For the second year running, Dave Bickers was to win the 250cc European Championship crown. In home meetings, he was now being supported strongly by Cheshire-based Alan Clough, but neither Dave nor Alan were entirely happy with the Greeves leading-link fork: on washboard going, such as the back stretch of Hawkstone Park, the damper units tended to work a little too well, and were not returning to normal before the next ripple jarred them again – so, by the time the end of the straight was reached, the build-up was such that they were almost solid.

'Couldn't they have telescopic forks?', they pleaded, but Bert would not budge and, in part, this was to lead to Bickers leaving the Greeves camp and moving across to Husqvarna. However, this was not before he had given Derry Preston-Cobb a tour of the Shrubland Park motocross circuit in a Ford stock car! The windowless Ford had had its doors welded-up, for rough-racing, and so the only way Derry could be inserted into the car was by a gang of men tipping the Ford on to its side, then sliding him in through the open roof. After the ride, they tipped it over again, to extract him!

The year 1962 saw Greeves moving into a somewhat unexpected field, with the announcement of a prototype 250cc road racer, listed as the Silverstone. Like the motocross machine, it featured a Greeves barrel on a Villiers Mark 34A lower end. Weight was 194lb and the price would be about £250. No world-beater, it was intended to give the club rider a reasonably cheap and quick (110mph was mentioned) little machine.

Time was to prove, also, that the Greeves Silverstone was a very tough and remarkably forgiving little cookie. It was adopted as the standard trainer of the Charles Mortimer Racing School, and stood up extremely well to the abuse meeted out by whole flocks of ham-fisted novices.

Moreover, in the hands of Gordon Keith, a Greeves Silverstone was to win the 250cc Manx Grand Prix of 1964. By that time, however, it had matured to a Mark II version, and other things had been happening elsewhere. Mainly, a January 1964 announcement had given the news that the first-ever all-Greeves machine would be ready for delivery from March onwards – and that Dave Bickers would be back in the fold to ride it in the 250cc World Motocross Champion-

Left: a 360cc Greeves Challenger scrambler Model 36; the Challenger was introduced in 1964 and was unique in that it was the first 'all Greeves' production. The machine featured a shell-moulded, light-alloy cylinder from the Invacar factory, cast around an austenitic-iron liner. This engine was also used in the Silverstone road racer model

Right: this 1961 Greeves roadster was powered by a twin-cylinder, two-stroke Villiers 2T unit. Greeves were never famous for their roadster models, however, as most of their success was gained in the field of trials and motocross. For example, in the 1961 Scottish Six Days Trial, Ernie Smith collected the best 150cc award for Greeves while Don Smith, on a 250cc Greeves, took the Best Newcomer cup. And on the motocross front Dave Bickers enjoyed much success on his scrambler

ships. Perhaps 'all-Greeves' was not entirely correct, because the full-circle flywheel and engine-shaft assembly was made by Alpha, of Dudley, and the gearbox was an Albion, but the description will suffice.

Known as the Challenger, the new bike dispensed with the channel-section cradle, the makers claiming that the engine-gear cluster was so stiff as not to need it. Paying a remarkable honour to the Greeves Challenger, Brittain's, the toy company, included a model of it in their catalogue. Giving the background of the Challenger, and of the Mark II Silverstone road racer derived from it, Bert Greeves remarked that, as time had gone by, the increasing power outputs of Greeves-built models had stressed the bottom-end assembly far beyond the limits for which it had been designed. It was becoming clear that a new engine,

from the ground up, was necessary. Quantities were not large enough for mass production to be contemplated but, by careful attention to detail, making every ounce of metal work in some way or another, it was possible for a small factory to compete with the big battalions. The Challenger and Silverstone featured a shell-moulded, light-alloy cylinder from the Invacar foundry, cast around an austenitic-iron liner. In road-racing form, the engine produced a healthy 30bhp at 7500rpm.

The Challenger cylinder barrel, grafted onto a Villiers bottom half, gave the Greeves trials machine a new lease of life, too, and, with the first experimental model, Garth Wheldon rode in, and won, the Terry Cups Trial. As an aside, yet another Challenger barrel found its way on to the engine of Derry Preston-Cobb's invalid chair. 'The fastest thing on three

Above: a 1977 Greeves Griffon Mark II on the production line at Greeves' factory at Benfleet, Essex. The Griffon was powered by a 380cc engine developing 44bhp

Below left: in 1965, Greeves produced this special police version of their 250cc model

Right: the 1977 Greeves Griffon Mark II scrambler used a 380cc, two-stroke, single-cylinder engine. The engine utilised an aluminium cylinder with single 'bridged' exhaust system and cast-iron liner. The gearbox was a four-speed unit which was designed by Greeves while the exhaust system was computer designed by Dr Gordon Blair. These machines, incidentally, were used by the Royal Artillery Motor Cycle Display Team during 1975

wheels, it was well able to out-drag a police Land Rover', said one who saw it in action!

This time, Bickers' entry into the 250cc World Motocross series was not marked with the same success as in earlier years but, on the home circuits, high-flying Bryan Wade was to keep the firm well in the picture. 'Wild Wade' was almost invariably pictured a full three feet off the ground, the bike headed this way and that at the same time. Very largely this was 'playing to the crowd', yet it got results. Others to get into the act included Badger Goss, Freddie Mayes, Chris Horsfield and, above all, Arthur Browning, who was to prove himself a star of the inter-time televised scrambles. By 1965, only two roadsters remained in the range, and these were the 197cc Sports Single, and the 249cc East Coaster (the latter powered by a Villiers Mark 4T

twin). Off the record, however, Greeves were doing quite nicely on police business. A batch had been supplied to the City of London Police. Another batch of 23, for beat-patrol work with the Staffordshire Police, were given extra 'plodability' by replacing the standard Villiers outside flywheels with the very heavy flywheels from Siba starter-generator sets.

Developed in the Scottish Six Days Trial, a new type of front fork, with external damper units, and stanchions which swept backwards at their lower ends, was adopted for 1966 on the Challenger motocross and Anglian trials models. Riders called them the 'banana forks', but they worked well enough, and Don Smith and the Adsett brothers were regularly to be found in the awards lists of national trials.

On the road-race scene, Reg Orpin evolved a special Silverstone for Gordon

Keith to campaign, which employed a light-alloy jacket welded around the Greeves cylinder barrel, a Velocette LE radiator and glycol cooling. A joint project between frame builder Eric Cheney, and the Greeves company, for a new Challenger having a duplex tubular frame and Ceriani telescopic front forks came to nothing, but Greeves themselves bowed to the wishes of the customers and, for the 1967 season, offered Ceriani forks instead of the 'banana-type' at the customers' option. By then, too, Greeves had moved into the higher-capacity class, with a 364cc twin-port version of the Challenger motocross bike, and a corresponding road-racer christened the Oulton. Malcolm Davis and John Pease joined the team. A new trail bike, exclusively for the USA market and named Ranger, went into production. In effect, this was the trials-going Anglian, with light-alloy Challenger barrel on a Villers bottom-end, equipped with lights.

However, Villiers were now nearing the end of the line as a supplier of engines and, in 1968, for the first time for fourteen years, the factory withdrew from the trials scene (they were to return in due course with the Pathfinder, powered by a 125cc Puch engine, but this model never did achieve the same degree of success and affection as did its predecessors).

Possibly an even greater surprise was the disappearance of the famous cast-light-alloy beam frame, for the new 1968 390cc motocross model, which made its debut at the Thirsk Motocross event, had a tubular frame. This model was the forerunner of the 1970s Griffon – except that when Albion stopped production of gearboxes, Greeves had, perforce, to design a gearbox of their own.

Also, to assist in engine design for the new Griffon, the services of two-stroke expert Dr Gordon Blair, of Queens University, Belfast, were enlisted; that explains why the 1977 machine was catalogued as the QUB Griffon. Incidentally, Greeves Griffon machines were used, by the Royal Artillery Motor Cycle Display Team, and had to withstand the constant punishment of trick rides.

In the 1970s the company diversified its interests and began to produce invalid carriages under a Department of Health & Social Security contract. Further grist was supplied to the mill by the wholesaling of accessories and these activities began to take priority over motor cycle production.

In April 1977 Derry Preston-Cobb followed Bert Greeves into retirement and it was not long before the company finally closed its doors for good. However, Greeves and Preston-Cobb had experienced the satisfaction of seeing their dreams transformed into reality.

HRD

Generous in its praise though it was, the obituary notice printed in the 1 May 1917 issue of *Motor Cycling* was wrong in one rather important particular. Lieut Howard Raymond Davies, that 'intrepid airman' (yes, it said exactly that) just didn't happen to be dead. For the second time within a couple of months, his plane had been shot out of the sky. But whereas on the first occasion he was able to make his way back to the British trenches, this time he had force-landed behind the German lines.

And Howard was to survive to become the only rider in TT history to win the Senior (500cc) race on a Junior (350cc) machine. What's more, he was to found a marque which, in an all-too-short existence of little more than three years, was to carve for itself a special niche in the motor cycling hall of fame.

Birmingham-born Howard Davies had taken up an apprenticeship with the newly-established AJS company on leaving school, but it was on a Sunbeam that, at 18 years old, he made his competitions bow, taking a vee-twin outfit through the 1914 Scottish Six Days Trial – until a broken frame forced his retirement. That same year, and still a few weeks short of his 19th birthday, Howard was a member of the award-winning Sunbeam team in the Senior TT, finishing joint-second with Oliver Godfrey (Indian).

His first job with the return of peace-time trading was as a sales representative for Amac carburettors, but 1921 saw him installed as racing manager of AJS, for which firm he had ridden, unsuccessfully, in the 1920 TT series.

This was certainly no desk job, and Howard got away to a good start by personally establishing new one-hour, two-hour, 50-mile, and 100-mile speed records at Brooklands, on the same 350cc AJS which he was to use a little while later in the Junior TT. He might have won that race, too, for he had established a comfortable lead when a puncture brought delay; even so, he struggled back up the ladder to finish second.

Then, with the same engine installed in another frame (AJS boss, Jack Stevens, didn't want to risk a fatigue fracture) Howard went on to score that history-making Senior TT victory.

But from that point on, luck deserted him, and in the next couple of years he suffered more than his share of machine troubles. It could be, of course, that he decided the best way to get a decent machine would be to build it himself – but anyway, in June 1924, the brand-new concern of HRD Motors Ltd was

Left: the Howard Davies 80, announced in 1924, was powered by a 344cc, single-cylinder JAP engine, with overhead valves and twin exhaust ports. In standard trim, the machine cost £84, but this is a racing version from 1925

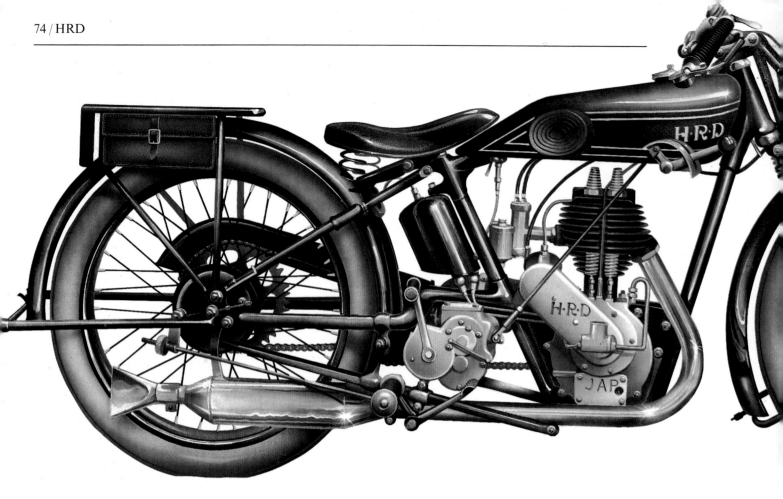

registered, with an office and works at Heath Street, Heath Town, Wolverhampton.

It sounded fine; except that the Heath Town premises actually comprised an adapted house. To help on the design side, Davies enlisted the rather controversial E. J. Massey, who had been involved with the Massey-Arran and Massey (these were separate and rival makes, incidentally) and, later, would join OK Supreme as a designer. Albert Clarke, too, came in as assembly fitter, and the three of them, working against time in an upstairs room, struggled to get the very first HRD completed; then they found it wouldn't go down the stairs, and the only recourse was to cut a hole in the floor, through which to lower it.

Time was indeed pressing. No word of the new venture had as yet been leaked to the motor cycle press, but a confident Howard Davies had booked stand space at the fast-approaching 1924 London Show, at which he hoped to show a four-model programme.

In the end, only three machines were made ready, and there followed a panic rush to Olympia. The building was already shut up for the night, and it was only by bribing a night-watchman to open up that Davies was able to get his bikes on to the stand, in time for the show opening next morning.

There was no doubt, however, that the HRD models were a sensation. The trio comprised the Howard Davies 90, which was a super-sports 500cc ohv with race-tuned JAP engine (and a kick-start as an optional extra!), the Howard Davies 80 with 344cc ohv super-sports JAP, and the Howard Davies 70/S, a 500cc side-valve model. Prices were, respectively, £94 10s, £84, and £66.

The specification was indeed attractive, embodying 7-in-diameter front brake, 8-in-diameter rear brake in a ribbed drum, quickly-detachable rear mudguard for quick access to the tyre, and a short auxiliary handlebar on which to mount instruments. Setting off the whole ensemble was a most attractively shaped saddle tank, in black with gold lining, specially produced to HRD's design by the still-extant tank making concern of A. J. Homer Ltd.

Getting the new make off the ground, *Motor Cycle* carried out a road-test of the 344cc Howard Davies 80 in late May, and their tester was fulsome in his praise. Said he: 'After 20 miles, the rider was beginning to think about getting a late entry in the TT!' Nevertheless the exhaust note was a bit naughty. 'It would not be desirable,' he warned, 'to accelerate violently under the nose of a policeman.'

Well, the possibilities of the TT had certainly not escaped the attention of Howard Davies, and he entered a two-man team of himself and Harry Harris (father of sidecar road racer, Pip Harris) for the 1925 series.

The Junior TT result was reasonably good – second for Davies, fifth for Harris – but there was better stuff to come. In the opening stages of the Senior TT, Howard Davies lay second to the redoubtable Alec Bennett; but then came time for refuelling, and slick pitwork gave Davies the edge. He took only 23secs to top up, to the 53secs spent by Bennett, shot into the lead, and from then on was never headed. That, despite the fact that with a combined weight of 487lb, Davies and his HRD were the heaviest pairing in the event.

Excellent publicity for the new make, of course, and there was more good publicity when Bert Le Vack took a 500cc HRD to Brooklands just before the 1925 London Show, batted round at over 104mph and set new flying mile and kilometer, and five-mile and five-kilometers world records.

Now, HRD could justify their advertising slogan of 'Leaders in Design and Speed'. Production was running at 10 to 15 bikes a week, and they had moved to larger and more efficient premises at Fryer Street, Wolverhampton. The Howard Davies 90 had now become the Super 90, with larger and even more stylish fuel tank, and the catalogue could now boast (and why not?) a full-scale TT Replica model.

Again HRD were represented in the TT races, but this time fate was against them. There was a new duplex frame, but the JAP engines were down on power by comparison with the opposition, and all that could be managed was Ken Twemlow's 11th place in the Junior race. In the following Senior battle, Howard Davies was holding third spot when he crashed,

but two other works team men – Clarrie Wood and Ken Twemlow – finished fifth and ninth, with Coventry private owner Sid Jackson (soon to find stardom in the new sport of speedway) in eighth place.

The new duplex frame was featured in the 1926 season HRD programme on the Howard Davies Super 90, which sold for a daunting £108 3s (or in 600ohv form, for £5 5s more). Those who couldn't afford that kind of money, but who still wanted to bask in reflected glory, could buy one of the new cooking-type ohv models – the 350cc HD65 at £68 5s, or the 500cc HD75 at £77 15s.

But as the 1927 season ran on, it was becoming clear that all was not well with the HRD company. 1926 had seen the General Strike, which hadn't done Britain's economy much good, and there wasn't the money around for top quality bikes such as those Howard Davies was marketing.

Nevertheless, the formidable Freddie Dixon was engaged to ride the works machines in the 1927 TT races and, in typical Dixon fashion, he adapted them to his own liking by fitting footboards, a windscreen, a backrest to the saddle, and similar oddball departures from standard.

Oddball he might have been, but Freddie could ride like nobody's business, and he won the Junior race in record time, with the second man 8½ minutes astern. In the Senior TT, Fred's gearchange linkage came adrift, but he rode on, swapping cogs as best he could, into a well-earned sixth berth. That event was Howard Davies' own last ride as a competitor, and it was sad that he should have to drop out with a split tank.

Dixon's victory should have boosted HRD business, but truth was that the company had travelled too far down the slippery slope. Space had been booked for the 1927 Olympia Show, and the 1928 models on the HRD stand included a Super 90 (now with a neat route-card holder attached to the tank top) with the price chopped from £102 to £94 10s.

It seems likely, though, that the machines on display were the only 1928 HRD models ever built, because before the Show closed its doors, HRD Motors Ltd had gone into voluntary liquidation. The Model 75 from the stand was later offered for sale by Life's Motors, of Southport, the company's main northern agents. But a small advertisement in the back columns of the motor cycle press in

Above left: one of several new models introduced at the 1926 Olympia Show was this 350cc side-valve sportster, the Howard Davies 60. It had a JAP engine, Burman gearbox and Druid front fork. The silencer style was used on all 1927 models. By 1927, however, HRD were in serious financial trouble

Below: although the HRD company folded in 1928 it was not the end of the HRD name. Some years later HRD became involved with the Vincent company and the HRD name was resurrected. Here P. Wilson, competing in the 1949 Clubman's TT on a 1000cc Vincent-HRD, sweeps through Greeba

March, 1928, wrapped it all up. Kings of Oxford were offering all five of the factory racing team models 'including Mr H. R. Davies' personal 350cc, capable of 96 mph', to be sold only to good, hardened riders who could do them proper justice.

Back at the Fryer Street works, only Harold Nock was left. The goodwill and manufacturing rights of HRD had passed to Ernie Humphries, of Humphries and Dawes Ltd (makers of the OK Supreme), and Harold Nock assembled, from parts in stock, the last few machines, affixing to their tanks a transfer modified to read 'H & D'.

Still, it wasn't the end. Waiting in the wings was a certain Cambridge graduate named Philip Vincent, with ideas of his own on how a motor cycle should be designed. But that is the start of another story.

Right: this immaculate 350cc HRD was seen in action at Hockenheim in 1977 when it took part in a demonstration race

Below: the legendary Freddie Dixon corners his 500cc HRD during the 1927 Senior TT at the Isle of Man. Dixon's gear change lever came adrift but he struggled on, changing cogs as best he could and eventually finished a well-deserved sixth. Earlier in the week, Dixon had ridden his 350cc HRD to victory in the Junior TT, winning the race in record time with the second man $8\frac{1}{2}$ minutes astern

James

Amid all the sound and fury of battle – the crump of exploding shells, the stuttering machine-guns, the swish of rockets – that characterised what has been described as The Longest Day, there came to many a British soldier struggling to establish a foothold on a Normandy beach, a homely and familiar note, the buzz of a lightweight two-stroke.

It could have been a little Royal Enfield. Equally, it could have been a 125cc Model ML James, of which nearly 300 were in action on the Normandy beaches during D-Day and thereafter. Some had been ferried across in landing craft, others had travelled with the airborne troops in their invasion gliders. Now, they were under the control of the beachmasters, scuttling across patches where heavier machines might have foundered, fetching and carrying, indi-cating the paths blasted through the enemy defences, and generally serving as mechanised sheepdogs.

The Model ML (the initials meant 'Military Lightweight') was by no means the James concern's only contribution to the war effort. With the introduction by Villiers in 1938 of the 98cc Junior auto-cycle engine, James had brought out their own version of a powered bicycle; it was well timed, for with the drastic fuel rationing of World War II, such an economical device was to prove invalu-able to those who could prove their need for independent transport. Between 1939 and 1945, almost 6000 machines were turned out, for the benefit of munitions shift workers, nurses and midwives, and others who had of necessity to be out and about at times when public transport was not available.

That was only part of the James war effort. Their works at Gough Road, Greet, was separated by a patch of open ground from the giant BSA plant and, like their BSA neighbours, James suffered considerable damage during the 1940 raids on Birmingham, but the scars were patched up, and shell cases, aircraft components, and similar war material continued to pour out of the factory.

Incidentally, a dozen or so rival makers were producing powered cycles (we would call them mopeds today) but, as yet, nobody had come up with a univers-ally accepted name for the type. All employed the 98cc Villiers Junior or, later, Junior De Luxe unit; but from the proliferation of Autobyks, Autoettes, Power Cycles, Powerbikes and suchlike, it was the James contribution – Autocycle – which caught on and became general.

It was in 1880 that Harry James, works manager of a Birmingham engineering company, took the bold decision to start out on his own as a maker of ordinary (that is, penny-farthing) bicycles. This was a bold decision indeed, for Harry was no youngster. However, he acquired a shop-cum-office in Constitution Hill, with workshop at the rear, and there he began the James Cycle Company, which title was to remain unaltered to the very end, 90 years later.

Trade flourished, larger premises became necessary, and 1890 saw Harry James installed in a bigger factory in Sampson Road North, Sparkbrook. Moreover, he could now afford to off-load some of the burden of running the company on to the shoulders of a manager, Charles Hyde.

However, Harry's connection with the firm which bore his name had now not much longer to run. In 1897 the James Cycle Company went public, and Mr James took the opportunity of retiring, leaving Charles Hyde in control. Unhappily, Harry survived to enjoy his retirement for only a few years more.

Thus far, production had been of pedal cycles entirely, but by the turn of the century several bicycle factories were toying with the idea of adding power to pedals. In 1902, Hyde took on an assistant. He was Fred Kimberley, a Coventry man who had been apprenticed to the Premier company and who had then gained some experience of early motor cycles at Hotchkiss, Mayo and Meek, whose Coventry-Eagle machines of the period used locally produced MMC engines copied from De Dion.

Fred soon persuaded Charles Hyde that James, too, needed a motor cycle in the range, and the outcome was a typical machine of the day, with a Minerva engine clipped to the front down-tube of a strengthened bicycle frame, driving direct to a pulley on the rear wheel by a twisted rawhide belt. The price was £55.

There was, too, an alternative model at the same price. This one carried its engine within the frame diamond and, by means of a short chain, drove a friction roller pressed against the rear tyre. It would seem, though, that the friction-roller version was not too successful, because the only machine shown in the 1903 catalogue is the Model T, the one with the clip-on 2½hp Minerva engine.

By this time the Werner Brothers, over in Paris, had discovered the most logical position for the engine – at the base of the frame diamond, where a cycle's pedalling gear was usually housed. However, the scheme was patented, and the James company had to find a way round by building a loop frame in which to house the power unit – which, for 1904, was a Belgian-made FN.

All this was fairly orthodox, but there happened to be, in the Birmingham area, a very astute inventor named P.L. Renouf. It had been he who, in association with Accles and Turrell, had vastly improved the De Dion powered tricycle design by moving the engine from De Dion's original position, at the rear of the axle, to within the wheelbase. This, of course, made the machine much more stable. The idea was taken up by Ariel and Swift.

To the James company, Renouf proposed a highly unconventional motor cycle in which the wheels were carried on stub axles. There were hub-centre steering, and a fuel and oil tank carried in front of the steering column. For riding comfort, the saddle was mounted on two long flat springs.

Understandably, the new machine was the sensation of the November 1908 Stanley Show. For the first time, the engine (86 × 90mm) was of the James' firm's own design and construction, and featured concentric inlet and exhaust valves. The rear axle was 'live', with the wheel on one side of the frame bearing and the belt-drive pulley on the other. Dogs on the axle permitted the machine to be started, on its centre stand, by means of a crank handle.

The procedure for getting under way was for the rider to withdraw the outer flange of the engine-shaft pulley, so leaving the engine running but no longer driving the belt. He then raised the centre stand and climbed aboard; by operating a pedal, the engine-pulley flange could then be closed. This served as a friction take-up, and the machine moved off.

By this time, Fred Kimberley was Managing Director, as, indeed, he was to be for fifty years. The General Manager was Selby Arter whose father, John Arter, had been the firm's accountant back in Harry James's day.

As with all too many an advanced design, the public marvelled but did not buy, even though *Motor Cycle*, in its show report, commented: 'Mr Arter, the manager, assures us that he has driven it seven or eight hundred miles with perfect satisfaction.'

The one-sided James could make other claims to fame. It was almost certainly the first motor cycle to be equipped with

Left: a James sidecar outfit of 1914; it was one of the first motor cycles produced purely for the commercial market and featured such selling points as drive chain, two-speed gearbox and multiplate clutch

Below: a vee-twin 500cc sidevalve James of 1928

Bottom: the first consignment of James motor cycles produced following the end of World War II. The bikes were civilian versions of the ML125 model

Opposite page: a 4½hp single-cylinder James of 1913

internal expanding brakes (whereby bronze shoes operated in a steel drum). And it introduced the staggered 'pine-apple' arrangement of cylinder fins that was to be seen on James-built engines for a number of years to come.

During the next couple of years, the 'safety' James underwent steady development. In its final form, for the 1911 season, it had an orthodox side-valve engine, conventional seat mounting, and a form of parallel-ruler front fork springing. The front tank was now for oil only, and a separate saddle tank contained petrol. The original type of belt drive, with the engine pulley serving as clutch, was still available, but at extra cost there was the more sophisticated alternative of a metal-to-metal clutch in the rear hub.

There would seem to be no logical reason why a machine with wheels mounted on one side only should not succeed. Scooters with such an arrangement were to be accepted quite readily in the years to come, but in 1911 the public

THE FIRST CONSIGNMENT OF JAMES MOTOR CYCLES

just wasn't ready for such a radical departure, and even the James people were losing faith, because flanking the 'safety' model at that year's London Show (by this time staged at Olympia) was a motor cycle of more orthodox appearance but which, nevertheless, was of extremely advanced conception. Its most noticeable feature was a two-speed countershaft gearbox incorporating a multi-plate clutch with alternate steel and bronze plates. Transmission was all-chain, with the primary chain housed in a cast-light-alloy casing, and the rear chain in a casing with detachable end to allow the rear wheel to be extracted.

That all-metal clutch was to remain a James feature right into the 1930s. It was, too, to find special favour among speed-

1955
JAMES 150 c.c. Cadet
Model J.15

way riders in due course and one, at least, was still being employed in league racing as late as the 1960s.

Indeed, 1911 was quite a notable year for James in many ways. In addition to the introduction of the new designs they had acquired a subsidiary in the Osborn company, of Tower Works, Newtown Row; this had been started by Fred J. Osborn, a famous racing cyclist, and was one of the earliest cycle firms to produce a lightweight two-stroke motor cycle. Renamed Osmonds (1911) Ltd, and transferred to the premises that had been erected three years previously at Greet, this was to provide a useful second-string label in later years.

By 1913, James had a two-stroke of their own, with the characteristic 'pine-apple' fin arrangement and a smart finish of two-tone brown. It partnered the 600cc 'big single', the engine of which had been made more compact by mounting the magneto behind the cylinder. Already on the stocks was yet another model, and this one was to be the firm favourite of many a rider in the next few decades.

Introduced in 1914, this was the 500cc Model 7 side-valve twin, with three-speed gearbox and, again, enclosed all-chain drive. However, war clouds were looming on the horizon, and soon production of the twin had to be dropped, so that Greet could concentrate on ammunition. The company was not asked to build machines for the British Army, but some twins were supplied to the allies for wartime use.

With the return of peace, the James came back to the market, but, before the company was fully back in its stride, the works were badly damaged by fire, and full production was not resumed until 1922. The first really new model was a 7hp twin, specifically for sidecar work, with interchangeable wheels. Under the Osmond name, there was a neat autocycle with the engine, like that of the P & M, taking the place of the front down-tube.

Through the 1920s, James prospered, offering the public a wide range of machines – two-strokes, side-valves, over-head-valves, singles and vee-twins. By 1928, there was an overhead-valve version of the 500cc twin, and like many another manufacturer, James caught the speedway bug. Their offering was a stripped and strutted version of the twin, and though its performance on the track was spectacular rather than speedy, it was adored by spectators mainly because, in the words of *Motor Cycle* speedway columnist, it was 'so sonorously vocal!'. The speedway twin was not a total flop, and in later years one example was to do quite a spot of cleaning-up at grass-tracks in the North London area.

For a while, James abandoned manufacture of their own two-stroke engines and, instead, employed Villiers units of 150, 172 and 196cc, but there was a return in 1932 with a James engined one-fifty. Meanwhile, the enterprising little Baker Motor Cycles company had been acquired, and this brought to the James programme the 'Baker Patent Brazeless

Frame'. Like Francis-Barnett, Frank Baker (who, earlier, had founded and operated the Precision works) had de-vised a frame employing straight tubes and a bolted-up construction. For a year or two, James continued to build bikes with the Baker name on the tank, but then replaced these by James models built under Baker patents. Frank Baker, himself, joined the sales staff of James.

Gradually, the manufacture of engines was dropped, and a lightweights-only policy took its place, with machines from 98 to 250cc, all employing Villiers units. The last engine to be built at Greet was something of an anachronism, for it was a 750cc vee-twin side valve with one-piece cylinder barrel and head; this was the power unit of the James Samson Handy-van, a commercial three-wheeler made until the mid 1930s, with a payload of 5cwt.

The return to peacetime production in 1946 saw James with a two-model range, comprising the Autocycle, and the Model ML 125cc, the latter out of Army service khaki and dressed in maroon and grey. Sport was just beginning to get under way again, and the James factory joined in with a trials team – all on Model ML one-two-fives at first – known far and wide as 'Three Normans'; they were Norman Hooton, Norman Moore, and Norman Palmer, and their exploits gained James much valuable publicity.

Naturally, the two-port Model ML was but an interim measure, and with the expansion of the Villiers engine range

JAMES *Cavalier*

came a wider choice of James roadsters and competition mounts. One of the best-known of these later Villiers engines was the unit-construction 197cc Mark 8E, with the aid of which a very competitive little trials model was devised.

In 1951, James was taken into the Associated Motor Cycles group, and in due course a range of machines employing 150, 175, 199 and 250cc engines made in the Woolwich factory of the parent AMC concern, was marketed. These were notable for the considerable use of pressed steel in the frame construction of such models as the Cadet, Cavalier and Commodore.

James joined the scooter movement, too, with a rather heavy-looking 150cc model in which the engine lay under the floor section, cylinder pointing forward. In fact this was a clever idea, because it gave a better weight distribution than was possible when, as in imported machines, the engine was mounted within the rear bodywork.

In the James, the whole of the underseat area could be used for parcel carrying. The frame, too, was ingenious, with its main members so widely spaced that they outlined the apron and floor, and, in consequence, served to protect machine and rider from the possible effects of an accident.

Several years before, Donald S. Heather of the parent AMC group had declared that scooters were only a passing craze. Eventually, even he had to admit that they had their advantages, but by the time James started work on their own machine it was already too late. Imported scooters such as the Lambretta and Vespa had gained too big a hold on the British market; with all their superior resources, not even BSA could make any impression and, anyway, in the eyes of scooter riders accustomed to the daintiness of Italian styling, the James was just too clumsy-looking. It achieved only minimal sales, and failed to recoup the company's outlay on bodywork press tools.

Under Norman Moore, the competitions department continued to thrive, and in the days immediately before the coming of the Bultaco, the Cotswold trials model – as demonstrated by riders such as Garth Wheldon – achieved a fair measure of popularity. The Cotswold had its scrambles counterpart in the Commando, and here Chris Horsfield was engaged to keep the James banner flying. (A decade earlier, there had even been some road-racing successes by a 197cc James which was prepared and ridden by Bill Lomas, but that was strictly a private venture.)

The factory bread-and-butter model was still the Cadet, now with 150cc AMC engine and a tubular-and-pressed-steel composite frame, and with an undamped coil spring to provide a measure of rear-end comfort. Higher up the capacity scale, the 199cc Captain retained a considerable following, and a mildly hotted-up version, the Sports Captain, was the preferred choice of youngsters who wanted to cut a dash with the girls. Topping the range was the remarkably handsome Superswift, which utilised the 250cc Villiers 4T twin.

Although they concentrated on the smaller-capacity end of the market, James were especially vulnerable to the new generation of lightweights which, as the 1960s advanced, began to flood in from Japan.

In an attempt to come to terms with the invaders, AMC formed a working partnership under the title of Suzuki (GB) Ltd. They even (thereby adding insult to injury) hived off a part of the James works, to serve as office, warehouse, and service department for Suzuki. Still, the Suzuki people did have the decency to use the back entrance to the plant, quoting Golden Hillock Road, instead of Gough Road, as the address.

Yet time was running out fast for James. The last new machine to carry the honoured name on its tank panels was another version of the utility 150cc Cadet, this time with the engine suspended from a large-diameter-tube backbone frame. It was an interesting design, but it only made little impact because AMC were now deep in the financial mire. In the ensuing crash, James disappeared. The factory was sold to a pump manufacturer, and, after a short while, even the outline of the James shield, which had graced the iron gates of the office entrance, had vanished.

Opposite page: the 150cc James Cadet Model J15 of 1955

Above: the 1959 James Cavalier 175 (left) and the James Commodore model of 1950, pictured on the right

Below left: the attractive James Sports Captain of 1964 had a 199cc engine

Below right: many of the James models were designed for the commuter market; this is the 122cc Cadet De Luxe of 1951

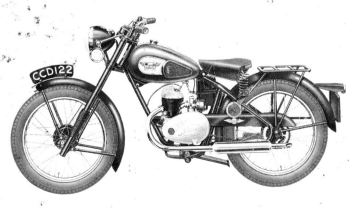

By 1914, when this 600cc, two-stroke single was made, the machine had been made more compact by repositioning the magneto behind the cylinder

Matchless

Unlike the history of so many other British motor cycles, the story of the Matchless commences in London, far away from the Coventry-Birmingham area which formed the hub of the infant British motor cycle industry. It is alleged that the first use of the Matchless trade name, as applied to two-wheel transport, occurred during the 19th century, when H. H. Collier commenced manufacture of pedal cycles bearing this name, in his Herbert Road, Plumstead, premises.

In due course Collier was joined by his two eldest sons, Charlie and Harry, to form H. Collier and Sons, and produce motor cycles. At first the engines were mounted beneath the front down-tubes, but the conventional position established by Werner was soon adopted.

Like many other manufacturers, they added a tricar to their catalogue during 1904, when this type of transportation caught the public eye, but it was short lived, due to the emergence of the sidecar; instead, the company concentrated its efforts on a vee-twin model, powered by a JAP engine. JAP were already involved with motorcycle racing at Canning Town and it was there that the two brothers became associated with H. V. Colver, a name to be associated with Matchless for two generations.

The 1905 vee-twin possessed two re-markable features, swinging-arm rear suspension and leading-link forks, which set the pattern for what was to follow some 50 years later. Certainly the machine was a success, for, on it, Harry Collier qualified to represent Britain in the International Cup Race, held in France. Although he did not win, Harry put up a good show and for the 1906 event his brother was invited to join him, on a similar mount. On this occasion, Charlie achieved the better result of the two, finishing in third place.

After the race, it is alleged, they travelled home with the Marquis de Mouzilly de St Mars, who had taken the place of the British team organiser at the last minute. A chance conversation in the railway carriage on the way home led to thoughts about a race in the Isle of Man, where machines would not be subject to the quite ridiculous weight limitation of 110lb applied by the continental race organisers. Realising that such a move would aid machine development, the Marquis became interested and offered to put up a Tourist Trophy for such an event. So, the TT was born, the world's greatest road race.

Having already guaranteed an entry if such an event were to take place, it is all the more fitting that Charlie Collier won the Single-Cylinder Class on his Match-less, at an average speed of 38.22mph. His machine was fitted with an ohv JAP engine and a B and B carburettor, which gave an overall fuel consumption of no less than 94.5mpg. The actual race winner was exhibited with pride on the Matchless stand at the 1907 Motor Cycle Show, accompanied by an announcement that a production replica would be added to the Matchless catalogue for the following season. Another addition to the catalogue took the form of a sprung-frame, vee-twin model and there was also a lightweight model fitted with a two-speed gearbox. As if that were not enough, there was a special racing model available too, based on the 120 × 120mm vee-twin JAP engine.

Building on its successes, the family business became a limited liability company, having already established a network of overseas agencies. Racing successes continued, Harry winning the TT in 1909, at 49.00mph and Charlie the year following, at 50.63mph. Their successes were by no means confined to the Isle of Man; following the opening of Brooklands during 1907, the two Collier brothers were just as well known at this venue – and just as successful. Prospects

Above: the first of a famous range – this is the original Matchless model of 1902

a design change that would be adopted by other manufacturers in due course. At the same time, the Company made use of the khaki/green finish that was to remain a characteristic of the Matchless motor cycle for many years to follow.

By now, an open-frame Ladies model was also in production, it having been decided that motor cycling was no longer an unseemly pastime for the fairer sex. As may be expected, the Ladies model used the single-cylinder lightweight engine.

In 1912 another significant step forward was taken, when the company decided to manufacture their own engine unit. A start was made with an 85.5 × 85mm single-cylinder engine that had some similarity with the JAP engine it replaced. It may be inferred that the engine itself was not a complete success, since within a couple of years the single-cylinder models, including the lightweights, were dropped from the catalogue. Instead, the company concentrated on their vee-twins, which were intended primarily for sidecar use. Of these, the model 8B attracted the most attention, having a three-speed countershaft gearbox, a kickstarter, fully enclosed chain drive, and an internal expanding hub brake in the rear wheel. This model was fitted with a Swiss-made proprietary engine, the inlet-over-exhaust MAG that enjoyed a good reputation for reliability. Rated at 8hp, the 8B model supplemented two other vee twins, one of which had chain-cum-belt transmission.

For the 1915 season, the 8B model was continued, with the addition of a new 8B/2 model that had detachable, interchangeable wheels. With the outbreak of war, these were now the only two models in the Matchless range, the 8B/2 only

looked good for the 1911 TT too, but on this occasion it was not to be. Although he was placed second, Charlie Collier was disqualified for taking on petrol during the race, other than at his pit. This was a great pity, as his placing would have split the all-conquering Indian team, who then achieved a 1-2-3 placing in the Senior Race.

The star rider of the Indian team on this occasion was a young newcomer, Jake de Rosier, who had his share of misfortune too. Because the eagerly anticipated battle between the English and the American rider had failed to materialise, a special three race challenge event was set up at Brooklands soon after; it has become one of the classics of motor cycle racing history. Sadly, this challenge too was none too conclusive, when both riders suffered troubles that made the final result indecisive. Although Jake won, technically, on a two to one basis, it was Charlie who later put the

'World's Fastest' record up to a speed in the region of 91mph.

By 1912, three-speed hub gears were coming into fashion and it was necessary to drop the spring frame so that they could be accommodated in a satisfactory manner. There was, however, the alternative of a six-speed model mainly for racing use, which employed an adjustable engine pulley and a moveable rear wheel to take up the belt slack. The arrangement used can be likened to a cross between the Zenith Gradua gear and that fitted to the Rudge Multi a year or two later. It was at about this time that the rear end of the top frame tube was curved to provide a lower riding position,

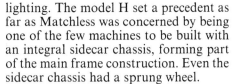

Opposite page, top: a Matchless Ladies' model of 1907; it had a step-through frame and used a single-cylinder engine

Opposite page, bottom: a Matchless machine-gun carrier of 1915; the sidecar platform was made up of ammunition boxes and the gunner could fire the gun from either side of the sidecar

Below: Charlie Collier poses on his Matchless after finishing fourth in the Senior TT of 1912; his brother, Harry, on a similar machine, had finished third

lighting. The model H set a precedent as far as Matchless was concerned by being one of the few machines to be built with an integral sidecar chassis, forming part of the main frame construction. Even the sidecar chassis had a sprung wheel.

For the next few years, the company concentrated on the production of vee-twins for sidecar use and it was not until 1923 that a single-cylinder model again appeared in the catalogue. This was the L2 model, a side-valve machine of 348cc capacity, with all-chain drive and internal-expanding brakes. The engine used was

standard specification, as did the more shapely petrol tank, which no longer fitted between the frame tubes.

The ohc model was not quite the success intended, developing only 13bhp at maximum revs, but it remained in production for several years more, albeit with a number of modifications.

Another innovation for the forthcoming 1925 season was the use of a vee-twin engine, of Matchless design and manufacture, for the large capacity twin specified for solo use. The engine was of 990cc capacity, the remainder of the machine closely following the design of the 590cc big single. The 347cc side-valve model was continued in production too, the engine having revised bore and stroke dimensions to coincide with those of the 69×93cc ohc model.

During 1926, H. H. Collier, the founder of the company, died; just two years later the company became Matchless Motor Cycles (Colliers) Ltd, when it went public. In the meanwhile, a 250cc lightweight model, fitted with a side-valve engine, had been added to the range. Known as the model R, it was the first to have an all-black petrol tank, relieved by gold lines. Surprisingly, the old, MAG-engined, vee-twin sidecar outfit still continued in production, with only very minor design changes. It was, however, coming to the end of a long and successful run, having established a first class reputation amongst those who relied implicitly on a sidecar outfit as their regular means of transport. It was only quite fundamental design changes that brought the run to a close, necessitated by the introduction of the shortened saddle tank and a higher steering head which combined to give the lower riding position that was by now being adopted.

An almost complete redesign of the Matchless range took place towards the end of the 1927 season and at the Motor Cycle Show of that year all the Matchless models were resplendent in their new guise, with white-panelled petrol tanks made pannier-wise in two halves and joined together by two nickel-plated steel strips. 1928 proved to be the last year of the ohc model which, though much more handsome looking than the original 1924 version, had been eclipsed in terms of performance by the Velocette and others which favoured the ohc engine.

The design changes were well timed, for they gave the range a new lease of life that saw them through the dark years of the depression. For the 1928 season, the range comprised the 246cc model R side-valve, basically unchanged apart from the use of a different silencer, the new 347cc, ohv Sports model, the standard 347cc side-valve model, the ohc model already mentioned, a new 495cc Super Sports model with fully enclosed push rods, and a continuation of the 591cc big

being continued for a further year. The manufacture of motor cycles for the civilian market was then terminated by the Government, and the Plumstead factory switched over to the production of munitions and aircraft parts, having the ability to make parts to a very high standard of accuracy. It was no coincidence that the Matchless trade mark had taken the form of two hands holding a micrometer.

Surprisingly, the company did not receive a contract for the manufacture of motor cycles for the armed forces, even though a so-called war model was available in 1917. This too was a vee-twin, with an 85×85mm engine, modelled along the lines of the earlier 8B/2. It was renamed the Victory model at the end of the war. When the production of civilian machines was again resumed during 1919, it supplemented the more famous model H sidecar outfit, which could itself be regarded as an updated version of the former 8B/2 model, with the addition of a swinging arm spring frame and electric

of Blackburne manufacture and the gearbox was a Sturmey Archer. One version was available with a Lucas Magdynette, the forerunner of the Magdyno. A big single of 591cc was added to the range for the 1924 season, the range of sidecar models being continued, one fitted with a vee-twin JAP engine and having a rigid frame.

Of more interest to the sporting fraternity was the new 347cc overhead camshaft model which, like the big single, had an engine of the company's own manufacture. The overhead-camshaft model had been developed with the 1923 Junior TT in mind, but had not been completed in time. An unusual and very distinctive feature was the location of the overhead camshaft drive, at the rear of the engine. This meant that the valve gear was arranged transversely across the frame and the carburettor was forward facing, with the exhaust pipe taken out on the left-hand side of the machine. As on the other models in the range, mechanical pump lubrication formed part of the

single. As far as the vee-twins were concerned, two versions were available, both of 990cc capacity. Needless to say, the single-cylinder sports models had twin exhaust pipes and silencers, in keeping with the trend of the times. It should also be mentioned that there was a sports version of the 250cc model R, known as the model R/S. Although having the same engine as the model R, it departed from the standard decor and followed the new specification. A year later, a new 250cc ohv model, designated the model R3, made its debut at the Olympia Motor Cycle Show. Another newcomer was the model V5, designed primarily for sidecar use and having a single-cylinder, 586cc, side-valve engine, fitted with a detachable cylinder head. These new models, and the various modifications made to existing models in the range, somehow instilled confidence in the Matchless marque, at the very time when many other manufacturers were fighting for their very existence.

For the 1930 season, the company took a very bold step by announcing the production of what, at first, looked like an in-line twin, but which was, in fact, a narrow angle vee-twin. Of 400cc capacity, itself a somewhat unusual size, the new Matchless was named the Silver Arrow and it bristled with many novel features, including valve operation via a single camshaft, skew driven from the crankshaft. All four valves were disposed vertically within the single casting that formed the two cylinder heads and the

inlet pipe was arranged to pass between the two cylinders, being cored out in the main casting. The exhaust manifold took the form of a separate casting and by bolting the oil tank to the front of the crankcase it was possible to dispense with external oil pipes. The frame itself had a triangulated rear section, which pivotted immediately behind the saddle tube in Silentbloc bearings. Its movement was controlled by compression springs between the rear frame and the top tube, with rubber 'bump stops' to iron out the effect of any severe shocks. Not unnaturally the machine proved to be one of the highlights of the 1929 Show, although unfortunately this was not reflected in a correspondingly high level of sales. As has happened on many occasions in the past, the general public was very conservative in its outlook, and hesitant to try anything that represents a considerable departure from existing practice. The relatively low capacity of the Silver Arrow did not help matters either, nor did the fact that it was very quiet running.

A year later, Matchless sprung another surprise, when they launched yet another new model, to complement the Silver Arrow. This was a narrow angle vee-four, known as the Silver Hawk that was just as revolutionary in design concept. This model used a built-up crankshaft assembly with a vertical shaft and bevel gears to drive the single overhead camshaft. The engine was, in fact, set across the frame, with the two pairs of cylinders

cast together. A similar type of spring frame to that used by the Arrow was employed and a four-speed Sturmey-Archer gearbox which, incidentally, was now fitted to the Silver Arrow as well, in place of the original three-speed version. Of 593cc capacity, the Silver Hawk created yet another show talking point, yet sales remained disappointingly low. Not even the attractions of the spring frame or the new handlebar mounted instrument panel could break down the sales resistance to a design that seemingly had so much to offer. 1931 was also the year of the sloping engine, as far as the single-cylinder models were concerned; this necessitated a change in frame design to pander to yet another of the latest trends. This was the year that the familiar chrome plated capital M appeared on the side of the petrol tanks, without the wings it was to grow later, in place of the name transfer used in the past. Chrome plate was by now beginning to replace nickel plating, as the beaded edge tyre had been replaced by the wired-on type a few years earlier. The vintage look was fast disappearing.

During 1931 the old-established AJS company, in Wolverhampton, fell on hard times and closed its doors, control of the company passing into the hands of Matchless Motorcycles. After a period of consolidation, manufacture of the AJS marque was recommenced at Plumstead, the various models retaining their original identity. Because the taxation system relied upon a weight limitation to

Above: the single-cylinder, 350cc Matchless G5 model of 1962

Left: introduced in 1930, the Silver Hawk engine was a V4 of 593cc

Opposite page: well known motor cycling writer 'Titch' Allan poses on the 398cc, vee-twin Matchless Silver Arrow of 1930 at the Stanford Hall Museum

pany was changed to Associated Motor Cycles Ltd. It was at about this time that the chrome plated M motif on the petrol tank 'grew' a set of wings. Through a continuous process of refinement, the G series Clubman engines (250, 350 and 500cc) reached a high state of perfection and in the case of the larger capacity sizes, featured hairpin valve springs and finned tappet covers as part of their standard specification. Some of these engines were sold to other manufacturers, such as Coventry Eagle and OEC, who incorporated them in their own cycle parts. At this time, the Matchless and AJS engines were virtually identical, the main distinguishing feature being the rearward mounted magneto in the case of the Matchless, and the forward mounted magneto of the AJS.

When World War II broke out in 1939, Associated Motor Cycles were in a much better position than their ancestors had been at the outbreak of World War I. The armed forces could use all the machines the company could manufacture and so production concentrated on the Matchless G3 design, much to the delight of the army dispatch riders who were more often than not relegated to the heavy, unwieldy side-valve designs made by rival manufacturers. Anyone fortunate enough to be issued with a Matchless G3 considered it was his lucky day.

Even better news was to follow. During 1941, Matchless motor cycles began appearing with an entirely new type of front fork that worked on the telescopic principle, the lower fork legs sliding within a pair of tubes attached to the steering head by a pair of yokes. Movement was controlled by internal compression springs of substantial diameter and there was a form of internal oil damping that constrained the movement so that road shocks did not cause the springs to take up a natural period of oscillation. Although the idea was not entirely new, both BMW and Norton having experimented with undamped telescopic forks in racing events before the war, the AMC approach to the problem was ingenious and had special merit. The design was patented under the trade name Teledraulic and from that moment onwards, the day of the girder fork was numbered. In a very short period of time, other manufacturers started work on their own designs, so that they would have a similar advantage when the war ended and the manufacture of machines for civilian use could again commence. Until then, Matchless Teledraulic forks were much in demand and if a pair could be salvaged from a crashed bike, there was no limit to the way in which they could be grafted on to all manner of different makes. Small wonder, for the introduction of the telescopic front fork represented the first major

segregate the different taxation classes of motor cycles, most manufacturers made strenuous efforts to keep their smaller capacity models as light as possible, Matchless Motorcycles included. They really excelled themselves with their 498cc model D/5 side valve, which tipped the scales at 220lb fully equipped, and was known as the Light Five-hundred. The saving effected by being able to tax the machine in the lightweight class made a very powerful selling point. The conventional, large capacity vee-twin that had earned the company such a fine reputation over the years had not been overlooked. Redesigned at the time when the entire range received attention, and redesignated the Model X, the 990cc side-valve remained the backbone of the Matchless range, right up to and including 1939.

By 1933, the black petrol tank had become standardised throughout the Matchless range, relieved only by the chrome plated M motif and thin gold lines. This was to prove the last year of manufacture of the Silver Arrow and although the Silver Hawk was to linger on for a further year or two this too ultimately suffered a similar fate.

Design tended to stagnate just a little

during this period, despite the introduction of the Sports models fitted with sloping engines, upswept exhausts and a Burman four-speed gearbox. It was not until the 1935 Show that Matchless Motorcycles entered another new era, following the introduction of their Clubman and Clubman Special models, with tuned engines, that had a particular appeal to the sporting fraternity. The basic engine layout and the design of some of the cycle parts set a standard that was to remain the hallmark of the Matchless (and AJS) motor cycle for a good many years to come. The G models had arrived. Although in the main they were fitted with ohv engines, the well-proven side-valve engine was by no means extinct. The G5 Tourist model was fitted with a 498cc engine of this type that had fully-enclosed valve gear and had been the subject of separate development attention. Of course, the 990cc vee-twin had not been neglected either. By shortening the wheelbase, it could be ridden equally well in solo form.

In 1938 the Company expanded yet again, when they acquired the manufacturing rights of yet another famous name – Sunbeam. Some reorganisation followed, and the name of the parent com-

improvement in the design of front suspension for something like 25 years.

During 1944, Harry Collier died, leaving his brother Charlie as the sole surviving member of the founders of the company. Then in his sixtieth year, 'Mr Charlie' as he was known within the works, still played a very active role, having a hand in many design projects. By the time the war was over, no less than 80,000 G3 and G3L models had left Plumstead for the armed forces, the G3L designation applying to the model fitted with the Teledraulic front forks. As in the case of World War I, the surplus military models were sold in lots by auction soon after the end of the war, passing into the hands of the public through numerous motor cycle dealers up and down the country. There was good demand too, for when the first civilian models appeared on the market they were virtually identical to ex-WD models except as far as the paintwork was concerned, but they were in short supply, and much more expensive.

With the resumption of private motoring and motor cycling, there was a tremendous resurgence of interest in sporting events, and many took part in competition events for the first time. Matchless were quick to bring out a trials model, based on the existing G3L design,

Above: the Matchless team lines up for the start of the 1949 International Six Days Trial. By 1949, the Matchless company was heavily involved in sporting activities, including trials, scrambling and grass track racing. Soon, with the coming of the G45 model, it was also to be involved in road racing

Left: the 347cc Matchless G3L competition off-road model of 1953

but having the necessary improved ground clearance, competition tyres and complete absence of lighting equipment. Soon, works-sponsored riders were very much in the news, especially Hugh Viney, who had an unparalleled run of successes on his Matchless in National trials. In scrambles events, Eddie Bessant and Basil Hall quickly made names for themselves, and on the grass tracks there were innumerable successful riders, including Jack Colver, an AMC employee and son of Bert Colver. It was the latter who had teamed up with the Collier brothers in the days of the Canning Town races, and remained with the company for the whole of his working life. His son followed in his footsteps, riding only AMC models, with no mean success, in South Eastern Centre events. Jack and his 137 riding number became an integral part of the grass track scene during the early post-war years.

In 1948, a 500cc vertical twin was

added to the Matchless range, unique in having a centre bearing for the crankshaft assembly and swinging arm rear suspension, controlled by oil-damped suspension units of the company's own manufacture. Of distinctive shape, the suspension units were known colloquially as 'jampots', a name that became part of the motor cyclists' language and later the title of the AMC Owners Club magazine. Initially, the twin was earmarked for export only, but within a couple of years, the G9 twin was available on the home market. By the end of 1951, the main distinguishing feature between the Matchless and AJS single-cylinder en-

Right: the famous Matchless G50 was introduced in 1958 and was virtually an overgrown 7R AJS. It had a single-cylinder engine of 500cc and was a direct rival of the Manx Norton of the time. The example photographed has been modified and now belongs to Martin Ashwood, who still races it. It had a duplex frame, rear Girling hydraulic dampers and a four-speed gearbox

Below: between them, the G50 Matchless and the 500 Norton were the mainstay of British road racing during the late '50s and early '60s. Here a very young John Surtees gallops his G50 during 1958

new G12 twin, and also a G12 scrambler. More significantly, the G45 racer had now been dropped from production and replaced by a new single-cylinder, ohc racer, known as the G50. It seems remarkable that the company took so long to develop what was virtually a stretched version of the very successful 7R AJS, when it was obvious that the G45 twin did not have the qualities that would make it really competitive against the all-conquering Manx Norton. Even if the G50 never achieved the record of success enjoyed by the 500 Norton, it often had the edge in short circuit events,

Left: close-up of the Matchless G80 engine. It was an overhead-valve 500cc, single-cylinder unit

Below: by 1958, Matchless had no less than seventeen models in their range. This is the G12 model, which was a revamped version of the G11 twin. It was powered by a 646cc, ohc, twin-cylinder engine. A more sporting version – the G12 CSR – was also available, as was a scrambles version of the G12

gines had gone, the Matchless engine now having a forward-mounted magneto. The Burman gearbox had been redesigned, and all bar the competition models were fitted with a swinging arm subframe, similar to that of the twin.

A surprise addition to the Matchless range was made at the 1952 Motor Cycle Show, when the G45 racing model appeared as a catalogue entry. Developed from the G9 twin, the G45 production model was based on the machine that had won the 1952 Senior Manx Grand Prix, in the hands of Derek Farrant. It heralded a welcome, and long overdue, return to road racing, as the company had not participated officially in this type of event since the Collier brothers made their last entry in the 1914 Senior TT. Many famous riders rode G45 Matchlesses during the years that followed, one of the most successful being Peter Murphy. It is also worth recording that Pip Harris experimented with one attached to a sidecar, but had to admit to defeat in the end because the usable power band was far too narrow for serious three-wheel use.

Charlie Collier died during 1954, at the age of 70. It was a sad occasion as his passing severed the remaining link with the early days of the company. In 1954, the full-width hub made its appearance as a new design trend and just a year later,

a 592cc twin, the G11 model, was added to the Matchless range. Now even the competition models had swinging arm rear suspension; the old rigid frame was no more.

It seems surprising, viewed in retrospect, that the Matchless range alone in 1956 comprised eight different models, including the newly added twin and the G45 racer. There was much going on behind the scenes too, since Associated Motor Cycles had acquired the Norton, James and Francis-Barnett marques at an earlier date, although each of the companies concerned still retained their individual identities.

One of the first moves towards consolidation occurred during 1956, when a two-stroke engine of AMC manufacture replaced the Villiers unit used previously in the larger capacity James and Francis-Barnett models. This was only the forerunner of what was to follow in later years. By 1958, the Matchless range had increased to no less than seventeen different models, which included a revamped version of the G11 twin – the G12 model which had a capacity of 646cc. An entirely new addition was a medium weight 250cc single, the G2, which had the unusual feature of a circular gearbox, housed within the main engine unit casting. There was also the G12 CSR model, a more sporting version of the

as the race results showed.

By 1965, the range had started to dwindle again as the result of some rationalisation, although a 750cc twin in both roadster and sports versions formed the most recent additions, replacing some of the older models. The engine unit used was that of the Norton Atlas and the free interchange of Norton and Matchless parts at this time provided ample evidence that the Matchless/Norton merger was now being implemented fully. All Norton production was now handled at Plumstead, the Norton works at Bracebridge Street, Birmingham, having finally closed during 1963.

Sadly, this last merger and the rationalisation of products that followed did little to help the flagging fortunes of the AMC Group and early in 1966 it was obvious that financial problems were presenting themselves. By the month of August that year, the management at Plumstead found they had reached the point where they could no longer carry on, and the bank was forced to appoint a receiver. Manganese Bronze Holdings, under the Chairmanship of Dennis Poore, came to the rescue and a new company – Norton Villiers Limited – was born.

Initially, the Matchless range was continued, albeit in a somewhat abbreviated form, Norton/Matchless hybrids with either 650 or 750cc engines forming the major part of the production run, but it was not to last. Following the evolution of the Norton Commando, every effort was made to get this new model into volume production and, as a result, the Matchless name faded into oblivion. Fortunately, there is little chance that the name will ever be forgotten, thanks to the remarkably fine range of machines produced over a span of something like 60 years. London pride counts for a lot.

Norton

James Lansdowne Norton, a citizen of Birmingham, was not really the sort of man one would expect to find involved in the manufacture of a highly successful range of motor cycles bearing his name. Deeply religious and an ardent supporter of the Salvation Army, his early apprenticeship to the jewellery trade seemed more in keeping with his upbringing and beliefs. Beneath it all, however, lay an intense interest in anything mechanical. If anything, his apprenticeship served only to heighten his desire to grapple with precision engineering problems and, in 1898, he founded the Norton Manufacturing Company, initially to provide components for the thriving bicycle trade.

It did not take long for him to become involved with the internal combustion engine, still in its infancy, and after conducting some experiments of his own, he became acquainted with Charles Garrard, the British importer of the French-made Clément engine. Garrard was fitting these engines into his own bicycle-type frames and marketing the complete machine as the Clément Garrard. James Norton followed suit, using his own frames, thus giving birth to the very first Norton motor cycle in 1902. Other designs followed, always using proprietary engines. This was a necessity, since the somewhat restricted production facilities at the tiny Bradford Street factory called for the purchase of as many 'bought out' components as possible. A lightweight model, known as the Energette, was fitted with a Moto-Reve engine, of Swiss origin, whilst the larger capacity models relied upon either a single or twin-cylinder Peugeot engine, that originated in France.

As has so often happened in the past, it was a win in the Isle of Man Tourist Trophy Races that helped the struggling company establish itself. Rem Fowler, a private owner, had purchased a Peugeot-engined Norton direct from the works, with the intention of entering it for the twin-cylinder class of the first ever TT race to be staged in the Island. James Norton agreed to accompany him, partly as helper and partly as pit attendant. As the history books show, Rem brought his Norton home into first place, at an average speed of 36.22mph over the rough 15-mile course. Although a total

of thirteen involuntary stops delayed his progress by something like 22 minutes, the other competitors had their troubles too, including the need to resort to the pedals that formed part of each machine's specification, when climbing some of the steeper inclines.

Encouraged by Rem's victory, James Norton decided it was time he designed and fitted his own engine. He quickly got to work, the outcome being a 633cc single-cylinder engine which he called the Big Four, on account of its nominal 4hp rating. A prototype machine fitted with this engine was completed in time to be exhibited at the 1907 Stanley Show.

James Norton himself decided to compete in the 1909, 1910 and 1911 TT races, but he did so without any luck, retiring on each occasion. It was in the last of these three events that he rode his new 490cc model, the forerunner of the ever popular 16H model that was finally phased out of production more than 40 years later.

Never enjoying the best of health as the result of a heart condition, James Norton had the ill-fortune to need a long convalescence following an illness he contracted while in the Isle of Man. He was sorely missed at the works and the business became generally run down, to the extent that liquidation seemed the only answer. Fortunately R. T. Shelley and Company mounted a rescue operation, having undertaken machining work for the Norton Manufacturing Company in the past. As a result, a new company was formed – Norton Motors Limited – with premises in Samson Road North. R. T. Shelley was appointed Joint Managing Director with James Norton, and C. A. Vandervell, of the CAV electrical concern, became Chairman. Production once again got under way, with the accent on the Big Four which could now be supplied with a matching sidecar.

It was around this period that D. R. O'Donovan appeared on the scene, having built up quite a reputation for himself through his record breaking exploits at Brooklands. His tuning abilities were

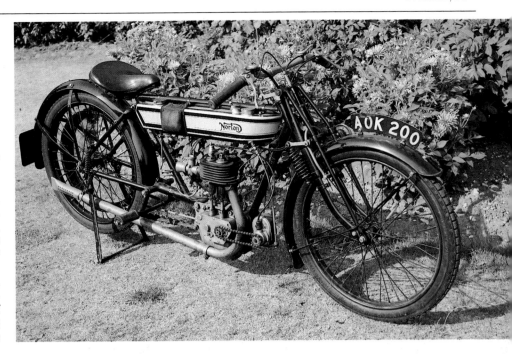

Far left: a 6hp Norton of 1907. It was powered by a Peugeot engine

Above: a single-cylinder 3½hp Norton tourer of 1912

Left: Norton TT winners both; Mike Hailwood (winner of the 1961 Senior event) poses with H. Rem Fowler, winner of the 1908 Senior TT

Below: a happy Alec Bennett is congratulated on his 1927 Senior TT win. He was riding the first of the new overhead camshaft Nortons. Also in the picture is Jimmy Shaw

such that the Norton factory sent him batches of engines which he tuned at Brooklands and then installed in a 'slave' frame and cycle parts so that their performance could be checked against the clock and certified. After certification, the engines were returned to Birmingham, where they were installed in standard production frames and dispatched to their respective purchasers. Two versions were available. The BRS, or Brooklands Racing Special, was certified to have covered the measured kilometre at Brooklands at a speed of at least 70mph, whilst the BS, or Brooklands Special model had to cover the same distance at least 5mph faster. In each case the customer was provided with a certificate which recorded his engine's performance, in either case a quite remarkable achievement for a single gear, belt driven model. O'Donovan's own machine, now preserved in the British National Motor Museum at Beaulieu, secured some 112 British and world records during the period before World War I. No wonder it was known affectionately as 'Old Miracle'.

When war was declared in 1914, Norton Motors was not in a position to be in the running for the supply, under contract, of machines for the armed forces. The company did, however, succeed in obtaining a smaller contract for supplying the Russian Government, and later the allied forces, when the Russian Revolution took place. The need to increase production necessitated a move to

new premises during 1916 and this marked the beginning of a long association with Bracebridge Street. After the Armistice of 1918, there was an outstanding need to meet the demand of the civilian market once more, so Norton Motors acquired all the ex-Army models they could lay their hands on, so that they could be refurbished and put back into service in civilian guise. Other manufacturers followed suit, for such was the level of demand at this time that prices reached an unprecedented high.

Supply eventually caught up with demand, and it once again became a sellers market, with the stabilisation of prices. As competitiveness increased between the many different manufacturers at this time, it was no longer possible to market what were virtually slightly modified pre-war designs. James Norton was not short of ideas, for a decade back he had originated a design for an overhead valve engine and had envisaged a desmodromic valve layout too. Other options included the reintroduction of the lightweight models and even a Norton twostroke. It was the overhead valve engine that won through in the end, however, the first example appearing at Brooklands early in 1922 as an experimental prototype. Rex Judd, another Brooklands rider of outstanding ability, who was O'Donovan's apprentice, rode it and raised the 500cc kilometre record to almost 90mph and the mile record to just over 88mph, a remarkable performance that augured well for the 1922 Senior TT.

Success, however, was not to be, the only ohv-engined Norton retiring on the final lap. Even so, the experience gained under racing conditions proved invaluable, and made the production overhead valve model, known as the Model 18, a very much better bike. The Model 18 made its debut at the 1922 Olympia Show, alongside the redesigned 16H and Big Four side valve models. Now catalogued as the Model 9, the single gear, belt drive model took its final bow at the Show, thus bringing to a close the end of the belt drive era.

In 1923, the overhead valve models put up a much better showing in the Senior TT, taking second, fourth and fifth places, and collecting the Manufacturers' Team Prize. George Tucker

Below: G. H. Tucker poses with his 588cc Norton sidecar outfit after winning the 1924 Isle of Man Sidecar TT. Standing behind the outfit are James Norton and Bill Mansell, two of the guiding lights behind the Norton fortunes in the early days

contested the first ever sidecar race, using an outfit powered by a special 588cc overhead valve engine. Even the production models made the news, when a stock Model 18 broke the 12-hour record at Brooklands under ACU observation and amassed eighteen world records in the process! Such a remarkable feat was rewarded by the presentation of the Maudes Trophy to the factory.

The Norton riders really showed their teeth during the 1924 season, having in

their midst a very promising rider by the name of Alec Bennett. On the Isle of Man, Alec won the Senior Race after a superb battle and George Tucker made sure of the sidecar race, after beating the same opponent. It is interesting to note that Joe Craig rode as a member of the Norton team in the Senior race, finishing twelfth, and that Walter Moore – previously the Douglas Chief Designer – passengered George Tucker. Soon after, he joined Norton Motors.

James Norton died on 21 April 1925, aged 56. It was unfortunate that he did not survive long enough to see his machines build up their imposing list of successes, for their run of wins had only just commenced. Although much attention had been given to racing, the standard production models had not been ignored. The Big Four and the new 588cc overhead valve production model were fitted with a four-speed gearbox of Norton manufacture for the 1926 season, the

Right: a 1938 500cc Norton to full 'Manx' specification, including light-alloy engine, and damper spring forks

Below: Jimmy Guthrie wins the 1934 Senior TT on his Norton 500

490cc models continuing with the three-speed Sturmey Archer gearbox that was a 'bought in' component. Phil Pike, a Norton dealer in Plymouth, saw to it that Norton won the Maudes Trophy yet again and for that matter, for a further three years in succession too.

1927 proved to be another landmark in the history of the company as it was during the year that Walter Moore unveiled his new overhead camshaft engine. Veloce Limited had already demonstrated the superiority of the overhead cam engine when they won the 1926 Junior TT with an engine of this type, the winner finishing over ten minutes ahead of the second place man. Moore's engine was very long and used a somewhat similar bevel drive arrangement for the camshaft, via a vertical coupling that ran up the right-hand side of the cylinder barrel. Of 490cc capacity, the engine employed the old familiar Norton bore and stroke measurements of 79 × 100mm. For the first time a full cradle frame was used, as was a saddle tank. Alec Bennett pulled off another Senior TT win riding one of these new models and another Norton rising star – Stanley Woods – raised the lap record to over 70mph before he was forced to retire. The

Norton team went on to notch up other victories in the various European Grands Prix, a happening that was to reoccur with almost monotonous regularity for many years to come.

At the 1927 Show, no less than thirteen different models were available, including a production version of the TT winner, catalogued as the Model CS1. There was also a cradle frame version of the Model 18, known as the ES2. 350cc versions of this latter model were projected for the 1928 Junior TT, but they proved underpowered and were replaced by a 348cc overhead cam model. Sadly, 1928 proved something of an anti-climax as far as racing was concerned and, for that matter, 1929 was much the same. Only on the continent were successes gained, although it should be noted that a Norton became the first 500cc model to cover one hundred miles in an hour during a record breaking attempt.

In 1930, the British motor cycle industry reeled from the slump that followed the historic Wall Street crash in the USA and many famous names vanished into obscurity. Fortunately, Norton Motors were in a strong enough position to survive, although Walter Moore departed, to join NSU. The vacant position of Development Engineer was taken over by Joe Craig, whilst Arthur Carroll set about the redesign of the overhead cam engine, to make it easier to maintain, without totally abandoning any of the original Walter Moore design concepts.

Thus began another era in Norton racing history, following the acquisition of riders of the calibre of Jimmy Simpson, Tim Hunt, 'Crasher' White, Stanley Woods, Jimmy Guthrie and Harold Daniell, to say nothing of Freddie Frith. So many racing successes were achieved during the years 1931–1939 that they would read like an extensive catalogue. Speeds rose continuously as more and more power was extracted from the overhead cam engine by Joe Craig and his backroom boys. In 1937, the first double overhead camshaft Norton engine made its appearance, to be followed by a spring frame of the plunger type, necessary to provide the improved roadholding that would accommodate the extra power. The overall design was somewhat rectangular and squared off in appearance, hence the derivation of the term 'garden gate' Norton. The only black spot during this period was the death of Jimmy Guthrie, which occurred as the result of a crash when he was leading the 1937 German Grand Prix.

Towards the end of the 'thirties, the foreign opposition was beginning to make itself felt, and the days of the single cylinder racing engine were numbered. Joe Craig did his utmost to uphold British prestige, coaxing something like 52bhp out of a 'works' 500 engine. The riders did their bit too, Harold Daniell

recording a quite remarkable lap at a speed of over 91mph during the 1938 Senior TT. The pace was beginning to tell and in 1939 Norton had to withdraw their official support from racing. Fortunately, there was hardly time to speculate on the future of racing due to more urgent matters of national importance. The shock of a BMW winning the Senior TT was soon forgotten when Britain declared war on Germany, and once again the production of motor cycles for the civilian market soon came to a sad and rather lengthy close.

Referring back to the standard production models, Norton policy had been one of steady improvement, applying useful experience that had been gained from the race tracks of the world. The range was much the same as before until 1932, when road-going versions of the works racers were added, in both 350cc and 500cc capacities. This was the beginning of a long run of the immortal International models, characterised by their large capacity petrol tank, soft soldered with a scalloped edge at the seams, wrap-round oil tank, and a downdraught inlet port, fitted with an Amal TT carburettor. They became the hallmark of the real enthusiast, who was very discerning in his choice. In 1938, it was the turn of the push rod engines to be cleaned up in terms of design, having fully enclosed valve gear and an altogether neater appearance.

Below: a single-cylinder 500cc Norton of 1923. The overhead-valve engine was reputed to develop 25bhp, enough to give the machine which weighed about 285lb, a top speed of almost 100mph

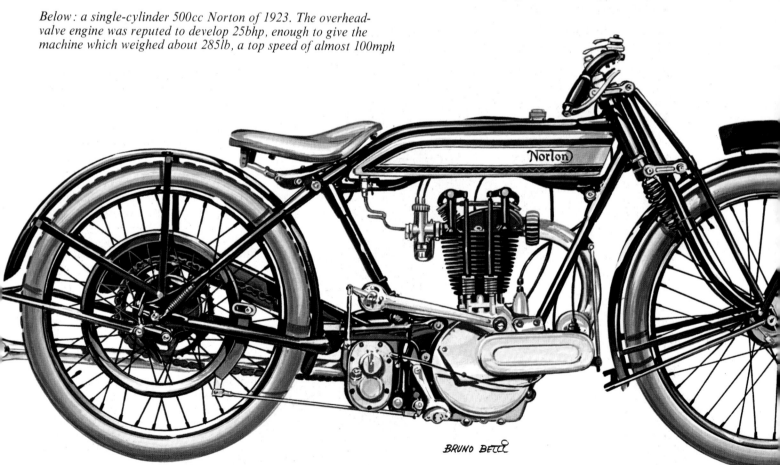

BRUNO BETTI

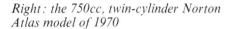

Above: the twin cylinder, 250cc Norton Jubilee model of 1958 was fitted with a three-quarter enclosed rear body section

Right: the 750cc, twin-cylinder Norton Atlas model of 1970

Above: a 750cc Commando of 1967; in time, the twin cylinder motor was enlarged to 828cc

Left: a 1954 works racer with an outside flywheel 350cc engine built by Doug Hele in 1961 and separate rear sprocket and brake

1939 was the spring frame year, a production version of the 'garden gate' frame being available for the two International models and the ES2. Those two old favourites the Big Four and the 16H side valve models were modernised too, for there was always demand from those who required a sidecar mount of outstanding reliability. Like most other manufacturers, Norton Motors had passed through the two-port period, where two chromium-plated exhaust pipes were considered an essential part of the specification of any machine, even though the changed cylinder head porting may have had an adverse effect on combustion, and hence performance and fuel economy. For the off-road enthusiast, there was a Competition Model, with upswept exhaust pipe, rubber saddle and knobbly tyres. It was

virtually a standard model fitted with these optional extras.

When the outbreak of World War II occurred, Norton Motors were in a much more favourable position than they had been just before the outbreak of World War I. Having the production capabilities, they were awarded a contract to supply the armed forces with countless numbers of the 16H model, now in drab khaki paint and without any chromium plated fittings. Although far from suitable for anything that involved off-road cross-country work, they gave sterling service and were used in all manner of climates, ranging from the heat of the African desert to the intense cold of the North. When eventually the war ended, a flood of ex-WD models came back on to the civilian market and, as had occurred during the immediate aftermath of World War I, they helped satisfy the initial demand until post-war production was resumed once more.

1948 was the telescopic fork year, the pattern having been set by AMC's Teledraulic fork design that was originated during the war. It was not completely new to Norton Motors, however, as a few of the works-prepared 1939 racers had prototype telescopic forks fitted, albeit of the undamped type. Soon the International models were reintroduced and with the advent of Clubmans racing they began to take the honours – until the BSA Gold Star came along.

It was during 1950 that the greatest innovation of all occurred, the introduction of the 'featherbed' frame on the works racers. Originated by the McCandless brothers in Belfast, it set an entirely new standard in handling characteristics and represented a major breakthrough in the design of such a vital component. A young man by the name of Geoff Duke was recruited into the Norton racing team about this time, to partner Artie Bell, Harold Daniell and Johnny Lockett.

Left: a 1963 Beart Norton 350, developed by Francis L. Beart and raced by Jimmy Guthrie and Joe Dunphy, amongst others.

Below: Norton engines have proved very popular power plants for sidecar motocross racers. Here, European Champion Robert Grogg is seen in action on his Norton outfit in Holland

Near right: the works John Player Norton team pictured at Imola

Far right: famous Norton star Peter Williams in action on the 750 Norton at the ultra-fast Spa circuit in 1974

Bottom right: Dave Croxford in action on his 750 Norton during 1973

It was a dynamic partnership and when Artie was forced to quit, after a crash terminated his racing career, Geoff had an incredible run of success that brought him several World Championships. The sidecar race was reintroduced to the TT in 1954, and it was Eric Oliver who carried off the World Championship in this type of event for several years too, riding the first Norton 'kneeler' outfit. So many British and Commonwealth riders contributed to Norton racing successes during this era that it is quite impossible to list all their names, let alone give credit where it is due.

Exports played a vital part in Britain's post-war recovery, and it was Francis Beart who engineered three successive Norton wins at Daytona during the years 1949–1951, against formidable opposition from the American nationals who were highly proficient in riding on loose surfaces. Francis was an old hand at tuning Nortons, as his earlier Brooklands exploits show, and his expertise often gave a private owner the upper hand when matched against the 'works' engines prepared by that legendary engine tuner Joe Craig.

The projected Norton multi was stillborn and inevitably the foreign fours dominated racing to such an extent that Norton Motors withdrew their official support from racing in 1955. This marked the beginning of the general rundown and despite the appearance of several prototypes, Norton's involvement with racing had virtually ceased completely by the time 1961 arrived.

A particularly sad note was struck during March 1957, when Joe Craig died in Austria, as the result of a motoring accident. He had retired at the end of 1955, only a short while after the death of C. A. Vandervell.

Reverting again to the production models, it was the introduction of the Dominator vertical twin during late 1948 that made the headlines. Of 497cc, it was designed by Bert Hopwood, formerly of Ariel and BSA. Originally supplied with plunger rear suspension, the conversion to the more efficient swinging arm layout occurred during 1953. Later still, the 'featherbed' frame was substituted, whilst the engine was gradually increased in capacity, leading eventually to the 750cc Atlas model. The old and well-proven 16H model was phased from production during 1954, severing a very long link with the early days of the company. Then, just two years later, a 350cc single was reintroduced, virtually a scaled down ES2 model.

In 1958, Norton Motors celebrated its Diamond Jubilee, and to mark the occasion, a new 250cc Jubilee twin was introduced – another Bert Hopwood design. It was followed during 1960 by a 350cc version, the Navigator. All was not well, however, and during mid-1962 the shattering news broke that Norton Motors was to be amalgamated with the AMC Group. This meant it would sever its long-standing association with Bracebridge Street when production was transferred to the Woolwich factory.

Even worse news followed. During August 1966, the AMC Group itself collapsed and an official receiver was appointed. It was the Manganese Bronze Holdings Group that came to the rescue and through the efforts of its Chairman, Dennis Poore, Norton Villiers Limited rose from the ashes.

A further relocation, at Andover, and the engagement of Dr Stefan Bauer during January 1967 led to the production of an entirely new Norton twin, the Commando. In effect, it was a modernised version of the original Norton twin engine, mounted in an inclined fashion in a quite revolutionary frame by using the Isolastic principle – a sophisticated form of rubber mounting designed to isolate engine vibration from the main frame.

Thus new lease of life was given to an engine that had first seen the light of day

almost 20 years earlier, giving rise to one of the very first Superbikes and the award of the title 'Motor Cycle of the Year' for five years in succession, by readers of *Motor Cycle News*. Initially, the engine capacity was 750cc, but it was later increased to 850cc and in its final stage, the Commando was fitted with an electric starter motor.

Alas, the Commando too soon reached the end of the line and by mid-1977, the last batch had been assembled and sold. Now only one machine carried the Norton name, a 50cc moped assembled from many Italian-made components, and known as the Easy Rider.

An all-new Wankel-engined machine was first seen and tried by the Press in 1974, the Fichtel & Sachs-based engine producing an impressive 65bhp at 8000rpm. However, its gestation seemed endless and in 1983– although NVT had sold some to the police – the bike had yet to reach full production.

One of the last Commandos to leave the factory, an 850cc model with electric start, the starter designed largely to assist the kick-start

OK-Supreme

Out around the famous Isle of Man TT circuit, enthusiasts were agog as the drama of the 1927 250cc race unfolded. In front on his Rex-Acme was Birmingham wonder-boy Wal Handley, but holding a consistent second place, and looking ready to pounce at any time, was Canadian superstar Alec Bennett, riding a JAP-powered OK-Supreme – a make new to the TT series. For lap after lap the battle raged, while playing a waiting game in third spot was the continental threat, in the form of Luigi Archangelli and his Moto Guzzi.

Five laps gone, two to go; but then came the news that Bennett was out of the running, and coasting in slowly from Craig-ny-Baa. What the crowd hadn't known was that the OK-Supreme's mechanical oil pump had gone on strike as early as the first lap and from then on Alec had been relying on the auxiliary hand pump. He had even set a new lap record at 64.42mph, a speed which would have put him third in the 350cc event, let alone the 250cc; but a piston can take only so much maltreatment before eventually crying enough.

OK-Supreme may have been a make new to the TT but OK machines, without the 'Supreme' suffix, had been around for a very long while. In fact it was in 1882 that Humphries and Dawes Ltd had set up shop in Lancaster Street, Birmingham, to produce bicycle components for the trade and, under the Criterion trade mark, complete bicycles for the discerning penny-farthing fancier. As early as 1899 they had had a tentative dabble in the motor cycle field, following up in 1906 with another attempt featuring an SOS (Smith's O'Saltley) engine which they themselves were manufacturing on Smith's behalf.

All the same, not until 1911 did the OK motor cycle earn anything more than local fame, because it was then that they first took space at London's annual Stanley Show, exhibiting a three-model range powered by 350, 500 and 600cc side-valve engines, from the recently-established Precision works of F. E. Baker. 'Humphries and Dawes', commented *Motor Cycle*, 'are capable of turning out a thousand bicycles a week, and now they are building motor cycles in no half-hearted manner.'

They raced them, too, and as with any

Left and above: this superbly restored machine, which is the property of the W. H. Fenby Collection on show at the Nostell Priory museum in Wakefield, Yorkshire, is an OK Junior of 1920. It is powered by a single-cylinder, two-stroke engine, rated at $2\frac{3}{4}$ hp, and has an Albion gearbox with hand-operated change. It was the forerunner of the famous OK Supreme model

British maker worthy of the name, OK entered the lists in the Isle of Man TT series. Equipped with Sturmey-Archer three-speed hub gear, a 346cc (70 × 90mm) OK-Precision plodded round in the 1912 Junior TT to finish third from last at a not very inspiring 28.51mph. For the following year, there were a couple of 346cc models, now sporting water-cooled Green cylinder barrels, and a fore-and-aft flat twin with overhead valve ABC engine. The team was out of luck though. One of the water-cooled models failed to start and the other dropped out with a broken rocker arm, while the ABC-powered version had all kinds of trouble during the practice period and was withdrawn.

By late 1914, the mainstay of the OK roadster range was a neat little 2½hp side-valve which employed an NSU engine and to cope with the demand Humphries and Dawes were erecting a fine new works situated in York Road, Hall Green.

Of course, the NSU was German and the outbreak of World War I put a sudden end to the supply. In any case, H & D were soon too busy making bomb fuses to worry about that, although they did have time to sketch the motor cycle they would offer when peace returned.

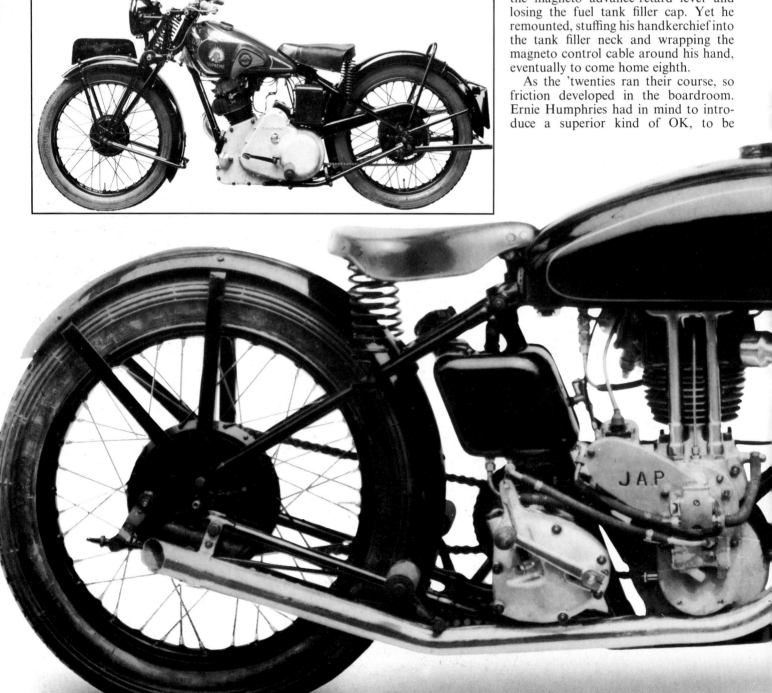

Unexpectedly, that model was to be an inlet-over-exhaust 348cc (60 × 60mm) flat twin in a duplex frame, but as 1919 dragged on and became 1920 the twin was still in prototype form and eventually it was dropped in favour of 246cc, 269cc and 292cc two-strokes, with Villiers or Union engines. For 1921 the two-stroke OK Junior employed what was alleged to be an engine of the company's own manufacture but which looked very Union-like.

One of the real characters of the motor cycle world, 'Black Ernie' Humphries was big, forthright (some would say rude), and very deaf. Still, it is to his credit that he spotted, and encouraged, a raw Birmingham lad with an ambition to become a road racer. Only eighteen years old, his name was Walter Handley, and Humphries gave him his chance in the 1922 Lightweight TT, on a machine powered by a special 250cc overhead valve Blackburne engine. True, Wal failed to finish – but before retiring he had set a new lap record for the class, on his first-ever appearance, and later the same year he was to bring victory to the OK marque in the Ulster Grand Prix.

Handley stayed with the OK stable for a couple more years, with mixed fortune, but none could deny his courage. In the 1923 250cc TT, for example, Wal came off at Windy Corner, after leading the race for the first three laps, breaking off the magneto advance-retard lever and losing the fuel tank filler cap. Yet he remounted, stuffing his handkerchief into the tank filler neck and wrapping the magneto control cable around his hand, eventually to come home eighth.

As the 'twenties ran their course, so friction developed in the boardroom. Ernie Humphries had in mind to introduce a superior kind of OK, to be marketed as the 'OK-Supreme', but Charles Dawes was more interested in the cycle side of the company. Matters came to a head in late 1926 and the partnership broke up. Ernie decided to go it alone, while Charles broke away to start the still-existing firm of Dawes Cycles Ltd. However, it did mean that capital had to be found quickly and this was achieved by selling the York Road factory.

Fortuitously, Velocettes were experiencing a boom, Alec Bennett having won the 1926 Junior TT on the new overhead-camshaft Model K, and the availability of the Humphries and Dawes place couldn't have suited them better. For a few weeks, until Ernie Humphries moved his newly-formed OK-Supreme Motors Ltd to a smaller factory in Bromley Street, Birmingham, both OK-Supreme and Velocette motor cycles shared the same home.

Not that there was anything especially supreme about the first machine to carry

Above: in the mid 1930s, much of the OK company's production was taken up with the Flying Cloud model. It was a cheap and reliable 250cc machine and the model photographed is of 1936 vintage

Far left: the OK-Supreme A/33 model of 1933 was powered by an overhead camshaft motor of 248cc

Left: the 500cc, JAP-engined OK-Supreme, as used in the Isle of Man Senior TT of 1934

that name. It was announced in January, 1927, and was just a 350cc side-valve JAP roadster, without even the snobbery of a saddle tank. However, Ernie Humphries now engaged the services of designer E. J. Massey, the man who had given the HRD such style, and soon more eye-catching models were under way.

One of Ernie Humphries' most sagacious moves was to sign Alec Bennett to lead the formidable five-man squad for the 1928 Lightweight TT. By now, Wal Handley was, ironically, the main opponent on a works Rex-Acme; but George Jones had designed a special cylinder head for the Supreme's 250cc JAP engine, featuring a down-draught inlet tract (novel, for the period) and squish-band combustion chamber. The new head, said those who should know, gave the OK-Supreme another 5mph.

As fate would have it, Bennett was the only one of the five to retire, with ignition problems. Frank Longman, however, took command right from the start, to give the factory its one-and-only TT victory, while Cecil ('The Count') Ashby, George Himing, and Vic Anstice brought three more OK-Supremes into the leading six positions.

Humphries did more than lure E. J. Massey from HRD. Late in 1927 he bought the moribund HRD company and, after selling off the remaining stocks of spares, raw materials, and machine tools, ended a profitable deal by disposing of the HRD trade-mark to newcomer Phil Vincent.

The surprise of the 1930 racing season was an entirely new 250cc OK-Supreme engine, designed by George H. Jones and Ray Mason and soon to become known as the 'Lighthouse' because the light-alloy tower housing the vertical camshaft embodied a small glass inspection window. Two bronze cams were carried at the upper end of the shaft, operating the valves through sliding tappets and bell-crank rockers.

Because OK-Supreme had no engine-building facilities, the manufacture was undertaken by Williams and James, of Gloucester, one-time makers of Saturn motor cycles. Ray Mason once confided that bronze cams were fitted to the proto-type engine so that the profile could be altered quickly as development continued; however, it was found that no wear took place, and so bronze was specified for production engines also.

In 250 and 350cc form, and supplemented by overhead valve JAP engines, the Lighthouse held sway for the next several years, to be replaced in time by a

more conventional Jones and Mason overhead camshaft design. A move to premises in Warwick Road, Birmingham, had taken place in 1934 but again there were no engine-building facilities and responsibility for the new unit was farmed out to Burman's, the gearbox manufacturing people.

In the mid to late 1930s, the overhead camshaft engine was offered in racing, sports-roadster and even trials trim but at last it found its own little niche, as a grass-track power unit. There were speedway-JAP grass models, too, and the OK-Supreme flag was kept flying high by riders such as Fred Hudson, wee Andy Mackay, and John Humphries, son of Ernie. On the roadster front, the cheap but reliable 250cc Flying Cloud earned a

Below left: the OK-Supreme N/38 model of 1938; it was powered by a single-cylinder, four-stroke, side-valve JAP engine of 500cc

Bottom: an OK-Supreme Road Knight model of 1935. It was fitted with a side-valve 600cc engine. Complete with sidecar outfit, the Road Knight retailed at £74. By 1935, however, the OK-Supreme company was nearing the end of its history

large following but now World War II was approaching, and John Humphries went into the Army.

The Warwick Road factory was closed and sold, and the aging but still astute Ernie Humphries concentrated his efforts on a subsidiary concern, Hughes Motor Fitments (originally, Hughes Sidecars), makers of seats, screens and other motor cycle accessories.

Most enthusiasts believe that OK Supreme died with the war, but that wasn't quite so because John Humphries, back in civilian clothes, built a batch of 346cc OK-Supreme-JAP, grass-track machines in 1946. The venture might well have blossomed into something bigger had not tragedy intervened. John Humphries was killed in a fall from a hotel window. For a while, his father continued the HMF business but then, approaching ninety years old, he was involved in a car crash from which he never fully recovered.

Right: the 1939 De Luxe model's 250cc engine was a pushrod-overhead-valve unit manufactured by OK-Supreme

P&M

Maybe it was something in the South Yorkshire air, that seemed to give engineers from that area the urge to cut loose from established precepts and plough an independent furrow. One such was Alfred Scott, who had interesting theories about two-stroke twins. Another was Joah C. Phelon, who saw no logic in the way that earlier manufacturers hitched on engines over the front wheel, over the rear wheel, or just any old where.

Joah reckoned otherwise. According to his philosophy a motor cycle should be built as a whole, with the power unit integrated into the design. To do that, the engine bolts holding the cylinder to the crankcase could be extended both at top and bottom, thereby permitting the engine to be used in place of the frame front down tube. Like most good ideas, Joah's was notable in its simplicity.

That was in 1900, when Phelon was in partnership with Harry Rayner in a small engineering business in Heaton Street, Cleckheaton, manufacturing special tooling and dies for the wire-drawing industry, and it was at the Phelon and Rayner works that a prototype was made. From the outset, the machine eschewed the usual belt drive and went for chain transmission.

However, Phelon realised that he had neither the capital nor the premises to produce the model in any quantity so, astutely, he journeyed to Coventry and offered the design to the established industry. Harry Lawson, of the Humber company, saw the possibilities and so a deal was negotiated, under which Humber would make and market the machine under their own name, paying Joah

Phelon a royalty of 7s 6d (37½p) on each. At the same time, the patents which he had prudently taken out would remain his property, and that allowed Phelon and Rayner to continue a token production of one bike a month at Cleckheaton.

Tragedy struck in 1903, however, when Harry Rayner was killed, in probably the first motor car accident in South Yorkshire. Almost at the same time, Phelon was approached by Richard Moore, whose brother owned a Phelon and Rayner and who had been greatly impressed by the model. Moore offered to join Phelon in partnership and so, in 1904, the business of Phelon and Moore was registered, on £250 capital and with a workforce of four men.

One of the first moves of the two partners was to patent, jointly, a two-speed gear system involving twin primary

chains and a selective clutch, and this was to remain a feature of P & M motor cycles right through to 1923. Humber, too, adopted the two-speed primary drive, but meanwhile they were developing machines of their own design and, soon, their licence agreement with P & M was allowed to lapse.

That left the Cleckheaton company out on its own, but development of the

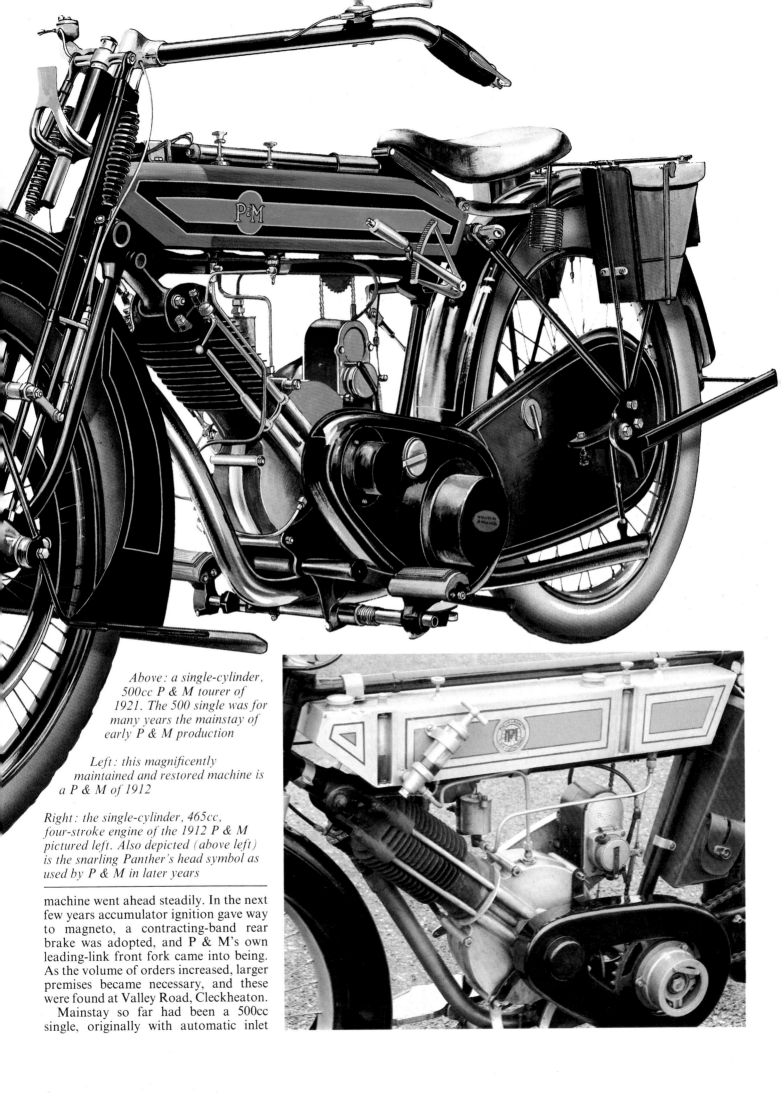

Above: a single-cylinder, 500cc P & M tourer of 1921. The 500 single was for many years the mainstay of early P & M production

Left: this magnificently maintained and restored machine is a P & M of 1912

Right: the single-cylinder, 465cc, four-stroke engine of the 1912 P & M pictured left. Also depicted (above left) is the snarling Panther's head symbol as used by P & M in later years

machine went ahead steadily. In the next few years accumulator ignition gave way to magneto, a contracting-band rear brake was adopted, and P & M's own leading-link front fork came into being. As the volume of orders increased, larger premises became necessary, and these were found at Valley Road, Cleckheaton.

Mainstay so far had been a 500cc single, originally with automatic inlet valve, but later with conventional side valves. Phelon and Moore, meanwhile, had been devising something new, in the form of a 770cc vee-twin, with the cylinders at 90 degrees to each other and the front cylinder, like that of the single, was especially designed to serve in place of a frame front down-tube.

Across in Europe the war clouds had been gathering, and it was P & M's bad luck that, just as the twin was ready for production, war between Britain and Germany was declared. Nevertheless, the war was not wholly bad luck, so far as Cleckheaton was concerned. During the War Office summer manoeuvres of 1913, a P & M had been undergoing evaluation with the fledgling Royal Flying Corps, and when that force (later to become the Royal Air Force) was put on a wartime footing, the 500cc P & M two-speeder was chosen as its standard transport.

In earlier years, Richard Moore himself had competed in local Yorkshire sport, but 1913 had seen, also, the first

International Six Days Trial, based on Carlisle, and Phelon and Moore entered a full three-man works team, on immaculately turned out roadsters, complete even to registration plates with polished, cast-light-alloy numerals. True, they didn't set the trials world alight, but they performed moderately well, gaining two well deserved gold medals.

With the return to peacetime trading, the vee-twin was shelved and again production concentrated on the 500cc side-valve single. One minor change was to the angle of the cylinder finning, but in general it stayed pretty much as before, until, in 1923, a 555cc sports model was added, retaining the double primary drive but adding a two-speed countershaft, to provide four ratios. Primarily, said the makers, the bike was for sidecar men, the rugged two-speed gearbox allowing extra-large cogs to be incorporated. Bottom gear, with a ratio of 17.5:1, would take a loaded outfit up the side of a house without even trying.

All the same, the bike was just an interim model, and for the 1924 season the 555cc side-valve was graced by a single primary chain and, for the first time, a proper four-speed gearbox.

Even more significant, during 1923 P & M had brought in Granville Bradshaw (famed designer of the ABC flat twin, and Bradshaw oil-cooled engines), and the machine which caused a real sensation when the doors of the Olympia Show opened was his work. It was still faithful to the P & M concept of using the engine as a frame member – but this was an overhead-valve model, with the push-rods neatly housed in a tube. Other features included the new four-speed gearbox, cast light alloy primary chain-case, and CAV Dynamag combined ignition and electric lighting. The price was £85, and the machine had a name; it was the P & M Panther.

Initially, the Panther was to have embodied Bradshaw's patented swirl-type inlet tracts in the cylinder head, but in

practice these proved difficult to manufacture, and production versions used a simplified inlet passage. Even so, the Panther was quite spritely and, for the first time, the manufacturers looked towards the Isle of Man. Ridden by Eric Headlam and Norman Hobson, two Panthers were entered for the 1924 Senior TT, but the result was far from happy. Hobson, a publican from the Isle of Man, first lost two gears from the box, then struggled on until, on Creg Willys Hill, he and Headlam collided, eliminating both models well and truly.

Undismayed, P & M tried again the following year, with Cecil Ashby and Tommy Bullus on the works models. This time Bullus finished fourth, which was very praiseworthy indeed for a rider on what was virtually a standard roadster, and in celebration the company added a TT Replica model to the range.

Granville Bradshaw was again engaged as a designer and, for 1927, he evolved a most un-P & M-like machine. Of only

Above: a 500cc, single-cylinder, four-stroke P & M Panther of 1924. Note the fully enclosed primary chain

Below left: messrs Sproule, Shaw and Drake, members of P & M's 1913 International Six Days Trial team, pose with their machines

Below: a P & M Panthette of 1927. These machines were designed by Granville Bradshaw and featured transverse vee-twin motors of 250cc, with unit construction of engine and gearbox

Bottom: another lightweight; this is the Villiers-powered Panther 250 of 1928

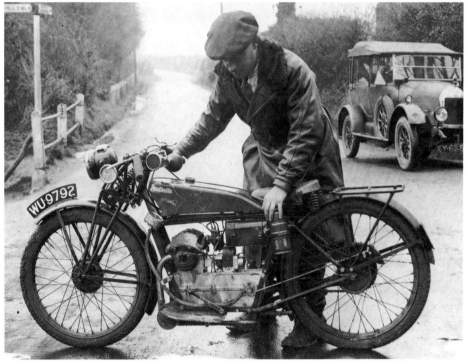

Top: a Red Panther model; this is the lightweight, single-cylinder 250cc Model 20 of 1935

Above centre: by the late 1930s, P & M's trading position had eased and they were able to introduce their Redwing range. This is the 600cc Redwing Model 100 of 1936. Also in the Redwing range were 350 and 500cc versions

Above: the Red Panther models were a result of the Depression of the 1930s. Built in 250cc and 350cc forms they offered good value for money. This is the Model 40 of 1939

250cc, this was the transverse vee-twin Panthette, with unit construction of engine and gearbox and the whole of the workings below crankcase mouth level encased on an unstressed, cast light alloy sump. The power unit was suspended by steel strip members from a stout forged-steel frame member which encompassed also the steering head.

Unfortunately, although the Panthette was ingenious it was also rather gutless, and it sold in painfully small numbers. Nor did the addition of a rather more handsome fuel tank for 1928 improve matters. Phelon and Moore had been banking on success and, in anticipation,

bought in a mountain of forged-steel frame members (some of which, so rumour has it, were still littering the works in the 1960s!).

To make at least some use of the surplus frame parts, P & M had perforce to introduce a range of Villiers-powered lightweights of 150, 196 and 250cc. These, like the big singles, now carried the Panther name badge.

Chief tester for the works in the early 1920s, Frank Leach had been becoming more and more involved on the design side, and the main 1929 introduction, a 598cc overhead valve Panther 'sloper' with a guaranteed 80mph performance, was his responsibility. So, too, was a stripped and very ungainly 500cc overhead valve speedway model – yes, a Panther speedway bike, still with the engine as the front down-tube! – but very little was to be heard of that particular venture in the passing of time.

The next machine from Frank Leach's drawing board was of far more consequence. This was the Model 20, a neat 250cc overhead valve machine with a sloping cylinder but departing from Cleckheaton tradition in employing an orthodox frame. It was announced in 1932, but by that time the hungry 1930s were upon the land, and P & M, like most firms in the British industry, were finding sales ever more difficult to come by.

In a pact of near-desperation, the firm worked out a deal with a big London motor cycle dealer, Pride & Clarke Ltd. Panthers would build the 250 (and also a companion 350cc model) for the lowest possible price, saving pennies here and there by, for example, reducing the thickness of the mudguard metal. To build the machine, the Cleckheaton works resorted to near-enough sweated labour, recruiting women for the assembly line from the even more badly hit woollen mills of the town of Bradford.

The outcome was the Red Panther, which in 250cc form sold for the incredible price of £29 17s 6d (there was even a period when, by specifying gas instead of electric lighting, the customer could buy it for £28 17s 6d). The 350cc Red Panther was priced at £39 10s, and for purposes of comparison it is worth remarking that the De Luxe 350cc Model 85 Redwing Panther, basically the same model but with a few more frills, was catalogued at a much more expensive £55 5s.

True motor cyclists despised the Red Panther as cheap junk, but bus drivers, factory workers, and others who needed reliable daily transport, bought it in their thousands. Only later, when Red Panthers were seen to be keeping going, day in and day out, with no more molly-coddling than an old greatcoat thrown over them in a back yard, did it sink in that this really was the greatest value for money that ever was.

A Red Panther even won the coveted Maudes Trophy in 1934! Awarded for exceptional demonstrations of a machine's ability, this trophy was well earned by a machine which was set a series of tasks at Brooklands. First, the tank was filled with fuel, and the bike ran until the tank was dry, returning 115.7 mpg at a 35.5mph average. Next, a lap of the track was made at high speed, the rider holding his hands away from the bars, to demonstrate the precise steering. Then there were stop-and-restart tests on a hill, both solo and with pillion, and standing and flying start quarter mile runs, finishing with a timed extraction of the rear wheel (which took 1 minute 16 seconds incidentally).

By the later 1930s the trading position had eased, and Panthers could offer a full range of Redwing models, 350, 500 and, of course, the 598cc Model 100. Ken Norris was using Red Panthers in trials, including the ISDT; Frank Whittle, with the big sloper, was contesting the trials sidecar field.

Again Granville Bradshaw was taken into consultation and, again, P & M developed a twin, this time a 600cc in-line vertical twin, in a frame with leaf springing similar to that of Bradshaw's earlier ABC. There was a side-valve model, too, and the spring frame was to be available also on the larger singles. It was not to be, however. For the second time, the coming of war killed off a P & M twin.

With the resumption of peace, Panther came back, with the well-loved 598cc 'Big Pussie' but, also, with a new range of vertical-engined 250, and 350cc singles, with their oil carried in a crankcase extension. For 1949 (by which time Dowty air-sprung telescopic front forks were a standard fitment) the roadster models were supplemented by 250 and

Above: Panther's rigidly-sprung Model 65 De Luxe of 1953 was powered by a single-cylinder motor of 250cc

Above: the 600cc Model 100 was a favourite with Panther enthusiasts for a number of years. This is the 1946 version

Above: in the 1960s, P & M started a concession for the French Terrot scooter but soon dropped it

350cc competition specials, known as the Panther Stroud models and campaigned in trials by Maurice Laidlaw, Bill Jackson, and others. On another hotted-up 350cc Stroud, Bob Dunn built up a useful reputation on the grass-track circuits of the west Midlands.

Frank Leach left the company, briefly, to become a manufacturer in his own right of the rear-sprung FLM (Frank Leach Manufacturing) 125cc two-stroke, but he was back at his customary desk in the middle 1950s, evolving a rather pretty little Villiers-powered scooter called the Panther Princess, which deserved a better reception than it received. Another Leach project was a Panther sidecar chassis, designed to bolt straight on to the big single; a spare wheel was included, and this could be used for front, rear, or sidecar.

Villiers-engined two-strokes rejoined the range, in 197, and 250cc single and twin-cylinder guise, in frames which featured Earles-type pivoted front forks.

Above right: the impressive Panther Model 100 of 1956 had a 600cc engine

Above: the Model 45 of 1959 was fitted with a two-stroke engine of 325cc

A concession for French-made Terrot scooters and mopeds was started – and dropped.

By 1964 the big single had grown to 645cc, and the 249cc Sports Twin two-stroke had been supplemented by an electric-start version with Siba Dynastart combined dynamo and starter motor. By now, however, the overall market in Britain for motor cycles was declining and for Panther the writing was on the wall. Essentially, the 645cc Model 120 single, with its separate engine and gearbox, and Lucas Magdyno electrical system, was of the 1930s; not even a total redesign, incorporating an alternator, and unit construction, would have saved it, even if P & M had had the finance to undertake such an operation.

Signs of the approaching end were only too clear. George Clarke Ltd, main London dealers for the big Panther, were offering the machines at £40 10s off list price by 1966. Even more ominous, Pride & Clarke were again selling a 'Red Panther', this time the 250cc Villiers twin in an all-over red coat of paint, for £149 10s. By 1967 the Panther was no more, the final batch of singles having to make do with second-hand, reconditioned gearboxes and Magdynos, Burmans and Lucas, respectively, having ceased production of these components. Sadly, hardly anybody noticed that the big cat from Cleckheaton had at last been put to sleep.

Above: Panther's 1967 range included this sporty 250, powered by a two-stroke Villiers engine. For this machine the name Red Panther was revived

Rex

had rounded the last corner, aiming to finish as the bike passed the flag. By the time Handley *did* get there, that tune was on its third lap.

In the next few years, the exploits of Wal Handley, who was eventually to become competitions manager of the factory, ensured that the name of Rex-Acme would be venerated everywhere. That same year, a couple of 250cc models had shaken the more established marques by finishing third and fourth in the 1923 Lightweight TT, ridden by Davy Hall, from Newcastle, and Reg Gray, from Doncaster. Wal Handley, a dour little Brummie who had first shown signs of latent greatness while serving an apprenticeship at the OK works, was recruited into the squad immediately after the TT. At the end of the week following the Belgian Grand Prix, he was at Brook-lands, setting a new British flying five-mile record at 79.94mph, and a standing-start ten-mile record at 78.42mph, on a 250cc Rex-Acme, tuned by Dougal Marchant. A week later, he was carrying the firm's colours in the 200-mile Brooklands endurance race. Before the season was over, he had added the Ulster Grand Prix to his growing collection of 'scalps'.

There was every justification, there-fore, for the Rex Motor Manufacturing Company Ltd to underline the Rex-Acme's racing heritage, by adding the Three Legs of Man to the badge on the fuel tank sides. In fact, the firm had been just as bold in the very earliest days of the British motor cycle industry. As *Motor Cycle* reported, in 1919: 'Rex was one of

A round the hairpin corner at La Source for the last time and down the hill to the pits came nineteen-year-old Walter Handley, newest recruit to the Rex-Acme racing team, and leader from the very start in this the 1923 250cc Belgian Grand Prix. Wal drew up at his pit counter to receive the congratula-tions of his helpers and well-wishers – a worthy winner, with nearest rival Geoff Davison (Levis) six minutes astern. How-ever, while the jollifications were in progress, somebody suddenly remem-bered something. The race, after all, was not yet over. The finishing line was a hundred yards farther on! Hastily, Hand-ley crammed his helmet back on his head and galloped down the road to restart his Blackburne-powered racer. Down swept the flag at last, and nobody was more relieved than the leader of the brass band which had struck up *God Save The King* in honour of young Walter as soon as he

Above: ideal for a family outing – the Rex forecar of 1904

Right: the three-wheeled Rexette of 1906

the pioneer makes which did so much to develop the industry at a time when it appeared to be in danger of becoming extinct by the apathy of manufacturers generally, around 1904'.

Oddly enough, Rex began in Birmingham in 1899 as motor car makers, and they were to stay in car and tri-car manufacture for several years to come. However, by 1900, they had found a new home at Osborne Road, Earlsdon, a Coventry district which was soon to house many more factories. That year, the National Show was held at London's Crystal Palace, and Rex broke new ground by exhibiting a 1¾hp motor cycle. What is more, the Rex was no static exhibit, and it proved to be the only bike to climb a particular hill in the Crystal Palace grounds without the need for pedal assistance.

Perhaps the company was fortunate in that two very enthusiastic brothers were in control, with Billy Williamson as managing director, and Harold Williamson as sales manager. Certainly, the Williamsons did not lack initiative and,

in the next half-dozen years, the Rex was promoted by vigorous advertising campaigns, and by the entry of machines in any kind of competition which would bring the name to public notice.

Harold Williamson himself rode in hill-climbs, such as the Willersey on the Cotswold slopes, or took part in long-distance rides; Frank Applebee carried the Rex flag in northern events. On the New Brighton cycle-racing track, the Baxter family (Edward Baxter, who was

to gain a posthumous VC in World War I, his wife and sister) staged a number of dashing displays of riding. However, it was probably the end-to-end record, from Lands End to John O'Groats, or the other way about, which seemed to fascinate Rex riders most. Arthur Moorhouse was just one of those who made an attempt (unsuccessfully, but that was of little consequence) on the record. The Bentley brothers had better luck in setting a new sidecar time, in 1910.

Right: Harold Williamson pauses at Perth during his record-breaking Lands End-to-John O'Groats run of 1904

Opposite, below: another record ride was attempted by Rex rider C. G. de Finney, who aimed at covering 56,000 miles in 1904, in as short a time as possible. Publicity attempts like these kept the Rex company's name in the public's eye

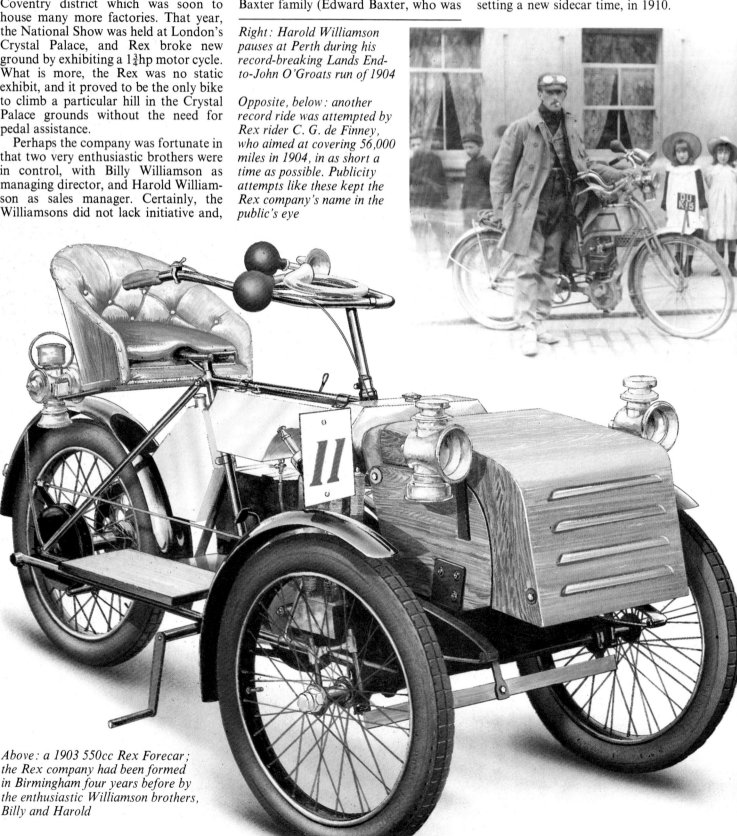

Above: a 1903 550cc Rex Forecar; the Rex company had been formed in Birmingham four years before by the enthusiastic Williamson brothers, Billy and Harold

An unusual feature of Rex engines of the 1900s was the square shape of the cylinder finning. From around 1903 onwards, the engines sat vertically in a well designed frame, and at first they were automatic-inlet-valve type, of 381cc, and drawing gas from a so-called surface carburettor incorporated in the expansive tinware which occupied most of the space between the frame tubes.

Design and development at the enterprising Rex works was galloping on apace and, within a couple of years, a 465cc side-valve and a 726cc, inlet-over-exhaust, vee-twin had come on the scene. By 1906, there were spring front forks, albeit rather clumsy looking affairs with the wheel spindle carried on a sliding member between double tubular stanchions. Yet, if the Rex looked a little odd, at least the forks were effective, and they gave Billy Heaton a comfortable ride into third place in the twin-cylinder class of the 1907 TT races.

Innovation followed innovation and, by 1909, Rex were experimenting with a racing 470cc two-stroke machine, having already explored the possibilities of a rotary-valve engine designed by G. Pilkington. Soon to become fashionable throughout the motor cycle industry, frames with the top tube angled downward at the rear to afford a lower riding position were standardised by Rex as early as 1908. Most eyebrow-raising of all, Rex were first in the field with a bike offered as cheaply as 25 guineas, and that

Above: Muriel Hind, pioneer lady rider, with her famous Rex twin – known as 'Blue Devil' – pictured in 1909. The bike is now in the Murray museum

was in 1907, when they were claiming 'No other maker's 50-guinea model is equal to the 25-guinea Rex'. A year later, Simms-Bosch high-tension magnetos had replaced coil-and-accumulator systems on all models.

Around 1910, motor cycle trials and hill-climbs had been enlivened by the appearance of a brave little lady named Muriel Hind, for whom the Rex works built a very special open-frame version of their 5hp vee-twin. This particular machine became a celebrity in its own right, earning the name *Blue Devil*. However, in the course of time, Muriel settled down and married another Rex rider named Reg Lord and, after several years, Reg extracted the engine from the old twin and used it to power a home made lawn mower.

That is where it was found, another thirty or so years on. Praise be, the discarded frame was still at the back of a garden shed at the Lord's home in Coventry. The frame and engine were reunited, and the *Blue Devil* can now be seen once again, in its entirety, at

Murray's Museum on the Isle of Man.

For the 1911 season, Rex took another bold step by dispensing with pedalling gear on all models, the range by now stretching from a 339cc single up to a 7hp twin, but behind the scenes a power game was being played, and an announcement in October of that year shook the motor cycle manufacturing world. The Williamsons, for so long at the head of Rex affairs, were out. Of course, it did not take either brother long to get back into action, Harold becoming sales manager of Singer, while Billy started his own make of motor cycle, the Williamson, using a big 1000cc water-cooled, flat-twin Douglas engine. The new man in charge of Rex was George H. Hemingway, and it soon became clear that he had no intention of letting the business slide.

By now, Rex were building a second marque, known as Rex-JAP, on behalf of the Premier Motor Company, of Birmingham, but for their own machines they stuck to engines of their own manufacture. The 1912 range was wider still, and could be divided into Tourist, Speed King and De Luxe variations on 499, 532, or 896cc themes.

There were other ventures under con-

sideration, too, such as a totally new 952cc vee-twin, with all-chain drive and roller main and big-end bearings, introduced for 1914. Further refined for 1915, the twin made a surprise appearance in the Buyer's Guide at £77 10s, with shaft-drive transmission, partnering another Rex novelty in the form of a 349cc two-stroke bike. Unfortunately, neither the two-stroke nor the shaft-drive twin reached the general public, because the Rex works had been switched to war work, and that did not include motor cycles – except for a batch of fifty vee-twins for the Russian Army, and a smaller batch for the *Daily Mail* to help the wartime distribution of newspapers from main railway stations.

First hint of post-war Rex plans came in January 1919, when it was hoped that a 4hp single and an 8hp twin would be available shortly. Indeed, the single (of 550cc) was a most interesting design, with mechanical lubrication, and oil carried in a sump extension. Other features included the use of light-alloy for the piston. Meanwhile, the Rex company's next-door neighbours in Osborne Road, the Coventry Acme Motor Company, had been quietly taken over. Acme ('The Machine of No Regrets') offered a JAP-engined 980cc vee-twin, and this was soon joined by a virtually identical 980cc Blackburne-powered Rex, yet not until 1921 did the marriage of names take place, the first model to carry the joint Rex-Acme label being a 350cc Blackburne job nicknamed *Impy*.

Gradually, Rex engine manufacture was tailed off and, from 1922, all Rex-Acme machines used proprietary engines, from the 170cc Aza two-stroke, up through 250 and 350cc ohv Blackburnes, to 293 and 550cc side-valve JAPs, and even a sleeve-valve 350cc Barr & Stroud.

Meanwhile, back to Wal Handley, who in 1925 became the first man to win two TT races in one week, these being the 350cc Junior at 65.02mph and the 175cc Ultra-Lightweight at 53.54mph. In addition, he had broken the 250cc lap record at 60.22mph. A year later, he was riding Rex-Acmes in the Senior, Junior and Lightweight TT. The Senior model, especially, was intriguing for it was a light 498cc vee-twin, on which he was second man home. On his Junior mount,

he was third, but the Lightweight machine failed. However, Lightweight TT victory was his again in 1927, and that year's haul of successes was to include (something rare for Wal Handley) a sidecar race victory in the Brooklands 200-miler.

By this time, too, J. S. (Willy) Worters, with a stable of Rex-Acme-Blackburnes, ridden by RAF pilot Chris Staniland, was helping to keep the name to the fore. Indeed, Worters' 250cc model was well able to lap Brooklands at 90mph and, in 1930, with Staniland up, was to win the 250cc Brooklands Championship at a speed of 90.22mph.

Yet, for all the honours won on the track, Rex-Acme were sliding downhill as the Depression took hold. As a desperate measure, a 172cc Villiers utility model was added, but in 1925 the famous Osborne Road works closed down. It was not quite the end, because the Rex-Acme name was bought by Mr Fulford, of the old-established Mills-Fulford sidecar company, and a new range of 174 and 250cc ohv Rex-Acme lightweights, using Abingdon King Dick power units, emerged from the Mills-Fulford factory at Stoney Stanton Road, Coventry.

The respite was but brief and, by 1933, Rex-Acme had disappeared from the market, taking the Mills-Fulford company with them.

Above: Wal Handley rounds Ramsey Hairpin during the 1927 Junior TT on his 350cc Rex Acme. He set a lap record for the race of 69.18mph

Above left: a 1927 Rex-Acme Blackburne; three years after this was built, Chris Staniland won the 250cc Brooklands Championship, using a similar machine.

Far left: the single-cylinder Blackburne engine of the 1927 Rex-Acme

Left: a 1914 vee-twin Rex sidecar outfit. The engine of 952cc, featured all-chain drive and roller main and big-end bearings

Below: a Rex fire-fighting motor cycle and sidecar combination of around 1914

The famous 1913 inlet-over-exhaust, 425cc vee-twin, designed by W. H. Guillon. One of its innovations was pressure-fed dry-sump lubrication, with a glass storage tank, clearly visible here

Royal Enfield

Like many other old established motor cycle manufacturers Royal Enfield had its origins in the pedal cycle boom of the late Victorian era. In the late 1880s a small firm, George Townsend and Company, of Hunt End – a hamlet two miles south of Redditch in Worcestershire – was marketing its own brand of pedal cycle, the 'Ecossais'. By 1890 the firm found itself in difficulties and was reorganised with new finance coming mainly from the Birmingham area.

George and Foster Townsend did not quite see eye to eye with their backers, however, and so left the business. It was here that Albert Eadie and Robert Smith were brought in to complete the reorganisation, the former being appointed managing director and the latter works manager. Both had had considerable experience of the cycle trade, Eadie having been manager of the cycle department of H. Perrey and Company of Birmingham and Smith having been assistant works manager at the Rudge Company in Coventry. Very soon after, the former Townsend concern became known as the Eadie Manufacturing Company and by the end of 1892 the 'Enfield' bicycle was being made.

In 1893 the Enfield Manufacturing Company Limited was registered, to market the bicycles being made by the Eadie Manufacturing Company and in 1896 the New Enfield Cycle Co was formed to take over the cycle manufacturing operations of both the Eadie Manufacturing Company and the Enfield Manufacturing Company. Within twelve months the word 'New' had been omitted from the title and the firm became the Enfield Cycle Co Ltd. In this same year the Eadie company moved to premises in Lodge Road, Redditch, leaving the Enfield company in sole possession of the Hunt End works.

By 1899 Enfield had made its first move into motor transport and was producing motor tricycles and quadricycles powered by De Dion engines. It was an Enfield quad that E. M. Iliffe entered and rode in the Thousand Miles Trial of 1900, with Walter Grew, manager

of Enfield's motor department, as passenger. Enfield then experimented with a heavyweight bicycle frame with a Minerva engine clamped to its front down tube and with drive via a rawhide belt to the rear wheel. This was followed in late 1901 by a machine designed by Jules L. Gobiet, a Frenchman who had originally come into the area to assist a fellow countryman named Guillaume to build bicycles. The 1901 Royal Enfield had the 1½hp engine clamped to the steering head and the drive was again by rawhide belt but crossed in this instance to ensure maximum contact with the engine pulley; this of course necessitated the engine to run 'backwards'. Other

Above: after a few false starts during the early 1900s the Royal Enfield company returned to full-time motor cycle manufacture in 1910 with this 2¾hp, vee-twin Motosacoche-engined machine

Left: Enfield introduced this 350cc, side-valve engine in 1928

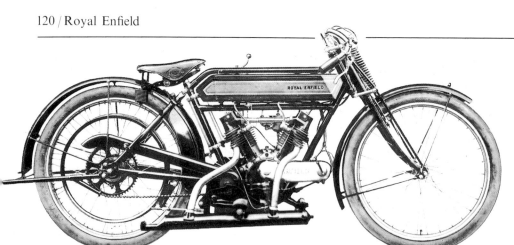

Left: eight of these works 347cc, vee-twin machines were entered in the 1914 TT races

Below: the road-going version of Enfield's 350cc model of 1914

Right: D. Alexander's Royal Enfield at Bray Corner, during the Isle of Man Senior TT of 1914

Below right: in 1912, Royal Enfield introduced this sidecar combination model – the 180. It was powered by a side-valve, 770cc JAP engine

features were a spray carburettor and a bronze connecting rod, which made separate bushes for the big and little ends unnecessary. During the next three years several different models were made, one had the oil tank incorporated in the crankcase (shades of things to come), another had final drive by bicycle chain while others had belt drive.

By 1904 Enfield had lost interest in motor cycles and turned its attention to the motor car trade. The Enfield Autocar Company was formed and although a few cars were built it was not long before the company was in trouble and in 1907 went into liquidation, the assets being acquired by Alldays & Onions of Birmingham who for a number of years produced the Enfield-Alldays motor car.

After the motor car debacle Enfield concentrated on manufacturing component parts for the motor cycle and cycle trade, both at Hunt End and at the new works at Hewell Road, Redditch, into which the company moved in 1907. In this same year the Eadie Manufacturing Company was acquired by BSA Ltd, and Albert Eadie relinquished his seat on the Enfield board of directors, leaving R. W. Smith in charge. It was not until 1910 that Enfield revived its interest in motor cycles and at the Motorcycle and Cycle Show of that year introduced a lightweight vee-twin of 2¼hp, fitted with a Motosacoche engine. This was quickly followed by a 2¾hp machine with an engine of similar design but now with a two-speed gear operating on a

similar principle to that of the Scott and the P & M, together with all chain drive. The company also offered a similar model with single gear chain which was driven via a countershaft.

The following year, 1912, saw the introduction of a model that was to become synonymous with the name Enfield. This was the 6hp sidecar combination, Model No 180, fitted with a 770cc vee-twin JAP engine, two-speed gear, all chain drive and the Enfield patent Cush-drive rear hub, which was to remain a feature of all Enfield models to come. Added to this was a fully upholstered wicker-work sidecar of 'torpedo' design. Early in 1911 the Enfield 'competition department' had been augmented by the addition to the staff of

H. V. (Bert) Colver who had had considerable experience in racing Matchless machines both in the TT Races and at Brooklands Track; it was undoubtedly he who laid the foundations of Royal Enfield's quite reasonable successes at those venues between 1912 and 1914. Unfortunately he only stayed with Enfield for just over twelve months.

In 1913 Enfield introduced its famous 3hp vee-twin solo mount, developed by W. H. Guillon from some of his earlier designs of 1911. The specification included overhead inlet valve and side exhaust valve and the engine was of 425cc capacity. One innovation was that the cylinder barrels were held onto the crankcase by a double clamp between the cylinders and a single clamp on each cylinder outside of the vee-formation. The major innovation was, however, that the engine was fitted with an automatic geared oil pump which fed oil under pressure to the big end bearing via a hollow crankpin and then returned the oil from the crankcase to a glass oil tank set below the saddle thereby giving fully automated dry-sump lubrication. It was with these models, scaled down to 350cc, that Enfield raced at Brooklands and in the TT Races, where, in 1914, F. J. Walker secured third place after a terrific scrap with the Douglases only to crash into a barrier after crossing the finishing line, receiving injuries which proved fatal.

In 1914 Enfield sprang a surprise by entering a single-cylinder, two-stroke machine at Style Cop Hill Climb. This prototype was fitted with a slide-valve actuated from the crankshaft to control the port opening, but as it proved to be expensive to produce the production models were fitted with a more standard type of engine of 225cc. The specification included the usual Enfield two-speed gear and this model continued with only minor changes for at least ten years. During World War I, Enfield supplied thousands of bicycles to the Armed Forces in addition to 8hp sidecar outfits fitted with Vickers machine guns; they also supplied solo 8hp twins to the Russian Government.

With the cessation of hostilities and the return of R. W. Smith's three sons from the Forces, Major Frank Smith again took up the position of assistant managing director, and Enfield was ready to supply the post-war market. The company did not, however, bring out a rash of new models and for 1919 offered the same three as previously, the sidecar combination, now fitted with an 8hp JAP engine, the 3hp twin and the 2¼hp two-stroke model. Before the end of 1919 the 3hp twin was phased out and production continued with just the two remaining models, a policy which was carried through until 1924. For 1921, however, a new 976cc twin of Enfield's own design, and built for them by the Vickers Company, was fitted to the company's successful sidecar combination.

By 1924 Enfield had decided to enter the 350cc single-cylinder market and catalogued a sporty 350, with overhead valve JAP engine. The company also offered a side valve version of the same model and introduced a lightweight, open frame, two-stroke suitable for the lady rider. Although Royal Enfield had featured in Reliability Trials from the earliest days of the sport there is no doubt that it was this excursion into the 350 single-cylinder class that marked the beginning of the marque's considerable and continued success in such events. For 1925 the range continued much the same although a sports two-stroke and a sports solo 8hp twin were added. The most important change in specification was that a Sturmey Archer three-speed gearbox, with hand controlled clutch, was now standard on all models except the two-stroke. The engine of the 8hp model had been redesigned and was now built at Redditch in Enfield's own works, as was the 350cc side-valve, single-cylinder engine that had been designed by Enfield designer E. O. Pardoe.

It was in the latter half of the 1920s that Enfield again tried its luck in the IOM TT races and for the 1925 Junior

Race the team acquired the services of Stanley Woods; unfortunately he retired with a broken handlebar when in fourth place with only one lap to go. In the 1927 Junior Race, Enfield won the Manufacturers Team Award when Reynard, Barrow and Burney finished fourth, seventh and eleventh respectively. C. S. Barrow also finished second in the Lightweight Race of 1928. After 1930 Enfield's interest in racing declined when it was realised that special machines were required to keep on the leader board.

The first 500cc single-cylinder model was introduced in 1927; it had a bore and stroke of 85.5 × 85mm giving 488cc, and this being half the capacity of the big twin meant that the same piston could be used. Included in the specification was a four-speed gearbox of Enfield's own design and manufacture. Gear changing was controlled by a single rod and a conventional quadrant gate but the system was found to be difficult to keep in adjustment. It was later replaced by a double quadrant gate and twin rods

the last to do so; from now on all models would feature the saddle tank arrangement. The following year this 488cc model was supplemented by a new 488cc overhead-valve engine with twin exhaust ports. The 350cc overhead-valve sports was also redesigned with the two-port exhaust arrangement. The frames had also been altered and now followed the lines of the 1928 TT frames. The 488cc models now had their petrol tanks finished in beige with attractive red panels and gold lettering.

1930 showed a deepening of the trade

depression and in an effort to secure its share of the market Enfield fielded eleven different models in its catalogue, but the financial results of the trading year 1930/31 were to show, for the first time since 1897, a loss – to the tune of £2000. By using reserve money, however, Enfield was able to pay shareholders a dividend of 5 per cent, which was more than some of its competitors could do.

Significant engine alterations had been made on the 1930 models, which now incorporated an oil compartment integral with the forward part of the crankcase,

which worked very well unless one tried to make a 'racing' change, when it was possible to engage two gears at the same time – with peculiar results!

For 1928 there was introduced a completely new 225cc, four-stroke, side-valve model, with bulbous saddle tank for the petrol and a separate oil tank below the saddle. Two of the two-stroke models and the 488cc side-valve retained the familiar 'flat' petrol tank but these were

Above: in the late 1920s and early '30s, Royal Enfield marketed their K models. These were big side-valve, vee-twin machines of 972cc. They were generally used with sidecars but were also delightful solo mounts. In 1935 such a model retailed for £65, with an annual tax rate of 45 shillings

and dry sump lubrication on the de-luxe models. Also on these models the petrol tank was chrome plated, with black top and side panels and white lettering. Enfield models were now being designated by letters instead of the previous numbers, and the de-luxe models were all fitted with inclined engines.

A new model, the 570cc side-valve was introduced for 1931 and the Model J de-luxe was uprated to 499cc by increasing the stroke to 99.25mm. A new design of duplex cradle frame was used on some of the models and a flange fitting carburettor was now standard. A last minute surprise at the Show was the introduction of a 488cc, four-overhead-valve model, the model JF; this was the forerunner of a similar type of machine which C. S. Barrow rode into eighth place in the 1935 TT, a splendid effort on a bike that was very close to standard but at the same time was reputed to be capable of 110mph. It was on this machine that the Enfield floating big end bush was first tried out before being revived in later

years to become standard practice. 1931 saw a break with the past with the death of Albert Eadie, one of the founders.

A small but significant change to the engine specification of the newly introduced 488cc four-valve LF Special in 1932 was that the pushrod tunnels were integral with the cylinder barrel and head castings. This model was produced as a sports special and featured foot operated gear change, pump carburettor and twin upswept exhaust pipes as standard. At

Top: a 1912 side-valve, 425cc model in action

Above: a corner of Enfield's road test department, pictured in 1927

the other end of the range was a model that caused quite a sensation. Known as the 'Cycar' it had pressed steel front forks and a pressed steel frame which completely enclosed the 148cc two-stroke engine and transmission and sold for twenty one guineas. Early in 1933 R. W. Smith died at the age of seventy seven years. Thus passed away the remaining founder of Royal Enfield. The chain, however, was not completely broken as his place was taken by his son, Major F. W. Smith who had been assistant managing director for many years.

The programme for 1934 included the 250, 350 and 500 sports models now designated as 'Bullets'. All had the push-rod tubes cast within the cylinder walls and now the magneto drive was by a train of straight cut gears instead of the previous chain drive. At the show, Enfield announced its new 150cc ohv, the Model T, possibly one of the very first ohv engines to have completely enclosed pushrods and overhead rockers. This model had a very good performance for its size and a very excellent fuel economy. The general design of this engine was so successful that eventually other models were built on similar lines.

The 500cc 'Bullet' for 1935 sported a three valve overhead engine, having two inlet valves and one exhaust valve. The previous four-valve head had shown a tendency to crack between the exhaust valve seats unless the head was made of alloy material, it was also difficult to enclose the four valves fully. The three-valve job was reliable but the performance did not compare with that of the four-valve model. The three-valve model was dropped for 1936 and the four-valve, known as Model JF, now with an upright engine, was reinstated. In this year also a number of Royal Enfield models were fitted with pressed steel forks which did nothing to enhance their looks and had a tendency to cheapen the product.

Above left: part of Enfield's production line at Redditch in 1933

Above: the unusual 148cc, two-stroke Cycar model of 1932

Below: Royal Enfield's Bullet model of 1933 had a 488cc engine, a four-speed gearbox and weighed 264lb

Early in 1936 Enfield introduced a super competition model based on the two-valve Model J; it could be had in either 350 or 500cc capacity. The engine was specially tuned and had a cylinder barrel of nickel chrome alloy, nitrided valves, hardened valve guides, and special valve springs. Competition tyres were standard, the frame was of short wheelbase and gave high ground clearance. The finish was certainly eye catching with a highly polished crankcase and lots of chrome plating on the mudguards, headlamp, wheelrims and the small two gallon tank, with red panels and gold lettering. The exhaust pipe was downswept with the large silencer sloping upwards in the manner adopted on the post World War II Bullet models.

Enfield had always supported, with much success, reliability and sporting trials since their return to motor cycle manufacture in 1910, some of their better known riders over the past years having been Harry Greaves, Fred Bicknell, Freddie Thacker and at the time of the introduction of the aforementioned model the legendary team of Len Holdsworth, Jack Booker and Charlie Rogers.

By 1938 the big twin model, the K and KX, was being offered to the home market in its 1140cc capacity. Although made in this form for several years it had been reserved for export only.

With the outbreak of World War II, Enfield supplied to the forces a number of 250cc sv models which were basically for training purpose, followed by the 350cc sv WD/C model and the 350cc ohv WD/CO model. An immediate pre-war development was the 125cc two stroke which was eventually supplied in considerable numbers to the Allied airborne forces, being carried in gliders or dropped by parachute enclosed in a special tubular crate.

With the return of peace Enfield offered the public a quantity of rebuilt ex-WD 350 sv and ohv models. These were apparently 'bought in' from the Ministry of Supply, stripped down and repainted in civilian colours. Most of this work was carried out at their Bradford-on-Avon works. For post-war production three models were available, the 125cc 'Flying Flea' two-stroke, the 350cc ohv Model G and the 500cc ohv Model J, the last being reserved for overseas sale only. Both the ohv models were now fitted with telescopic front forks, the two-stroke model still retaining its rubber band front suspension.

At the Colmore Cup Trial in February 1948 the Royal Enfield team consisting of Len Holdsworth, Charlie Rogers and Jack Plowright were mounted on prototype 350cc machines which incorporated

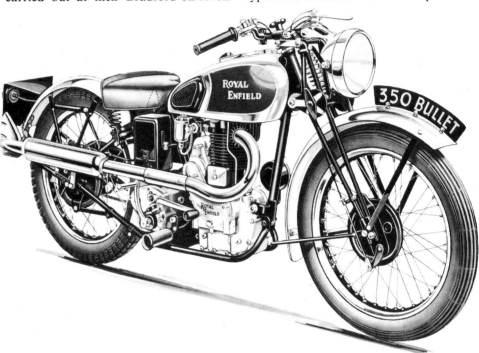

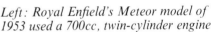

Above: a 350cc Royal Enfield Bullet of 1937. The Bullet was also available in 250cc form

Left: Royal Enfield's Meteor model of 1953 used a 700cc, twin-cylinder engine

swinging arm rear suspension, a new engine with alloy cylinder head and the gearbox bolted to the rear of the crankcase. The machines heralded the arrival of the post-war Bullet.

The new Bullet in its road going form was at the show in November 1948, as was a new 500cc ohv vertical twin, which had separate cylinder barrels and heads, a one piece forged crankshaft with 'bolt up' alloy connecting rods, chain driven twin camshafts and coil ignition together with rear springing and telescopic forks. Early in 1949 it was announced that the 350cc Bullet would be available in Trials or Scrambles specification to order. In the 1948 International Six Days Trial, Enfield had machines in the teams which won both the International Trophy and the Silver Vase. This was followed in 1949 by Enfield's inclusion in the winning Trophy team and in 1950 and 1951 they secured Manufacturers Team Awards.

By 1949–50, Enfield realised that it was missing out on the 250cc market and so for 1951 introduced the 250cc ohv Model S51 which was virtually the reincarnation of the pre-war 250cc ohv model but with the addition of telescopic front forks. By the end of 1952 that young trials star, Johnny Brittain, had firmly established himself and Royal Enfield in the trials world by winning the Scottish Six Days Trial, the Welsh Two-day Trial and finished the year with the best solo performance in the British Experts Trial; and just to prove it was no fluke he won it again in 1953. At the Motorcycle Show in November 1952, Enfield introduced three new models for the following season, the 150cc Ensign two-stroke, the 500cc Bullet and the 692cc ohv twin cylinder Meteor. Early in 1954 three competition models were available in either trials, scrambles or short circuit racer form, in 350 or 500cc capacity. The same year saw the introduction of a new 250cc ohv, the Clipper, and all models now had their headlamps and the uppermost part of the forks enclosed in an alloy 'Casquette'.

A new style frame was introduced on the Bullet and Meteor for 1956 and the electrical system was reorganised by fitting a Lucas RM14 alternator on the engine shaft for lighting and battery charging. Ignition was attended to by a Lucas rotating magnet type of magneto.

Enfield broke new ground for 1957 with the introduction of a completely new 250cc ohv model, the Crusader. The engine bottom half was of singular construction having virtually four separate compartments to house respectively the gearbox internals, footchange mechanism and Lucas generator, primary drive and timing gear and lastly the engine mainshaft and flywheels cast as a one piece construction. The connecting rod was of split big end type with white metal plain bearings. Seventeen inch wheels and deeply valanced mudguards and a fully enclosed rear chain made for a tidy and compact machine.

In co-operation with one of the motor cycle weekly magazines, Enfield produced the prototype of a fully enclosed streamlined model which became known as the Dreamliner. Tests carried out proved it to be highly satisfactory from a point of view of speed, general handling and fuel economy. It was considered, however, that the cost of production and its rather futuristic design would not appeal to the motor cyclist of the day so an abbreviated design of frontal enclosure was made and became known as the Airflow.

Late in 1958, the 350cc Works Replica Trials model was announced and, as its name implied, it was a replica of the machines that had been ridden so successfully by the works riders. Today it is a much sought after vintage model.

Top: Royal Enfield introduced their 500cc Bullet model at the London Motorcycle Show of 1952. This is a 1956 version.

Above: a Royal Enfield tank badge

Above right: John Hartle (seated) discusses the single-cylinder, 250cc Royal Enfield with Geoff Duke in 1964

Also introduced in this year was the 692cc Constellation which was virtually a sports version of the Super Meteor. Another model also introduced was the Meteor Minor of 492cc capacity which was more or less a updated model of the 500 Twin. For the 1962 season Enfield introduced a completely new model the Crusader Super-5, powered by a sports version of the Crusader engine to which was added a five-speed gearbox and a new design of leading link telescopic front fork.

The year 1962 was to leave its mark on the history of Royal Enfields for in April Major Frank Smith died at the age of seventy three. He had joined his father, R. W. Smith, in the company in 1909 and became joint managing director with him in 1914. On the death of his father in 1933, Major Smith became sole managing director which post he held until his retirement from the board in 1960 when he became chairman of the company. His passing severed a direct link with the past history of Royal Enfield. Later in the year Enfield's directors recommended that share holders accept a merger offer from E. & H. P. Smith Ltd, the holding company of a large group of Midland engineering firms.

At the end of 1962, Enfield announced a even bigger and better twin, the 736cc Interceptor developing 52bhp at 6000rpm which gave over 100mph maximum and easy cruising at 85 to 90mph.

At the beginning of 1963, as a result of the merger, Enfield found itself with a new board of directors with Leo Davenport, of past racing fame, together with Major Vic Mountford, operating as joint managing directors.

Billed by the Press as the fastest British 250, the Continental GT introduced for 1965 was a instant success. With its bright red tank, swept back exhaust and a top speed of 90mph it appealed to the younger riders.

For some time Enfield had been developing a racer fitted with a Villers Starmaker engine. This was later replaced by a new engine consisting of an Alpha bottom half and a Royal Enfield cylinder head, barrel and piston which had been developed by Herman Meier. The services of Geoff Duke had also been retained in a advisory capacity.

November 1964 saw the untimely death of Major Vic Mountford who had joined Royal Enfield in 1928, working his way through the sales department to become cycle sales manager in 1933. After wartime service with the Worcestershire Regiment he re-joined Enfield, was made general manager in 1947 and appointed to the board in 1959.

At the Earls Court Show of 1964 the centre piece of the Royal Enfield stand was the 250cc production 'racer' with the Alpha/Enfield two-stroke engine. The engine was mounted in a low built duplex tube frame with leading link front fork, transmission was via a five speed Albion gearbox and the rear hub and brake were by Oldani. Price tag was £350. The Enfield range now offered consisted

of nine 250cc models ranging from the Turbo Twin through the Crusader and Continental to the Racer; the two final models were the 350cc Bullet and the 736cc Interceptor twin.

During 1965, Royal Enfield tried very hard to hit the jackpot with their works entries of the racer but all to no avail and by the end of the racing season they had

decided to call a halt. A great pity because Gordon Keith achieved a maximum of 125mph in the 1965 TT, a speed reputed to be faster than any other British 350.

In 1967, the long history of Royal Enfield came to a end, the machinery and stock were sold off and the Redditch factory disposed of. For a short while production of the Interceptor was continued at the Bradford-on-Avon works.

The Enfield name did not die, however, for Enfield India continued production of the 350 Bullet, under a licence agreement forged in the 1950s. Known as the Madras, the bike was even imported into Britain.

Above: by the end of 1952, Royal Enfield's young trials star Johnny Brittain had established himself and his Enfield as a powerful force in the sport by winning the Scottish Six Days Trial and the Welsh Two Day Trial. This is his magnesium-engined 350cc model of 1949, with its famous HNP 331 registration number

Left: many people suppose that the 'super-bike' is a recent invention, but Royal Enfield could claim to have built a superbike as far back as the mid 1960s. This was the 736cc Interceptor model, capable of well over 100mph

Rudge

Travellers around Coventry city's elevated Ring Road cannot help but notice that at one spot (named Rudge Ringway, although the nameplate is difficult to find) the road runs alongside a very substantial factory. On the roof of that factory, nowadays occupied by the General Electric Company, there is a square, brick-built tower with white painted sides; and when the rain lashes against the tower two huge black letters make a ghostly appearance through the white paintwork, on one panel a big 'R', and on another an equally gigantic 'W'.

The explanation is that the works, actually situated in Crow Lane, were formerly the home of Rudge-Whitworth Ltd, in the eyes of motor cycle enthusiasts possibly the saddest casualty of World War II.

Not that the Rudge began in Coventry nor, for that matter, did it die there. For the start of it all we must travel to Wolverhampton in 1868 where, in a

workshop behind the Tiger's Head Inn of which he was the innkeeper, Dan Rudge had begun building velocipedes, forerunners of the bicycle. Old Dan was not only a good workman, but he had an inventive brain and within a few years he had patented such worthwhile features as ball-bearing wheel spindles, and adjustable ball-bearing cycle pedals. He died in 1880, but by that time he had built up quite a considerable business.

Shortly afterwards, the business was bought from Dan's widow by one George Woodcock, a very shrewd Coventry lawyer who already held interests in several other bicycle manufacturing companies. Among these were Smith and Starley (who were making Ariel cycles and Europa sewing machines), and Haynes and Jefferies, and Woodcock now merged all three companies into a new combine with the rather clumsy title of 'D. Rudge and Company and the Coventry Tricycle Company'.

Above: the first of the really famous Rudges was the Multi, introduced in 1912. It was known as the Multi because of the multiplicity of gear ratios offered

Smith and Starley had housed the sewing machine part of their operation in modest premises called Trafalgar Works, Crow Lane. Nevertheless, Crow Lane was chosen by Woodcock as the headquarters of the new company and, of course, over the years it was to be extended, demolished, and rebuilt in step with the expansion of production. From 1885, after Woodcock and a few friends had launched a private limited liability company, the latter part of the firm's name was dropped, and the more manageable title of D. Rudge and Company Ltd was adopted.

But the story was certainly not one of sunshine all the way, and by the early 1890s Rudge were heading for the rocks. There were several reasons for this. The home cycle market was showing signs of having reached saturation, while the once-lucrative American trade had dwindled to nothing, in consequence of the establishment of the USA's own cycle industry. In addition to this, the Rudge company was sadly missing the guiding hand of George Woodcock, who had died after a short illness.

A few miles away in Birmingham, however, the sun still shone brightly on the business of Charles H. Pugh Ltd, manufacturers of screws and ironmongers' sundries, of Whitworth Works, Rea Street South, Birmingham. Pugh had been supplying cycle fittings and stampings to other manufacturers for some while and now, in 1891, they were to enter bicycle manufacture themselves by forming the Whitworth Cycle Company, with Charles Vernon Pugh as managing director and John Vernon Pugh as works manager.

The new Whitworth bicycles needed a trade-mark, and that same year the device of an open red hand superimposed on a bicycle wheel was duly assigned to 'Charles Henry Pugh, of Birmingham, screw and velocipede manufacturer'. Just why such a design was chosen is a mystery that has puzzled researchers into Rudge history for many a year, because the Pugh family were of Welsh stock, and had no apparent connection with Ulster, of which province the red hand is also

the badge. The fact that Rudge were to introduce, many years hence, a very potent motor cycle known as the Rudge Ulster is pure coincidence.

Be that as it may, the Whitworth cycle business flourished. It became a limited company in 1893, and because the need for larger premises was becoming urgent, talks were instituted with the ailing Rudge Cycle Company Ltd (as it now was, following yet another financial reshuffle). Agreement was reached which resulted in the formation of Rudge-Whitworth Ltd in October, 1894.

The headquarters of the new company would be at Crow Lane, Coventry, but there was little doubt that the reins would be firmly in the hands of the Pugh family. Meantime, the original Charles H. Pugh Ltd business was to continue at Rea Street South, as a source of parts and sub-assemblies for Rudge-Whitworth in addition to manufacturing specialities in their own right. Here it may be said that this arrangement lasted well into the 1920s before the Birmingham branch (by that time mainly concerned with making Atco motor mowers) became wholly independent. It still exists, today a member of the Qualcast group.

Involvement of Rudge-Whitworth with motor cycles was, at first, rather oblique in that Charles V. Pugh came to an arrangement with Werner, of Paris, to market Werner motor cycles in South

Africa through the Rudge-Whitworth distributing network based on Johannesburg. Not until mid-1910 did the Coventry factory produce an experimental machine of Rudge's own design. It was a 499cc (85 × 88mm bore and stroke), with inlet over exhaust valve layout, and from the prototype there evolved the first production models of 1911.

These featured the same inlet-over-exhaust engine, refined in detail and now with a starter pedal coupled by chain to a sprocket outboard of the timing chest. From the start, a dropped frame top tube afforded a low seating position; there

was a girder-type front fork with enclosed centrally-mounted spring, and as a protection against rust the sweeping handlebars were coated in black celluloid. Indeed, the enclosed central spring, and the black-coated handlebars were to survive right to the end of the company's motor cycle production.

Rudge were not slow in showing what the new machine could do, and in 1911, Victor Surridge gave a demonstration by completing laps of Brooklands at an average of 61.39mph. Months

Left: Cyril Pullin poses on the 500cc, single-cylinder Rudge Multi on which he won the Isle of Man Senior TT of 1914. His time for the race was 4 hours and 32 minutes which was an average speed of 49.50mph

Far left: a close-up of the single-cylinder, 500cc engine of the Rudge used by A. Gulling at the BMCRC Brooklands meeting in 1914

Rudge Multi

The Blue Riband of Motor Cycle Sport.

The unapproachable perfection of the Rudge Multi was demonstrated in the 1914 Isle of Man Senior Tourist Trophy Race. Mr. C. G. Pullin, on a 3½ h.p. single cylinder machine, secured first place, doing the 225 miles in 4 hrs. 32 mins. 48 secs. His average speed was more than a mile an hour faster than that of the 1913 Winner.

The Catalogue which illustrates and describes the Rudge Multi is sent post free by

Rudge-Whitworth, Ltd.
(Dept. 201), Coventry.

London Depots: 230, Tottenham Court Road (Oxford St. End), W.; 23, Holborn Viaduct, E.C.

By Appointment Cycle Makers to H.M. King George

R262

Left: in 1919, Rudge introduced a 998cc vee-twin Multi model which, when equipped with the Multi gear, was also known as the Multwin

Above: this poster was used by the Rudge company to advertise its impressive victory in the 1914 Senior TT by its 3½hp, 500cc model

later Surridge did better by setting a new Brooklands lap record of 66.47mph, his Rudge becoming the first 500cc machine to pack sixty miles into one hour. A rival manufacturer was to better Surridge's one-hour record, but by October the same record was back in Rudge hands, now raised to 65.45mph.

Tragically, it was not Surridge who regained the record, but Stanhope Spencer. For the 1911 TT races, the first to be held over the full mountain course, Rudge had entered a four-man squad, but during one of the practice sessions Vic Surridge crashed in Glen Helen, earning a black page in Isle of Man history as the first rider to be killed in the TT series. Only two riders finished, with Stanhope Spencer the better of the pair.

On the mainland, Rudges had been doing well enough in trials and hill-climbs, with Cecil Burney and Alan Hill the most prominent performers. More-over, there was a further boost for the factory when Stanhope Spencer established a new world motor cycle record, by covering the flying mile at 72.5mph in August, 1911. Nevertheless, it was be-coming obvious that the Rudge needed the added refinement of a change-speed gear system.

To this point all production Rudges had been single-gear, although NSU two-speed gearing, the Mabon variable gear, or Phillipson adjustable driving pulleys could be specified. The Rudge engine-

Above: a 250cc Rudge similar to this machine was used by Graham Walker to win the 1930 Lightweight TT

Above right: A.E. Taylor, a member of the 1922 Rudge Isle of Man TT team

Right: a close-up of the single-cylinder, 750cc Rudge Multi engine of 1919

Far right: a 500cc Rudge single of 1926

Below: G. Watson Bourne used this three-speed Rudge in the 1922 Senior TT

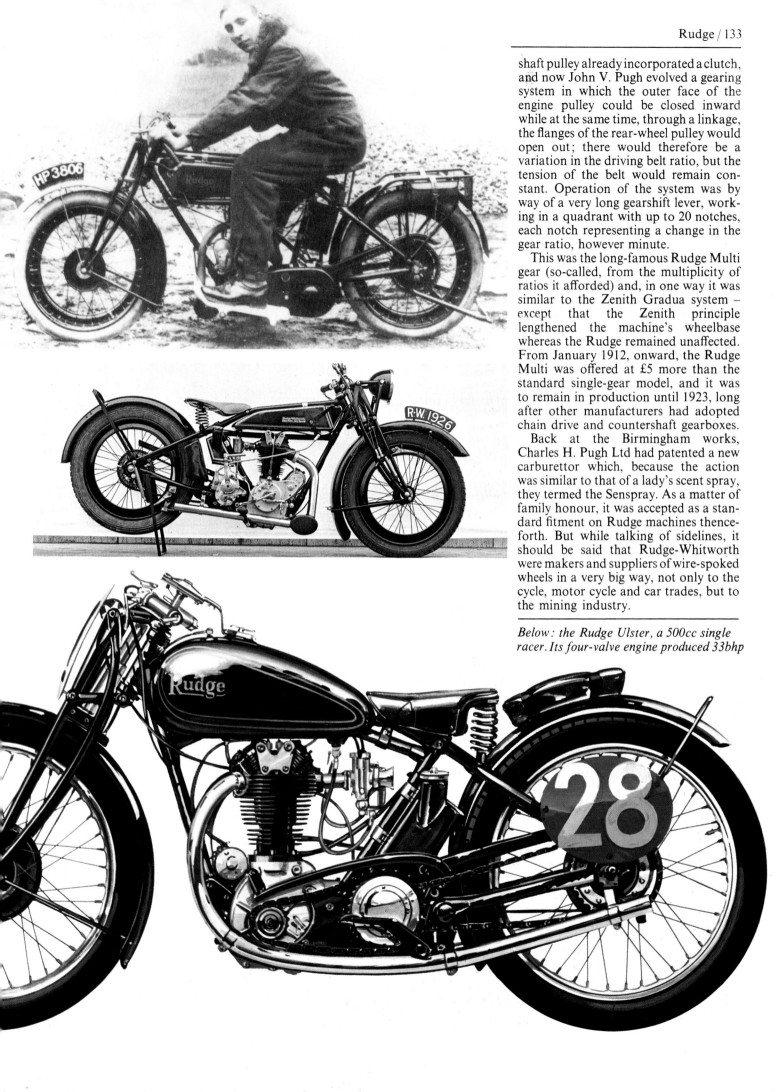

shaft pulley already incorporated a clutch, and now John V. Pugh evolved a gearing system in which the outer face of the engine pulley could be closed inward while at the same time, through a linkage, the flanges of the rear-wheel pulley would open out; there would therefore be a variation in the driving belt ratio, but the tension of the belt would remain constant. Operation of the system was by way of a very long gearshift lever, working in a quadrant with up to 20 notches, each notch representing a change in the gear ratio, however minute.

This was the long-famous Rudge Multi gear (so-called, from the multiplicity of ratios it afforded) and, in one way it was similar to the Zenith Gradua system – except that the Zenith principle lengthened the machine's wheelbase whereas the Rudge remained unaffected. From January 1912, onward, the Rudge Multi was offered at £5 more than the standard single-gear model, and it was to remain in production until 1923, long after other manufacturers had adopted chain drive and countershaft gearboxes.

Back at the Birmingham works, Charles H. Pugh Ltd had patented a new carburettor which, because the action was similar to that of a lady's scent spray, they termed the Senspray. As a matter of family honour, it was accepted as a standard fitment on Rudge machines thenceforth. But while talking of sidelines, it should be said that Rudge-Whitworth were makers and suppliers of wire-spoked wheels in a very big way, not only to the cycle, motor cycle and car trades, but to the mining industry.

Below: the Rudge Ulster, a 500cc single racer. Its four-valve engine produced 33bhp

At the request of sidecar enthusiasts the standard 500cc ioe engine was supplemented by a 750cc version, and by 1913 total motor cycle production was running at approximately 80 machines a week. The early months of that year had seen Rudge riders collecting their customary tally of honours at Brooklands and elsewhere, and everything seemed set fair for the Isle of Man TT. No fewer than twelve Rudges were in the line-up, the biggest contingent from any factory, and they were headed by talented rider-designer Cyril Pullin.

That year, for the one and only time, the ACU ran the TT as a two-day event over thirteen laps. The end of the opening lap saw four Rudge riders heading the field, with Frank Bateman as race leader. In those days, however, the track across the mountain from Ramsey to Creg-ny-Baa was little more than a three-ply farm lane, and as the field approached Kate's Cottage Bateman's front wheel caught in a rut, and he was thrown against a roadside rock at 70mph, dying from his injuries shortly after.

Even then, the race might have been a Rudge victory, because in the closing stages the lead was held by Ray Abbott. Perhaps it was excitement, or maybe it was just exhaustion, but Abbott came into the final corner with his Multi gear in high instead of low, and stalled the engine. He got going again, but by then the race was lost – by just five seconds. There was no such mistake the following year, Cyril Pullin winning the 1914 Senior TT at the speed of 49.50mph.

John Pugh had been experimenting

Above: the 1930 Isle of Man TT Rudge team lines up for a group photograph

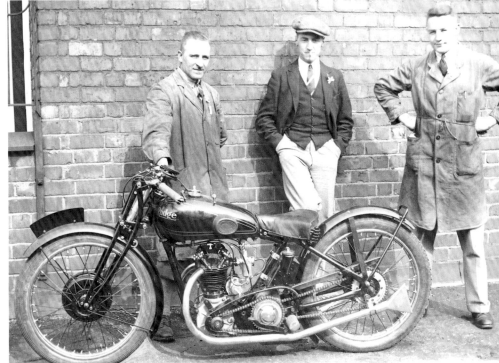

Top right: Walter Handley in action during the Senior TT of 1932

Above right: messrs Mott, Handley and Tyrrell Smith with the 1932 250cc racer

Right: some things never change; can this immaculate 500cc speedway racing Rudge really have been built as long ago as 1928?

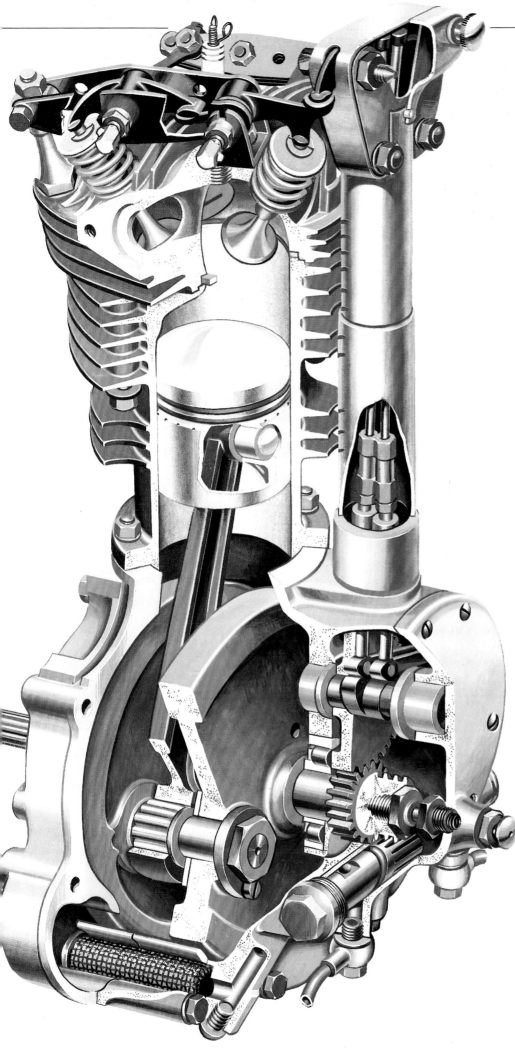

with a 998cc vee-twin, but before it could be put into production the shadow of war had fallen across Europe. Rudge bicycles, in service green, were chosen as the standard mount of the British, French, Belgian, and Russian armies, but in the main the works were occupied with other military contracts, and motor cycle production had to be set aside.

And so it was 1919 before the 998cc twin (which, when equipped with the Multi gear was known as the Multwin) entered the Rudge catalogue. The 499 and 750cc ioe singles returned, too, and production began to creep upwards. But the sad truth was that belt drive, and with it the Rudge Multi, was by now hopelessly outdated. John Pugh began work on a three-speed gearbox, and a twin so equipped appeared at the 1920 London Show, followed in the spring of 1921 by an all-chain-drive 499cc single.

It was by no means enough. The immediate post-war boom had long since spent its force, and now there were too few customers to be shared among too many manufacturers. In the hope that a sales increase would follow competitions success, Rudge reinstated a racing programme, but to little effect. However, the gloom was lightened a little by the exploits at Brooklands of Bob Dicker and Bert Mathers, with a gearbox-equipped 998cc twin in both solo and sidecar trim. The haul included the Brooklands 24-hour sidecar record.

Only just in time, a replacement for the superannuated inlet-over-exhaust engine arrived. This was the 'Rudge Four', not a four-cylinder machine but a single, available first as a 350cc, but later with the alternative of a 500cc engine, with four overhead valves and a four-speed gearbox. Public response was immediate, and in 1924 the total output of the factory was double that of the previous year.

The company returned to full-scale racing in 1926, using pent-roof four-valve engines that were little different to the standard road-going jobs.

For 1927, racing manager George Hack opted for an all-out effort. For the first time the Rudge entries had saddle tanks, and there were coupled 8in-diameter drum brakes instead of the flat-rim brakes of earlier years. The new cylinder heads had splayed instead of parallel exhaust ports, Amac carburettors replaced the old Senspray type, and on alcohol were capable of 100mph.

Rudge's sales department joined in with a publicity campaign which included distribution, to TT visitors, of many hundreds of dark green handkerchiefs bearing the slogan: 'When you see a Rudge go by, cheer and wave your hankie!' Oh, it was all great fun; except

Left: cutaway of the single-cylinder, four-stroke, 250cc Rudge engine of 1931

that, alas, all three machines retired with mechanical trouble.

All was not quite lost, though. On test, the TT engines could turn out a healthy 28bhp at 5200rpm, and after only minor modifications they were sent out to reap a successful continental harvest, including second places in the Belgian and Ulster Grands Prix, and third at the German Nürburgring circuit.

Previously with the Sunbeam company, Graham Walker came to Rudge in 1928 as sales manager, doubling when necessary as works road-racer. In that year's Senior TT he was holding a three-minute lead on the last lap, with only nine miles to go to the finish, when the big-end bearing seized. It was a disappointment, but glory was to come in full measure before that season was over.

After a wheel-to-wheel battle with Charlie Dodson (Sunbeam), Graham won the Ulster Grand Prix by 200 yards – but that wasn't all. His winning speed was 80.078mph, the first time any road race anywhere had been won with an over 80mph average. It was to give the UGP the proud title of 'The World's Fastest Road Race'. And it was to give the Rudge company a name for the subsequent works-replica racers that was to live in history, the Rudge Ulster.

The Ulster Grand Prix win heralded Rudge's best-ever racing era. Walker won the Ulster again in 1929, in which year Ernie Nott won the Dutch TT and Tyrell Smith the German and Czech Grands Prix. A new short-track sport had reached Britain from Australia, and riders such as Smiling Jim Kempster and Arthur Willimot were broadsiding their short-wheelbase Rudges through the cinder turns to offer effective opposition to the Douglases and Harley-Davidsons.

In the Rudge four-valve engine, however, the layout was 'pent roof', with the inlet and exhaust valves arranged in parallel pairs. It was a convenient arrangement, but not necessarily the best for efficient filling and combustion.

Still, Rudge decided to have a go in 1930. The original concept was George Hack's, who combined the duties of race-shop chief and development engineer, but the detail design work was left to Frank Anstey (in later years chief designer for Villiers), and he solved the problem of the valve operation by using just two pushrods and a chain of rockers across the top of the cylinder head.

One of the new engines was to be entered for the 1930 Junior TT, ridden by Tyrell Smith, and accordingly a machine was built, together with what was judged to be a suitable supply of spare parts. Almost at the last moment, however, John Pugh decided that there would be a full three-man works team, the other two being Graham Walker and Ernie Nott.

That threw the works into a panic, because the race was only weeks away, and the only radial-valve engine that had even fired was the hack road-mileage prototype. Nevertheless, three machines were built, even though it had meant using up all the stock of spares, and were duly shipped to the Island.

Elation came the first morning of practice, when Tyrell Smith whistled round in a time that (unofficially) beat the lap record handsomely. But the elation died shortly after when, having stripped the engine for routine inspection, the Rudge mechanics found that both piston bosses were cracked. The cloud over the camp grew greyer yet when, after Walker and Nott had practiced, the piston bosses of their engines exhibited ominous cracks.

On the third practice morning, George Hack gave Tyrell Smith instructions to go flat-out from the start and rip off three non-stop laps, just to see what would happen. Again the engine was stripped, but at least the piston cracks seemed little worse than before. George did some calculations, and declared that the pistons would last for eight laps before breaking up completely, and since the race was only seven laps long, it was considered that that left something in hand.

New pistons were fitted for the final morning's practice session, and the riders were told to go out and do just *one* lap each, to bed things down. One from eight left exactly seven, and if Hack's calculations were right, there would then be nothing in hand whatever.

Nor was that the only worry, because that final morning Graham Walker's engine had seized, bending the connecting rod and tearing the cylinder from its base flange. The only source of spares was the road-mileage development bike, and the connecting rod and cylinder were removed and installed in Graham's.

When the race got under way, Charlie Dodson and his Sunbeam proved to be the danger man, as had been anticipated, and Tyrell Smith was given the job of going after him, in the hope that the Sunbeam's engine would blow up. That is exactly what did happen, and in the final stages of the race Tyrell Smith was the leader, with Walker and Nott coming through to sit in second and third places.

Later, the three machines were stripped for official examination. On Graham Walker's engine the piston not only had cracked gudgeon-pin bosses (as had the other two models) but there was a

back, to finish fourth.

With the financial position worsening rapidly, Rudge now went into proprietary-engine manufacture, offering the 250, 350 and 500cc four-valve engines (and even a 175cc version, never seen in their own programme) under a Python label. The Python engines were soon to be seen in Cotton AJW, Grindlay-Peerless, and various other frames, including some from European factories.

For all the troubles, the roadsters were progressively improved. The 1932 range brought cast-aluminium primary chaincases, and a centre stand worked by a long, easy-lift hand lever. These and other features could not stave off impending bankruptcy, and in March, 1933, an official receiver was appointed; at the

Above left: as a result of Graham Walker's superb victory in the Ulster Grand Prix of 1928, the company's sports 500cc machines were thereafter called Rudge Ulsters – a name which has now become part of motor cycling history. This is a 1933 model.

Left: a 500cc, single-cylinder, four-valve Rudge Special of the 1930s

Above: Harold Hartley on his 500cc Rudge at the 1939 Senior TT; he eventually finished in 29th position

Right: members of a Palestine motor cycling club touring Britain on their Rudges, pause at the factory in Crow Lane, Coventry

ghastly slit all the way down to within a quarter-inch of the skirt base. George Hack had been dead right. The bike would never have travelled more than another mile or so!

In normal times, the tremendous TT success would have resulted in soaring sales of the corresponding road-going models, which by this time embraced a 250cc, 350cc, and several variations on a 500cc theme. It was just Rudge's typical misfortune that they should find road-racing form coincidentally with the onset of the deepest trade recession the world had ever known. Design and development of the racing engines had cost a stack of money of which there was now little hope of recouping.

Even so, a 250cc radial-valve racer was introduced in 1931 (there was also an experimental 250cc radial valve vee-twin, but this was not proceeded with) and, ironically, the beefiest character in the whole Rudge squad, Graham Walker, collected his one and only TT Trophy by winning the Lightweight TT, with Tyrell Smith as runner-up. It was very nearly another 1-2-3 for Rudge, because Ernie Nott had been leader on the last lap until a tappet slackened off and he dropped

same time the racing department was closed down. There would be racing Rudges in 1933 and 1934, but these were private entries, running under the banner of the Graham Walker Syndicate.

To his credit, the receiver tried to make the company viable rather than put it into liquidation, and the range was updated both in looks and by the adoption of such features as a positive-stop gearchange pedal – on the left (the reason for

compact factory adjacent to the main EMI plant at Hayes, Middlesex.

The transfer took place during 1938, and although the Rudge range as advertised for the 1939 season was of necessity on a smaller scale, behind the scenes a new design project had been put in hand, and this included a totally new 350cc overhead-camshaft engine. A two-valve 250cc Rudge had been on acceptance trials with the British Army, and

Below: a Rudge Special of 1938. It was powered by a single-cylinder, four-valve, 500cc, four-stroke engine
Right: the power house of the 1930 500cc TT replica machine. The picture shows Frank Anstey's neat method of controlling four valves with just two pushrods

this, it was said, was that Graham Walker couldn't operate a gear pedal with his injured right foot).

The final blow came with the death of John Vernon Pugh in 1936. Control of the company's destinies passed to the Gramaphone Company Ltd, manufacturers of radio equipment and records under the HMV trade-mark. In fact this was a rescue operation, and HMV had every intention of making a go of their new acquisition. Development continued, and totally-enclosed valve gear was introduced for 1937. Also, Britain had chosen Rudges for the 1937 International Six Days Trial 'Vase B' squad (they won!) and the quickly-detachable rear wheel developed for the ISDT models was now to be listed as an optional extra for the 500cc Ulster, Special, and Sports Special.

Gradually, sales began to pick up, but not to the extent that would keep the big Crow Lane factory fully occupied. Accordingly, HMV (by this time known as EMI) decided to condense the Rudge business, moving it south to a more

now came the happy news that it would go into service immediately.

Regrettably, though, Rudge plans were to be disrupted by war yet again, and only 200 of the Army-model 250cc bikes had been completed before the entire factory was requisitioned for the production of radio (and, later, radar) equipment for service use. In the last months before World War II, one new Rudge had been introduced, but this was a utility autocycle (grandfather of the moped) with a Villiers two-stroke engine.

Production of the Rudge autocycle was passed across to the Norman cycle works at Ashford and, eventually, the manufacturing rights of Rudge machines were acquired by Raleigh, who already owned the rights to Rudge bicycles. However, the EMI-built Rudge works at Hayes did have one final fling in the two-wheel (or, in this case, one-wheel) world because it was there, in the 1950s, that the little Cyclemaster power wheel was manufactured under contract. It was an incongruous postscript.

Scott

Alfred Angas Scott was no ordinary man. Possessed of many attributes – an outstanding inventor, a very talented engineer, a gifted artist and an accomplished pianist – to name but four of his talents, it is indeed tragic to find that he died when only 48 years old. Typically, his death was caused by little more than a severe cold that developed into pneumonia when he refused medical attention, and all because he insisted on driving home in wet clothes after a pot-holing session, one of his favourite pastimes, around Ingleton.

Alfred was born in 1874, the tenth son and a twin, in a family of twelve children. His birthplace was a sizeable Victorian house in the Manningham district of Bradford. When he left school, Alfred became apprenticed in the world of marine engineering and it was his work with large steam engines that had much influence on his engine designs in later years, as events will show. Initially, he became very interested in the bicycle and he applied for his first patent in 1897, when he developed a caliper brake. A year or two later, it was the internal combustion engine that intrigued him,

possibly as the result of assisting one of his elder brothers to perfect a single-cylinder gas engine which he had designed and built. Alfred became very interested in the two-stroke engine, which was still hardly a viable proposition, and it was not long before he had designed and built his own vertical twin engine, which he fitted to the frame of his Premier bicycle – a convenient test bed. The engine was rated at 2hp and was mounted in front of the steering head so that it drove the front wheel by direct contact with the centrally disposed flywheel. Later, the engine was moved back behind the steering head, from which drive to the rear wheel was arranged by means of a twisted leather belt to a countershaft and thence to the rear wheel by chain and sprockets. On occasion, the engine was removed from the bicycle and fitted into a boat named Petrel, which Alfred used on the River Clyde whilst holidaying in Tighnabruaich. It was this prototype design that led to his successful application for a patent during 1904, thus making the vertical twin, two-stroke engine a reality. An outstanding feature of the engine was the centrally-disposed

flywheel mentioned earlier, fitted with 180° overhung cranks to which the slim section connecting rods were attached. Scott had found during his marine engineering days that it was necessary to keep the cylinder axes as close together as possible, to eliminate the rocking couple that is inherent with this design of engine.

1908 was another year of significance. It was during this year that Scott had another patent application granted, for a design of frame that relied upon an arrangement of triangulated tubes, all of which were straight. He had a hatred of cranked rear frame members, especially those designed to give clearance for the belt drive transmission of that era. Scott's frame design became as much his trade mark as his engines, and it remained virtually unaltered until 1930. In 1908 he also patented a greatly improved engine, of 333cc capacity, with water-cooled cylinder heads and a simple, but very effective, two-speed gear. Having what seemed to be a very promising prototype design on his hands, it now appeared opportune to commence the manufacture of machines that would be marketed bearing his name.

Below: by 1910, Alfred Scott had formed his own company to build his two-stroke specials. By then the capacity of the twin-cylinder engine had been increased to 450cc

Below right: a 1911 Scott; by this time the engine capacity had again been increased, this time to 486cc. In addition, a water-cooled block was now fitted, as was a honeycomb type radiator

first public appearance at the Bradford Club's Wass Bank Hill Climb, he came away with a shield and a gold medal. Three weeks later he won no less than three gold medals in the Coventry MCC's Newham Hill Climb. The press attended this latter event and also the trade, so that the promise shown by this new machine did not escape attention.

Development work continued at the newly-rented premises in Grosvenor Street, Bradford, where the production of Scott motor cycles recommenced under the direct control of the inventor. The target was one hundred machines, embodying many improved features that included a radiator of Scott's own design, and a kickstarter – the first occasion on which such a device had been fitted to a motor cycle. Frank Philipp, a cousin by marriage, road tested the first few mach-

Below: Alfred Scott's first six bikes were built in the premises of the Bradford engineers Ben and William Jowett in 1908. The bikes were water-cooled, two-stroke twins, of 333cc

ines off the production line and later became a 'works' rider, together with Eric Myers, another Bradfordian. Outwardly, the newer models differed little in appearance from the Jowett-made originals but, because the earlier engines were underpowered, the engine capacity was now increased to 450cc. The colour purple figured prominently in the company's catalogues and was also used for the cylindrical petrol tank that surrounded the saddle tube, surmounted by two silver bands. Purple was the colour of Scott's sister-in-law's favourite dress and it was she who had inspired the use of the two silver bands as symbolic of two stroke. The familiar index number AK222 used in the catalogues represented the local registration prefix, then two-stroke, two-speed and two-cylinder. Scott had his own personal number, AK 775, which became a familiar sight in competition events.

A Scott ridden by Eric Myers was

With no capital, financial backing or production facilities, Alfred Scott came to an arrangement with two Bradford motor engineers, Ben and William Jowett. It was on their premises that the first six Scott motor cycles were built, but production came to a halt when the Jowett brothers decided to concentrate on the development of their own light car. So, the Scott Engineering Company was born, when Alfred and several close friends raised the necessary capital for him to set up on his own, which seemed the only alternative.

Already his machines were gaining quite a reputation for themselves. When a Scott ridden by Alfred himself made a

their induction cycle, he designed and patented a rotary valve, which he fitted in place of the transfer port covers. Frank Applebee joined the team as third man, but again their luck was out. The rotary valve sprocket was not keyed to the taper on the drive shaft and inevitably the timing slipped during the race. Not, however, before Frank Philipp had set the fastest lap at 50.11mph. Later in the year, Frank featured in a publicity stunt, when he made one hundred successful ascents of Sutton Bank in $7\frac{1}{2}$ hours, being delayed only by an eighteen minute stop to repair a puncture. The hill itself had a gradient of one in four at its steepest point, yet there was no need to add water to the radiator during the entire session. Engine refinements continued and,

entered for the 1909 TT, but a spill on his seventh lap caused Myers' retirement. Undeterred, Scott made two entries for the 1910 event, for Eric Myers again and for Frank Philipp. Although a complicated formula had been implemented by the ACU in an attempt to curb what seemed to be a threat from the two-stroke engine, Philipp finished ninth and Myers 24th, the latter after a spate of punctures and endless plug troubles. Even if they did have to race in the twin-cylinder class, with a falsified capacity of 640cc (the formula necessitated multiplying the true capacity by 1.32), the Scotts were beginning to show their real capabilities. Needless to say, they were not proficient in speed events. Jesse Baker was making quite a name for himself in reliability trials on his privately-owned Scott, enough to merit some factory support towards the end of the year.

It was in 1911 that some further changes in engine design were made, increasing the capacity yet again, this time to 486cc. A water-cooled block and cylinder head were now employed as was an improved radiator of honeycomb construction. Although the Scott team missed the Team Prize in the ACU's Six Days Trial, Jesse Baker came away with a gold medal. Meanwhile, Scott was working on the machines he had entered for the 1911 TT, to be run for the first time over the Mountain circuit of $37\frac{1}{2}$ miles. Knowing that the engines of the race machines needed better control over

externally, the machines had a much cleaner appearance. Some attention was given to the carburettor at this time which, although still based on Scott's original 1904 design, represented a considerable improvement. Even so, it was never as good as one or two of the proprietary makes and was eventually replaced after 1914.

Having learnt his lesson from the 1911 TT, Scott redesigned the race bikes so that the rotary valve was gear driven, increasing the compression ratio slightly at the same time. Only two machines were entered for the 1912 event, Applebee and Philipp being the riders. Other deviations from the specification of the standard road models included water-cooled cylinders only, twin spark plugs for each

cylinder and an extra-large petrol filler cap. Philipp was soon out of luck during the race, when his rear tyre came off the rim and relegated him to an eventual eleventh place. Applebee, unaware of his partner's fate, set a cracking pace, and won the race at an average speed of 48.69mph. This was the first occasion on which a two-stroke had won a TT and on which the winner had led from start to finish. This was the breakthrough Scott needed. Orders came flooding in and it was soon evident that production would have to be increased to cope with demand. With no extra room available at the Mornington Works in Grosvenor Street, the Scott Engineering Company went public, to help finance the purchase of land at Shipley for the erection of a new factory. The year ended well when the three members of the Scott team each won a gold medal in the ACU's Six Days Trial. They missed the team prize, however, which went to their arch rivals, P & M, based in nearby Cleckheaton.

The 1913 models on show at Olympia,

during late 1912, had water-cooled cylinder barrels and air-cooled heads. A curious exhibit was a Scott in solo form, fitted with a Laird-Menteyne machine gun, a sign, perhaps, of the approaching hostilities in Europe. It was claimed that almost 550 machines had been manufactured at the old Mornington Works that year, an increase of some 250 machines over the previous year, all attributed to the 1912 TT win.

It was a newcomer to the Scott team, Tim Wood, who won the 1913 TT, when Applebee and Norman Longfield (a substitute for Philipp, who was recovering from an accident) were both forced to retire. He won after a very hard challenge from a Rudge rider, A.R. Abbott. On this occasion the race machines had been fitted with an improved rotary valve and a new type of throttle, although in general appearance they did not differ much from the standard production models – a move in keeping with Scott's own principles. Now a Scott had won the Senior TT for two years running and had

Far left: Tim Wood and Frank Applebee pose with the Senior TT Scott of 1914

Below: a Scott two-speeder of 1911. This particular machine has an engine capacity of 532cc, a feature of the 1912 model which suggests that this bike was modified during its early life

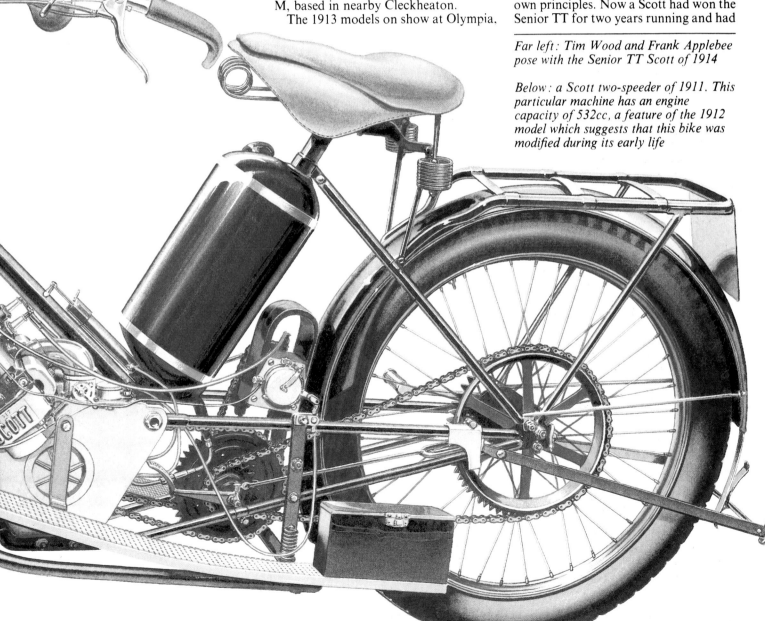

made the fastest lap for the third year in succession, an impressive performance.

For 1914, the production models were fitted with drip feed lubricators to give more even oiling, a centre stand and heavier gauge forks – more suitable when a sidecar was to be fitted. An XL-All saddle improved rider comfort. It was during this year that Scott inaugurated the infamous Scott Trial, initially for Scott employees only and those from Eric Myers' premises in Bradford. The honour of the very first win went to Frank Philipp. As far as the TT was concerned, Scott evolved an entirely new design of race machine. Although still employing a central flywheel fitted with overhung cranks, that is where the similarity with the earlier designs ended. Induction and transfer cycles were controlled by an adaption of the Corliss valve, used on the large steam engines at one of the firms where Scott served his apprenticeship. There was also a new design of carburettor, a gearbox built in

Above: the three-wheeled Scott Sociable was designed and developed after World War I. It was powered by a twin-cylinder, two-stroke engine

Below: Harold and Willie Wood in action in their Scott Sociable at Bluehills Mine during one of the classic Lands End Trial events

unit with the engine, with the gear cluster eccentrically mounted to facilitate chain adjustment, and twin pannier petrol tanks to maintain a low centre of gravity.

In the race, Tim Wood provided the main challenge but he was forced to retire when his magneto called it a day, a malady later traced to a shorting cut-out button. Frank Applebee managed 25th place, and H.V. Prescott, a newcomer to the team, faded out on his third lap. On paper, a Scott should have won, but in reality, all they achieved was the fastest lap speed once again – for the fourth year in succession.

Before further attention could be given to the design of the race bikes and other matters, Britain was at war with Germany and there were other problems of more urgency. Scott himself became very involved in the design of a Scott sidecar outfit fitted with a machine gun and in next to no time, a prototype was inspected in London by (Sir) Winston Churchill. An order for three hundred such outfits resulted, to be divided between the Admiralty and the War Office. Sadly, the machines had their shortcomings under active service conditions and Scott switched to an entirely different project, divorcing himself entirely from the motor cycle activities. His aim was to develop a form of three wheel guncar, in effect a tricycle with two wheels at the rear and one at the front, arranged in the form of a triangle, the front and the offside rear wheels being in line. Although a curious looking vehicle, it had extreme stability and the manoeuverability of a sidecar outfit. A twin-cylinder, two-stroke engine provided the motive power, with a friction band clutch and a countershaft, three-speed gearbox. Although the engine was similar in some respects to the motor cycle engines, rotary induction valves were used with independent cylinder barrels that were water-cooled but quickly detachable. The guncar project was handled in a separate building off Manningham Lane, known as the Springfield Works. Despite intensive testing, the anticipated War Office contract never came and when the war ended, Scott forsook motor cycles entirely, so that he could market a three-wheeler, based on the guncar concept and to be known as the Scott Sociable. He sold his interest in the Scott Engineering Company and formed the Scott Autocar Company, with premises at Lidgett Green, near Bradford. From now on, he would manufacture the Sociable only.

The motor cycle company continued under new management, initially making an updated version of the pre-war model, then extending the range into a number of

Right: E. Mainwaring leaps his Scott at Ballig Bridge during the 1928 Senior TT

variations on the basic theme. A Binks three-jet carburettor helped to improve performance and more generous mud-guarding gave better weather protection to the rider. It was in 1920 that the Scott team scored its first really major success in the ACU Six Days Trial, when they won the team prize and six gold medals. The first post-war TT was held in 1921, but of the four Scotts entered (similar in some respects to the ill-fated 1914 models) only two finished, in seventeenth and 22nd places. It was not until 1922 that their turn came, when, riding machines based on the new Scott Squirrel, they won the team prize and finished third, fourth and ninth. The riders respectively were Harry Langman, Clarrie Wood and Geoff Clapham – immortal names in the history of the Scott. At the end of the year, a new three-speed Scott made its debut, using a gearbox of conventional design and a multiplate clutch operated by lever from the handlebars.

Back at Lidgett Green, Alfred Scott was fighting a losing battle with the Sociable. Despite its many attributes it looked very odd, a fact even he acknowledged by referring to his own

vehicle as 'the crab'. Sales proved disappointing and when the Austin Seven came along, the fate of the Sociable was sealed. Scott himself died before the project came to an end and never saw his creation pass into oblivion, to become one of motor cycling's curiosities. The motor cycle company was not in too good health by this time either, and badly needed another TT win to help bring in new orders. A very near miss in the first ever Sidecar TT of 1923 didn't help, Harry Langman crashing while leading on the last lap. All the team could salvage was Jack Watson-Bourne's eleventh place in the Senior race. Harry did his best to make amends by winning several later speed trials with his TT solo, and also both the Welsh TT and the Ulster Grand Prix.

A three-speed Squirrel appeared at the 1923 Show as did a 596cc model with a detachable alloy cylinder head, reflecting experience gained from the 1923 TT models, but it was in the 1924 Senior TT that the development paid off. Harry Langman, using a long-stroke engine, with a non-detachable cylinder head, finished second, at an average speed of

Below: a Scott Flying Squirrel of 1949, which used a 596cc engine; this particular model is now in the Glasgow Transport Museum. Flying Squirrel production came to a halt in 1950

Right: a close up of the engine of the 596cc, two-stroke twin of 1961. The bike consisted, in effect, of a Flying Squirrel engine in a new swinging arm frame unit. It was not a sales success, however

Below right: a gaggle of Scott machines line up at the start prior to a race specially organised for Scotts at Cadwell Park in 1946. The eventual winner was number 72

61.24mph, only a little slower than the race average of the winner. The trials riders went from strength to strength too, offering formidable opposition in many of the 'open' events. The new Super Squirrel, fitted with a 68.25mm square engine, made its debut late 1924, to become available in both 498cc and 596cc capacities. It became one of the most revered of all the Scott models.

By 1925 the four-stroke was beginning to offer too much of a challenge in speed events, and the Scott gradually faded from the scene, despite Harry Langman's epic fifth place in the Senior race of that year. The cycle parts were no longer capable of handling the higher speeds, while the engine was getting a little fragile too. As far as the standard production models were concerned, the Flying Squirrel series of late 1925 re-activated an interest in the Scott marque, having an optional TT full-frame tank, and a mechanical oil pump mounted on one of the crankcase doors. A better, three-speed, gearbox and the repositioning of the magneto also represented

Below: this is the J.C. Scott Special of 1952; it was a Scott-engined off-road machine built and developed by John Catchpole, a dedicated Scott enthusiast

substantial improvements. Now it was time for Scotts to shine in the 1925 Amateur TT, a clubman's version of the TT itself, run over the same course. Noel Mavrogordate made a habit of creeping onto the leader board, and finished seventh in the 1926 event. Later in the year the Scott Trial was reorganised, to become an open event run under the auspices of the ACU. As the year closed, the new Flying Squirrel went into production; it was virtually the 1926 TT model, with the option of a 498cc or a 596cc engine.

G. Limmer and D. de Ferranti pulled off second and third places respectively in the 1927 Amateur TT but this did little to help the company, which was now faced with financial problems. Somehow, they managed to get through the lean years of the depression that followed and they even became involved with dirt track racing through Frank Varey and Wilf McClure. Perhaps it was the advent of the beloved TT Replica model of 1929 that helped, or even the Sprint Special of a year later. Certainly it could not be attributed to the 'cheap' 298cc single that was manufactured for two years only (1929–30) or the ill-fated Trivan, designed for commercial deliveries.

In 1931 an Official Receiver was appointed and the company was in dire financial straits for a while. Albert Reynolds, a Liverpudlian Scott enthusiast, came to the rescue, purchasing some of the Scott production which he customised and sold initially as the Aero Scott and later as the Reynolds Special. Different forks, twin headlamps the choice of a spring or a rigid frame and a restyled radiator represented the main

departures from the Scott norm. Needless to say, Scott plans for an ambitious 650cc vertical twin were dropped, although the company did find time to prepare two special 'Grand Prix' models in 1933 for the Manx Grand Prix of that year. Another development project was in hand too, a three-cylinder two-stroke, initially of 747cc capacity but later increased to 986cc. Designed by William Cull, the new model had many ingenious features, including a swash-plate oil pump and an Elektron crankcase with three detachable crank chambers and a built-up 120° crankshaft. It was exhibited at the 1934 Olympia Show, but never went into quantity production. Cull also designed a twin-cylinder, air-cooled aircraft engine for the Flying Flea aircraft.

In 1938, the company became involved in the manufacture of an autocycle, using a 98cc single-cylinder engine of its own manufacture. This was the Cyk Auto, which used a worm and pinion drive to the bottom bracket. It was towards the end of the year, however, that the most sensational news broke – of the imminent manufacture of the Clubman's Special, a specially tuned 596cc model, available with either a rigid frame or plunger rear suspension. Either model was capable of over 90mph and had special cylinder wall oiling. They represented the ultimate in Scott engine development, while retaining good mechanical reliability. Alas, World War II brought an abrupt end to their manufacture.

Production of the 596cc rigid frame Flying Squirrel continued after the war, firstly with girder forks and a twin brake

for the initial half dozen or so, then with Dowty telescopic forks of air suspension type. In 1949 coil ignition replaced the Lucas Magdyno system used previously, having a crankcase door mounted dynamo of the 'pancake' type, and a distributor. Sales were not up to expectations however, and less than a year later, production came to a halt.

Matt Holder, of the Aero Jig and Tool Company in Birmingham, brought about a revival when, in 1954, he announced a new version of the Scott. In effect, it was the old Flying Squirrel engine unit in a new swinging arm frame, based on some earlier prototype designs. There was even talk of a new engine, with flat top pistons,

to be known as the Swift. The new model went into production during June 1956, using the original 596cc engine unit; the 498cc Swift engine never progressed beyond the prototype stage. Despite an appearance at the 1961 Show the new Scott had limited sales prospects and this, allied with limited production, caused it to fade away gradually until it became to all intents and purposes extinct. Another manufacturer took up the basic theme and went his own way, using new materials and no small amount of redesign, and so, alas, yet another famous name faded from the scene and with it, a sound that no other machine has ever emulated.

Above: in 1958, Scott introduced their new Swift model. Although the 498cc engine was of entirely new design, it was based on the traditional Scott layout. The Swift never went into production

Below: the experimental 344cc Scott racer of 1965

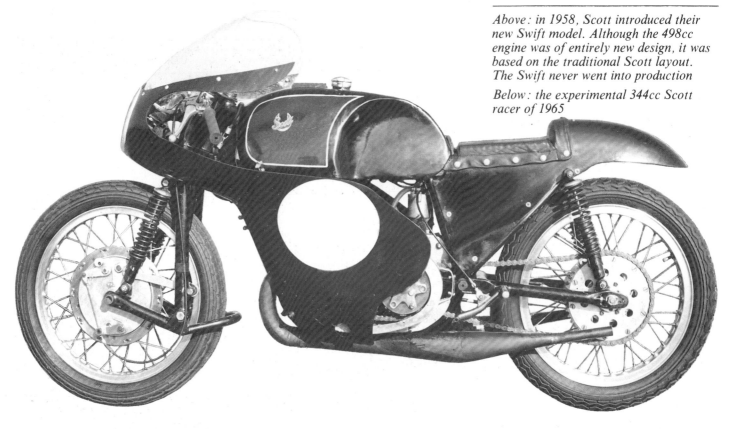

Sunbeam

Latecomer to the field of motor cycle manufacture, John Marston waited until 1912 before introducing the elegant Sunbeam; yet it was a brave gesture, at that, because John was already 76 years of age and had been in business on his own account since 1859. Indeed, the claim on the front of Sunbeam catalogues was 'Established in 1790', the Marston family having been among the first in Britain to perfect the art of japanning, the application of a high-gloss baked finish to metalware.

The Sunbeam trade-mark was first applied to kitchen utensils and japanned metal goods, and perhaps it was only natural that, when John Marston turned his attention to pedal cycles in the late 1880s, they should quickly earn a reputation for the excellence of the paintwork. An experimental Sunbeam car was built in 1899, but the first powered Sunbeam to be put into production, two years later, was a very odd vehicle indeed. The invention of a Mr Mabley Smith, it resembled a sofa on wheels – and those wheels were arranged with one at each side amidships and single wheels fore and aft. Power was provided by a single-cylinder De Dion engine. The Sunbeam-Mabley was not a passing eccentricity. Selling at £130, it was produced in fair numbers, and it is on record that no fewer than thirty turned out for a club run in 1902.

Soon, Sunbeam car development began to follow more orthodox paths and, after famous designer Louis Coatalen joined the firm in 1909, the four-wheeler side was to go on to international glory. By that time, however, it had split from the original John Marston Ltd company and, while still sharing the Wolverhampton industrial complex known as Sunbeamland, was now operating as the Sunbeam Motor Car Company Ltd.

Rather stately machines with a deeply glossy all-black weatherproof finish, Sunbeam pedal cycles were always advertised as 'The Gentleman's Bicycle' (although there was an open-frame, lady's model also), and were renowned for their total enclosure of the driving chain in 'The Sunbeam Patent Little Oil Bath', a close-fitting metal casing.

It was from the pedal-cycle factory that the first Sunbeam motor cycles appeared in 1912 and, although the prototypes had an unfamiliar green-and-silver tank finish, by the time production began, the machines had adopted the same all-black finish as seen on the bicycles. Weatherproofing extended to all-black handlebars and front-fork springs and fittings. Wheel hubs, spokes and rim centres were black, too, and only the outer edges of the front wheel rim, on which operated the bicycle-type stirrup brake, were plated. In fact, John Marston, and his right-hand-man, Thomas Cureton, had pulled off something of a coup in securing the services of John E. Greenwood, designer of the Imperial Rover, and Greenwood's masterpiece was a 347cc (75 × 79mm) single with Hoffmann roller-bearing mains and big-end and all-gear drive to a Bosch magneto carried behind the cylinder. Crankshaft balance was effected by the unusual method of making the internal flywheels eccentric. From the beginning, trans-

Below: this superbly restored machine is a 2¾hp Sunbeam of 1913. It was powered by a single-cylinder engine of 347cc

mission was all-chain, with both primary and final-drive chains enclosed in the now-famous 'Little Oil Bath' for longevity. There was a two-speed countershaft gearbox with input on the left and output on the right and, to provide smooth riding, a friction-faced slipping clutch was incorporated in the engine sprocket. Other advanced features included a dropped top tube (to afford a low saddle position), multi-plate clutch and a divided-axle rear wheel mounting to permit the tyre to be removed without disturbing the final-drive chain and casing.

John Greenwood evidently believed in trying things for himself, and the first two Sunbeam three-fifties to appear in public were ridden by himself and by Tommy de la Hay in the ACU Autumn Trial of 1912. For the record, Greenwood gained a gold medal for the only non-stop run by a 350cc machine, but Tommy had an unlucky stop due to failing to turn on the petrol tap.

Priced at £63, the 'Gentleman's Motor Bicycle' duly made its appearance at the 1912 London Show, its deep black finish enhanced by lettering and lining in genuine gold leaf. In all, 843 examples of the three-fifty were to be made during 1913 but, in June of that year, it had gained a companion in the form of a 770cc vee-twin powered by a JAP engine and driving through a newly designed three-speed Sunbeam gearbox, again with cross-over drive. The twin, too, carried the magneto at the rear (in fact, on a bracket clamped to the seat tube), and both chains were totally enclosed. That summer, the Sunbeam began to make its presence felt in open competition work, successes including a 1-2-3 in the Coventry and Warwickshire Club trial, two gold medals in the London–Edinburgh Trial, the team award in the Irish End-to-End Reliability Run and class wins at Style Cop hill-climb. Enterprising private owners had even taken Sunbeams to the very top of Snowdon and Ben Nevis, the highest peaks in Wales and Scotland. Significantly, too, a youngster named Howard R. Davies had gained a first-class-award in a Birmingham hill-climb.

Also from the drawing board of John Greenwood, in September 1913, there came the first 500cc single, generally similar in layout to the successful 350cc model, but employing the three-speed gearbox of the 770cc JAP twin. The new machine was entered for the 1914 Senior TT, the manufacturers claiming that 'absolutely standard' engines were fitted. So they may have been, but the frames were non-standard, being rather shorter in the wheelbase and carrying the engine a shade lower. Also, the TT models had a separate oil tank on the seat tube (instead of carrying oil in a compartment of the fuel tank) and both brakes were arranged

to operate on the rear wheel. Their riders were Vernon Busby, Tommy de la Hay and young Howard Davies, and the outcome exceeded the Sunbeam company's hopes. Davies finished equal-second with Oliver Godfrey (Indian), Busby was eleventh, de la Hay was thirteenth and Sunbeam won the Manufacturers' Team award. Well, not quite . . . A little while later, the race organisers did a recount and awarded the team prize to somebody

Above: Tommy de la Hay in action on his 3½hp Sunbeam during an ACU-organised one-day trial in 1921

Right: in 1913, Sunbeam introduced a vee-twin JAP-engined machine of 770cc. This is a 1914 example with a Mills-Fullford sidecar

Below: this single-cylinder model was raced in the 1921 TT by R. Brown

else, but that was a minor matter.

World War I was now not so very far off, and the conflict was to find Sunbeamland busy with the manufacture of Short seaplanes and Avro fighters, while the car company contributed Sunbeam aero engines. Yet motor cycles were certainly not forgotten, and a special version of the 500cc single was produced in quantity to meet a French Army contract. Rather to the disgust of old John Marston and his engineers, the contract called for belt final drive – a backward step but, if that was what the French wanted . . . In addition, the fuel tank was provided with three compartments instead of the usual two, the extra one carrying paraffin (kerosene) in view of the inevitable wartime fuel shortages.

In 1915, an Abingdon King Dick-engined vee-twin was added, and a year later there was a 1000cc twin powered by a Swiss-built MAG unit. Legend has it that John Marston insisted on all engines from outside suppliers being stripped on arrival at the Sunbeam works, then re-assembled with all the care he demanded in the construction of his own engines. However, old employees of the factory confess that this was indeed just legend, just part of the Sunbeam mystique which insisted also that visitors to the works were never allowed to see the enamelling shop where, it was said, that beautiful deep black finish was obtained by the

application of no fewer than nine coats of paint, each being flatted down before the next was added.

The original 347cc two-speeder was discontinued after the outbreak of war. A few of the twins were used as machine-gun sidecar outfits, while others were equipped with sidecar-ambulance bodies and were used for ferrying wounded men across rough territory to the nearest point at which a conventional ambulance could take over.

Alas, almost coincidental with the return of peace in 1918 came the death of John Marston at the age of 82, followed within the year by his son Roland. The double blow was too much for the remaining members of the Marston family who, faced with the need to find money to pay off colossal death duties, had perforce to sell the still privately owned firm of John Marston Ltd. The purchasers were Noble Industries Ltd, a munitions consortium which was seeking suitable investment properties. To their credit, Noble Industries (which was eventually to become Imperial Chemical Industries) had no intention of interfering with Sunbeam production and, keeping a low profile, they continued to build the cycles and motor cycles under the familiar John Marston Ltd name. Meanwhile, works manager Thomas Cureton, too, had died, and to replace him Noble's brought in Sidney Bowers – who, in any case, was steeped in Sunbeam tradition.

With the 1920s, Sunbeam motor cycles entered on a new and even more illustrious phase, illuminated by a string of competition successes. Their riders included Tommy de la Hay, George Dance, Alec Bennett, Graham Walker, Charlie Dodson and, especially in the sprint and hillclimb fields, a Staffordshire market gardener named George Dance. Dance didn't usually compete in road races but, nonetheless, he produced the fastest lap in the 1920 Senior TT, an event won at record speed by his team-mate, de la Hay. Two years later, Alec Bennett set new race and lap records in giving the Sunbeam camp their second Isle of Man Senior TT victory.

So far, the machines used had been basically standard side-valve models, latterly the illustrious 'longstroke' which earned its nickname by featuring a 77mm bore and 105mm stroke. Maximum speed was around 75mph, and there were those who considered the model to be the best side-valve single ever built. Perhaps it was, but now the Sunbeam designers were turning their attention to overhead valves and, in 1923, they produced both 350 and 500cc versions. With one of the three-fifties, George Dance came close to scoring a Junior TT victory, only to break a valve on the Mountain stretch while leading with one lap to run. In compensation, he went record-breaking, hoisting the 350cc one-hour figure to 80.24mph and the two-hour to 70.52mph.

Above: Staffordshire market gardener and works Sunbeam team rider George Dance poses on his side-valve, long-stroke, 500cc Sunbeam racer before the start of the 1921 Isle of Man Senior TT

Left: a 499cc, side-valve Sunbeam 'Light Tourist' model of 1925

George also fitted one of the 493cc ohv units into a light frame with a small wedge-shape fuel tank, and with this potent model – often timed at around the 90mph mark – he became absolutely unbeatable at sprints and hillclimbs all over the country.

It was in 1924, too, that Graham Walker joined the gang as Sunbeam competitions manager and, for the first time, the overhead-valve Sunbeams were seen in continental road racing. An overhead-camshaft model was added for 1925, with shaft-and-bevel operation of the upstairs mechanism and hairpin valve springs; that the ohc models didn't feature strongly in race results was more a matter of bad luck rather than weak

Right: the early Sunbeam racers were sidevalve machines, but in 1923 the company turned its attention to overhead valves. This is the 500cc, ohv racer

Below: in 1925, Sunbeam marketed this 492cc sports model for £86. It was powered by a side-valve engine

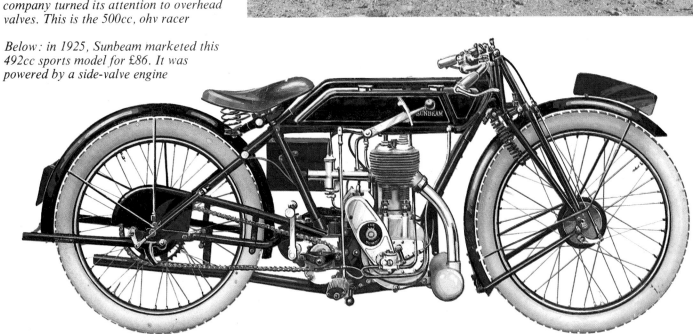

design but, be that as it may, the factory decided to drop the idea and revert to pushrod ohv operation for the following season. Now, Graham Walker got into his stride, collecting the Ulster Grand Prix (new team-mate Charlie Dodson won the 350cc class) and, over the spectacular Nürburgring circuit in Germany, the Grand Prix d'Europe. Nor were Sunbeam successes confined to the racing circuits, because the marque was becoming equally well known in reliability trials, in the hands of solo men such as Eddie Flintoff, and sidecar exponents like Peter Bradley.

By now known as the Model 90, the 493cc ohv Sunbeam reached its peak in 1928, with Charlie Dodson winning the Senior TT after a battle with Graham Walker (who by this time had transferred to the Rudge stable). Charlie's feat was all the more remarkable because, at an earlier stage in the race, he had come off when an inattentive spectator wandered

across the roadway. That year, the Sunbeam factory had fielded an international TT team, with Luigi Archangeli of Italy and F. Franconi of Switzerland providing the necessary backing to Dodson; once again, Sunbeams collected the Manufacturers' Team award.

On the racing front, the Sunbeam success story continued. Dodson again won the Senior TT in 1929, at record speed and with a record lap, and, together with Alec Bennett and Digger Simcock, claimed the team award for the third successive year.

That 1929 Model 90 of Dodson was a marvellous piece of work, with deep cylinder-head finning, hairpin-spring valves set at 90°, a very stiff I-section connecting rods and flywheels in which the weight was concentrated in the rims. However, an era was passing, and it was to prove the last pushrod, two-valve engine ever to power a Senior TT winner.

The truth was that Sunbeams had been neglecting the roadster side and, although the superlative finish and the tradition of never wearing out still remained, the catalogue models were, in fact, falling behind contemporary fashion. The firm

was among the last to switch over from the old flat fuel type to the saddle pattern demanded by current taste (oddly enough, the other major Wolverhampton factory, AJS, showed a similar reluctance). It was, too, the very last to abandon the time-honoured, side-spring Druid front fork in favour of the centre-spring girder pattern which afforded the machine more wheel movement.

Around 1930, the tag-line, 'A subsidiary company of Imperial Chemical Industries' began to appear, just now and then, in John Marston advertising. It could be that the Wolverhampton factory was being shown a touch of the whip, but this was no time for the launching of new designs and, as the trade recession began to bite, so the range was trimmed to just four models – the 493cc ohv Model 9 tourer and Model 90 sports, 492cc side-valve Lion (the old and much-loved 'longstroke') and a new cheap 344cc ohv which carried its oil in a specially

Above: this is Sunbeam's Lion model of 1936. It was fitted with the single-cylinder, side-valve, 492cc engine

designed crankcase extension.

After a while, the firm began to recover, and there were new and sleeker models (some with chromium-plated tanks) such as the 'Little 95', virtually a 250cc version of the sporting five-hundred. Another excursion into the 250cc field was a light tourer with a train of gears driving a high-mounted camshaft from which short pushrods operated the overhead valves. As the 1930s ran on, so the famous 'Little Oil Bath' chain enclosure was discarded, and the cross-over Sunbeam gearboxes were replaced by Burman boxes incorporating positive-stop foot gear change.

True, Sunbeam competition glory was now a thing of the past, but the roadsters were well on their way back to public esteem when, in 1936, there came the surprise news that Sunbeam motor cycle production was to be transferred from Wolverhampton to the Plumstead, London, premises of the new owners, the Matchless concern. Matchless had al-

ready bought AJS four years earlier, and now Matchless, AJS and Sunbeam were to come together under the new title of Associated Motor Cycles Ltd.

One of the first acts of the new combine was to explore the old Wolverhampton works, to discover what new models John Marston Ltd had had in the pipeline. Unhappily, there was but one, the unit-construction side-valve with coil ignition and a squish-type combustion chamber, and designer Dougal Marchant claimed that he, not the company, owned the rights to it. For the next season or so, there was, understandably, little change in the Sunbeam range, as AMC consolidated their new acquisition. Then, sud-

denly, there appeared a totally new range of Sunbeams, with vast timing covers behind which lurked chain drive to high-placed camshafts. Not everybody liked them, and there were those who thought the name 'Sunbeam', in scrawling script across the timing cover, was too undig-nified for a machine of such a heritage. It seems likely that the design, which was made in 250, 350 and 500cc form, had in fact been put in hand originally for a series of models to be built under the AJS trademark. However, AMC were quite evidently keen on building a range in which detail design and finish took precedence over cost and that, at least, was in line with old John Marston's very strict principles.

Too bad that the new breed of Sun-beams had but a few short months in which to gain public acceptance, for war was again imminent, and production was ended in favour of 350cc G3 (and, later, G3L) Matchless singles for the British Army. One more Sunbeam was to be built, in 1940: a 750cc ohv vee-twin with sidecar-wheel drive, it was a prototype built for Army consideration, but never put into production.

As the war ran into its closing stages, so a series of Sunbeam advertisements began to appear in the weekly motor cycle press. 'The post-war Sunbeam design,' they read, 'has been finalised. But readers are invited to submit their ideas on various aspects of design.' It was a useful forum, through which motor cycle-starved servicemen could let them-selves go on the subject of dream

Above: a close-up of the single-cylinder, 500cc Sunbeam of 1927. It used the old favourite side-valve engine developed several years previously. The versatile Sunbeam company was, at that time, also building ohv and overhead camshaft models

machines. The really interesting thing was, however, that the advertisements were issued, not from Plumstead, but from Small Heath, Birmingham. Yes, the Sunbeam name had changed hands again, and BSA had hired Erling Poppe (at one time a partner in the Packman and Poppe company, but in more recent times a designer of Dennis trucks) to evolve *the* super-de-luxe machine of all time. What emerged was the first completely new motor cycle of the post-war years, owing nothing to any machine that had gone before. This was the S7 Sunbeam, built at BSA's branch works at Redditch, Worcestershire (from which, in earlier years, had come the immortal 250cc 'round tank'). It had an all-light-alloy, 487cc, vertical-twin, overhead-camshaft engine mounted in line with the frame, and shaft final drive to an underslung worm at the rear spindle.

There were big, fat 4in-section tyres at front and rear and, to add to the riding comfort, the saddle had its own compensated springing system. A pancake dynamo was built into the front of the engine, there was a choice of mist-green or black as the colour scheme and the telescopic front forks were supplemented by plunger springing at the rear. Oh, it was a beauty, there was no doubt of that. One model was presented with due ceremony to Lord Montgomery of Alamein, and at the London Motor Cycle Show so great was the crush of spectators pressing forward to see the new Sunbeams (in-

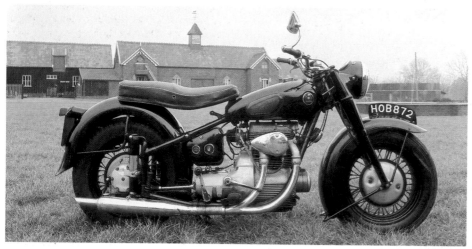

cluding the 'Monty' model) that the show stand collapsed amid the splintering of wood and the tinkling of glass.

BSA had promised a sports version, with the valves set at 90°, but it has to be recorded that the straight-twin Sunbeam had, quite literally, an Achilles heel. The worm drive to the rear wheel was incapable of transmitting the power of the sports engine. Indeed, the gear casing of the tourer grew almost unbearably hot after a longish run, and so the makers resigned themselves to only a modest performance. That wasn't the only snag.

A batch of S7 Sunbeams from the first production quota was rushed out to South Africa, to serve as a police escort during King George VI's visit but, such was the vibration, that they had all to be returned to the factory. At that stage, the engines had been bolted directly into the duplex tubular frame, and the vibration cure was to insert rubber engine mountings. That explains why, thereafter, all Sunbeam twins had to have a short length of flexible metallic tubing inserted into the exhaust pipe.

It had to be admitted that the S7 looked

Above: the S8 Sunbeam of 1948. It was a development of the S7 model and was fitted with a vertical twin engine of 487cc, which featured an overhead camshaft. Final drive was by shaft

Left: a Sunbeam S7 of 1947

a whole lot heavier than it really was and, to overcome some of the sales opposition, BSA added a lighter-looking version, the S8, which made use of the BSA A10 twin's front fork and wheels. Even so, sales were never very high and, by 1957, the straight-twin Sunbeam project had folded. Two other ventures, a 250cc single and a water-cooled 650cc straight-four, never got beyond the prototype stage. Yet this wasn't quite the end. Scooters were booming, and BSA joined the race with a 175cc two-stroke single and a 250cc ohv twin. As scooters went, they weren't at all bad (even though they could have been so much better in some respects). However, the manufacturers chose to label them as BSA Sunbeams, and even graced the front of the apron with the traditional sun-and-rays badge dating back to the earliest of John Marston days. How many Sunbeam traditionalists died of apoplexy at the sight is not recorded . . . FG

Triumph

There is a subtle irony in the fact that what was to become Britain's most successful motor cycle, and what remained the only large-capacity British machine in quantity production in the late 'seventies, should have been launched by a pair of German immigrants.

Siegfried Bettmann was no penniless European immigrant of legend. His parents were wealthy and a university education ensured that he spoke English and French as fluently as he did German.

Indeed, his talent for languages gained him his first job, that of a translator with a London publishing company, on his arrival in England in 1894. In turn, this brought him into contact with overseas manufacturing companies and by late 1885 young Siegfried was in business on his own account, as a reasonably successful import and export agent.

The imports were of sewing machines and to balance the trade he decided to take advantage of the bicycle craze then sweeping Europe, exporting British-made machines obligingly built for him in Birmingham by William Andrews. At first, these bore a 'Bettmann' trade mark – but that didn't sound British enough and, soon, they were being sold as 'Triumph', a name chosen because it was recognisable in most languages.

As the business grew so the import of sewing machines was discontinued, and Triumph bicycles began to appear on the home market, too. Their success was such that the name of S. Bettmann and Company was changed, to The Triumph Cycle Company.

In 1887, with trade improving all the while, Bettmann took on another German immigrant, Maurice Schulte, as junior partner, and the joint decision was made that the company should abandon the practice of merely fixing Triumph transfers on to bought-out bicycles and, instead, manufacture the machines themselves. Schulte was despatched to Coventry, to prospect for a suitable factory.

He found one, a former ribbon-weaving works in Much Park Street, and soon activities were transferred from London to the new premises. Manufacture began with capital of only £650, of which £500 had been subscribed by Bettmann's parents and the other £150 by relations of Maurice Schulte. However, two Coventry businessmen, Albert Friedlander and Alderman Thomson, were instrumental in raising more funds, and within a few years Triumph had become a limited liability company, with capital of £45,000 (much of it provided by the Dunlop tyre company).

Schulte was a trained engineer and he foresaw that there was a market for a powered two-wheeler. His first idea was to build, under licence, the German Hildebrand and Wolfmüller machine, going so far as to import an example and teach himself to ride it, for evaluation purposes, at Coventry cycle stadium. The scheme came to nothing, as did a plan to build Beeston Humber motor cycles and motor tricycles. The motor cycle, agreed the partners, was as yet too crude and it would be best to wait a couple of years longer.

Top: the earliest Triumph machines were fitted with proprietary engines such as Minerva, Fafnir and even JAP. This is a Triumph model of 1903 and is powered by a single-cylinder JAP engine of 2½hp

Left: C. L. Mere poses on his 3½hp Triumph prior to a race in 1908

Far left: this Triumph roadster of 1910 had a single-cylinder, side-valve, 3½hp engine with single speed and a hub clutch

Centre left: a close-up of Triumph's single-cylinder, 3½hp, 499cc engine of 1912

Left: H. F. Lamb in action on his 499cc Triumph at Quarter Bridge during the 1913 Isle of Man Senior TT

Below: a Triumph TT model of 1914. It used a single-cylinder, four-stroke engine of 499cc which was rated at 3½hp. Final drive was direct by belt. The engine had been developed from the 450cc unit originally introduced in 1907 and was of Triumph's own design, unlike a number of engines used on earlier Triumph models

The impetus came with the introduction by Minerva of Belgium of a neat, and reasonably reliable, little power unit, designed to be clamped to the forward side of a bicycle's front down-tube driving direct to the rear wheel by a twisted rawhide belt. Using the 1¾hp (66 × 70mm bore and stroke) Minerva engine, equipped with surface carburettor and suction-operated inlet valve, the first Triumph motor cycles were announced in 1902.

For the following year a more technically advanced Minerva engine was fitted, now with both inlet and exhaust valves cam operated and with a spray carburettor replacing the dubious surface type. The machine remained typically pedal cycle in design, with the engine as an afterthought, but something was in the offing, and 1904 saw the first real Triumph motor cycle, with the engine – now a 3hp Fafnir producing peak power (such as it was) at 1800rpm – mounted vertically in a recognisable motor cycle frame. There was also a forecar, employing the same power unit, and a lightweight, but with the clip-on engine – now a British-made 2½hp JAP.

Nevertheless, Triumph had been doing little more than put out feelers in various directions and for 1904 they decided to take the plunge and go into the fray wholeheartedly with a machine that would be totally Triumph in design and manufacture. The scheme was Schulte's but drawing-office work was left to Charles Hathaway, who produced a simple but effective 298cc engine (with dimensions of 78 × 76mm) of side-valve design, with the crankshaft carried on ball bearings.

The front fork was still unsprung but strengthening struts had now been added to the fork blades. Unusually, too, the frame featured two front down-tubes in tandem, an arrangement which looked strong but was in fact soon to give trouble. With accumulator and trembler coil ignition, the price of the 'three horse' was £45. For a further £5 a magneto-equipped version could be supplied. Production climbed to five machines a week.

Bettmann and Schulte were alive to the publicity value of demonstration rides and they consulted 'Ixion' (the Reverend Basil H. Davies), famous columnist of the weekly magazine *The Motor Cycle*, arriving at a scheme whereby 'Ixion' would ride two hundred miles a day for six days, on routes radiating from an Oxford base, and all under the eye of an officially appointed timekeeper.

The machine chosen was the magneto version and it was equipped with the first prototype of the celebrated Triumph fore-and-aft sprung front fork, another design by Charles Hathaway, patented in his name. Unhappily, the test didn't go well. The engine gradually lost power (a subsequent examination showed very rapid wear of cylinder and piston rings) but, worst calamity of all, the tandem front down-tubes broke on the Friday, the fifth day of the test, with almost one thousand miles already covered.

Undaunted, Schulte arranged for the same engine to be installed in a new single-down-tube frame over the weekend and, come Monday morning, 'Ixion' was off again, to begin the test all over again. This time, fortune smiled and by the end of six days a total of 1279 miles had been covered – thanks to 'Ixion's' nightly chore of stripping the engine and grinding-in the valves.

At least the Triumph works were willing to learn from experience, and the 1906 machine was a vastly better job. A metallurgist had been consulted, resulting in better metal being employed in the valves, piston rings and cylinder; the frame was now of the single-down-tube pattern; and the horizontal-spring front fork had been refined.

In a very real sense, this was the machine which revitalised the entire British industry. Because of the shortcomings of the early motor cycles, the general public had largely lost interest, but here at last was a truly reliable machine. That year, the Coventry factory produced five hundred complete Triumphs, but in addition a branch works had been established at Nuremberg, Germany, and Coventry-made engines were there installed into locally built frames.

Already, the firm was outgrowing its Much Park Street works, and in 1907 there came a move to new premises in Priory Street. In the course of the years, the Priory Street works were to extend both upwards and outwards. The original Much Park Street site, however, was not abandoned and became the service and competitions department, and the headquarters of Triumph's second-string cycle company, Gloria Cycles, where cycles

Right and far right: two views of a superbly restored Triumph Model H of 1919. The machine has a single-cylinder engine of 550cc. Some 30,000 of these bikes were supplied to the British and Allied armies during World War I and after the war the Model H remained a mainstay of Triumph production for a number of years

Below right: a view of the Triumph works at Priory Street, Coventry, in 1915

and Gloria sidecars were manufactured.

To jump back a year, at the Dashwood (West Wycombe) hill climb of September, 1906, a Triumph ridden by Frank Hulbert, formerly a partner in the Hulbert-Bramley Motor Company, had made a surprise appearance, cutting seven seconds off the hill record. In fact, the machine was the prototype of a new 3½hp (450cc) model, which was to replace the 'three horse' in the 1907 range.

The exterior appearance of the newcomer was much as before, but internally stamped steel flywheels with cast-iron rims were featured. Over 1000 were to be built in 1907, and yet a successor was already under way; this was a development of the machine Coventry publican Jack Marshall had ridden into second place in the 1907 Isle of Man TT. The bore had been enlarged from 82 to 84mm, increasing the capacity to 475cc, but a production change was that the cylinder was cast from a brass pattern, so ensuring greater uniformity of cylinder and fin thickness. Another innovation was a twin-barrel carburettor of Triumph design and make, which was to remain in the range until well into the 1920s.

Marshall's racer had dispensed with pedalling gear but, although pedals were retained on the standard tourers, a 'TT Model' with shorter wheelbase and no pedal mechanism was added to the range. A three-speed Sturmey-Archer rear hub gear was catalogued at extra price, as was a variable-ratio driving pulley, although this last was something of a misnomer. The ratio could not be varied with the machine on the move, and to change from high (4 to 1) to low (6 to 1) gear meant adjusting the pulley with a spanner and shortening the driving belt.

Triumphs were now on the crest of a wave, and the 1908 TT Race (single cylinder class) saw Jack Marshall welcomed home as winner, with more Triumphs filling third, fourth, fifth, seventh and tenth places. Sales success followed racing success, and in 1909 a total of 3000 machines left the Priory Street factory, many of them fitted with the newly introduced Triumph rear hub multi-plate clutch.

Once again the TT was used as a testing ground for the next season's model, the 1909 race machine being

Above left: members of a Belgian police force squad in 1921

Above: in 1921, Triumph introduced an overhead-valve, 500cc engine. It was the work of Harry Ricardo and Frank Halford

increased in stroke to 86mm, to produce a capacity of 499cc. That became the standard 1910 production model, and it was with one of these, single geared but with the multi-plate hub clutch, that Albert Catt, a Northampton leather merchant, staged an endurance run that was incredible in its conception, bearing in mind the still primitive machine, the lack of roadside services, and the untarred roads of the time.

The target Catt set himself was 2000 miles in six days – not in mid-summer, but in gloomy November. The weather conditions he encountered ranged from snow and ice to fog. On one day's run he collided with a cart parked without lights across a main road. At dawn on the final day his engine seized due to fluff blocking the oil pump seating, but he stripped and repaired the machine himself at the forge of a nearby flour mill. Just before midnight he clocked off with 1882½ miles completed, instead of the 2000 miles for which he had hoped.

Six months later, Catt set out again, this time to cover 2400 miles in six days. All went well, but the arduous rides, with a virtually unsprung machine on narrow tyres over rough roads, left him with a permanently damaged heart.

Around 1910, Maurice Schulte began to get ideas about vertical twin engines and experimented with a French engine in a Triumph frame. Three years later, Triumph's own vertical twin was in existence in prototype form – a side-valve 600cc with horizontally split crankcase, and a longitudinal camshaft driven by skew gearing from the middle of the crankshaft. Rather surprisingly, the two pistons did not rise and fall together, as in subsequent Triumph vertical-twin design, but rose and fell alternately.

World War I brought experiments with the twin to an end, but in any case

the factory was soon to have quite as much work on hand as it could comfortably handle. The neat little 225cc two-stroke known as the Triumph Junior was another 1913 development. The Junior had no clutch or kickstarter, but a two-speed gear built in unit with the engine and operated by cable from a handlebar lever. The designer was, once again, Charles Hathaway, with Frank Hulbert as development rider.

For 1914, the roadster machine was increased in capacity yet again, this time to 550cc, and in single-gear form the model filled the first British Army order for despatch-rider duties. However, an improved version was on the stocks, and in late 1914 it went into production. Equipped with three-speed Sturmey-Archer gearbox, it was the immortal Model H, of which some 30,000 were to be supplied to the British and Allied Armies before the war was over.

Moreover, the Model H was to continue in peacetime production and remain the mainstay of the Triumph line for several years to come, flanked by the 225cc two-stroke Junior. Whereas the Model H used chain primary, and belt final drive, a new all-chain-drive machine entered the lists for the 1920 season. Even at this comparatively late date, chain-driven machines were regarded with some disfavour by the general public, because unless some form of shock absorber was provided the transmission was much harsher than that provided by the vee-belt. Triumphs, however, had thought of that; the newcomer was the Model SD (Spring Drive), with a large-diameter coil spring shock absorber outboard of the clutch.

By 1920 the German branch works was back in production, building models basically similar to those produced in Coventry, but with minor variations (for

example, the two-stroke was 269cc, instead of 225cc as in Britain). Gradually, however, the Nuremberg factory moved towards autonomy, and by 1929 the last link with Coventry was broken. Motor cycle production, latterly of small two-strokes, ended in 1957; typewriter production followed, and the company is now merged with Adler, another former motor cycle firm now manufacturing office equipment.

Back to Coventry, and the sensation of 1921 – the first overhead-valve Triumph. The cylinder head incorporated four overhead valves; the light-alloy piston was another innovation. The lower-end assembly, and the frame, were still basically Model SD, but the cylinder head was the work of Harry Ricardo, with Major Frank Halford (later to earn fame as an aero-engine designer) as development engineer and test rider.

Coincidentally with Ricardo's work on the Model R, Triumph's own engineers had been engaged on a new racing 498cc side-valve machine, and for the 1921 Senior TT there were two three-man Triumph teams, one on the side-valves, and the other on 'Riccys'. Perhaps it was too early to expect much of the four-valver, only one of which finished, but Jack Watson-Bourne was fifth on a side valve, and Fred Edmond recorded the fastest lap before dropping back with a split oil tank.

Ricardo and Halford continued developing the engine, with Frank Halford taking time off to break the world

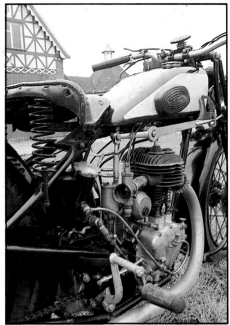

Above: this 1929 Triumph has a 550cc side-valve engine and is now on display in the Easton Farm Park motor cycle collection in Suffolk

Above right: a close-up of the engine and saddle tank of the 1929 550cc Triumph

flying-mile record at 83.91mph, and cracking the one-hour and fifty-miles records for good measure. For the 1922 Senior TT, the unit had a larger bore and shorter stroke, permitting the use of bigger valves, and the exhaust ports were splayed instead of parallel.

That year, the factory decided to give a brilliant young Coventry rider named Walter Brandish their backing – and the firm's confidence was certainly not misplaced for, although Walter finished in second place, he had ridden with top gear inoperative since the end of the third lap.

Naturally, Walter was again chosen for the 1924 Senior TT, but during one of the practice sessions he fell heavily, breaking a leg at the left-hander still known as Brandish Corner. It was the last occasion on which Triumphs relied on the four-valve Ricardo; another racing engine was already on the stocks, this time a two-valve model developed and raced at Brooklands by Victor Horsman.

Back at Coventry, the Triumph company was spreading its wings. Maurice Schulte had left, and the new manager, Colonel Claude Holbrook, favoured a move into car production. Accordingly, Harry Ricardo was asked to design a suitable engine and, in 1923, the first Triumph car (a 1393cc open tourer) emerged from the Priory Street plant.

Also in 1923, the Triumph Junior two-stroke was enlarged from 225 to 250cc and, for the first time was given a clutch and kick-starter. Nevertheless it had only two more years to live, and it was dropped

after 1925, retaining belt drive and the famous fore-and-aft front fork to the end. In the meantime, the firm had introduced a very advanced little unit-construction 346cc model, the LS, with gear primary drive, an all-metal clutch, and internal expanding brakes at front and rear. For no good reason it failed to catch the public fancy, despite a reduction in price by the manufacturers.

What was needed, reckoned Siegfried Bettmann, was a machine of the simplest possible design, compatible with a reasonable performance, capable of being both made and sold very cheaply. The outcome was the Model P, a 494cc side-valve with which the Triumph company were to bankrupt half the small-production manufacturers in Britain. The fact that a new model was on its way from Coventry had been common knowledge in the trade – but the actual selling price was not, and Triumphs kept that a dead secret until the doors of the 1924 London Show were thrown open. Only then was the new model seen to be wearing a sensational placard, giving the price as £42 17s 6d, the cheapest five-hundred ever offered.

It was made possible by planning an initial run of 20,000 machines and placing contracts for the necessary bought-out parts accordingly. Taking a few short-cuts in design, such as running the valves directly in the metal of the cylinder head, instead of in valve guides, and fitting the front wheel with an asbestos-rope band brake derived from a Triumph bicycle, helped make the cost extremely competitive.

One competitor had been George Bell, manufacturer of the 350cc Barr and Stroud-engined Banshee. 'When I saw the price of the Model P,' recalled Mr Bell recently, 'I knew there was no way in which we could compete, because the

Banshee was costing us £45 in raw materials alone. So I closed the Banshee works, went to the Triumph factory and told them: "You have put me out of business. What do I do now?". They told me: "If you've any sense, you'll start here, on Monday". And, in the end, that's exactly what I did!'

The Model P was almost certainly the best-selling motor cycle of all up to that point, and by May of 1925 production was running at the hitherto unheard-of rate of 1000 machines a week. Later that year an improved version, with a drum front brake, valve guides and other minor changes, began to come off the assembly line. Sales continued at a high level right into 1926, augmented by other related models (the N, the Q, the QA, etc) which were really just refinements on the Model P theme.

Top of the range by this time was the 498cc two-valve sports model based on the Victor Horsman design, heading an eight-model parade for 1927. However, the car side of the company had a new model too, the Triumph Super Seven, and in order to get this safely launched the motor cycle programme was slashed to just four bikes for 1928.

Saddle tanks came in with the 1929 range, which was back to eight models, including a new C-range family with basically the same bottom-end layout. The 1930s slump, however, was just over the horizon, and soon Triumphs, like other models were trying desperate measures to keep the works occupied. Potential customers had little money either, and so small two-strokes of 150 and 175cc were brought in (there was even a 98cc Villiers-engined machine but, shame-facedly, Triumphs marketed that under their Gloria name).

The larger models were continued, however, and a new range of 350 and

500cc singles with foot-change gear-boxes, including the semi-enclosed Silent Scout model, was put in hand. For the small-machine man, A.A. Sykes designed a very nice little 150cc, single-cylinder, overhead-valve model.

Val Page (famous for his work at JAP and Ariel) joined the Coventry company in 1932 and immediately set to work to create a new Triumph image, evolving new side-valve and overhead-valve singles of modern appearance, topped by an entirely new semi-unit-construction 650cc vertical twin with double-helical-gear primary drive, dry-sump lubrication, and a one-piece crankshaft.

To publicise the new twin, Harry Perrey took a 650cc Triumph sidecar outfit through the 1933 International Six Days Trial, winning a silver medal, then immediately staged a Brooklands test in which, with a team of riders and despite foggy conditions, the same machine covered 500 miles in 500 minutes.

However, the parent company felt that their destiny now lay in the manufacture of cars, and a move was afoot to close down the motor cycle side of the business. Fortunately, Ariel chief Jack Sangster heard the rumour, moved swiftly and closed a deal under which Triumph motor cycles would continue at Coven-

try, but under new management.

In charge of his new acquisition, Sangster placed Edward Turner (hitherto known as the designer of the Ariel Square Four), and Turner's first move was to add glamour to the existing Triumph range. Basically, they were still the Val Page models, but it was surprising what a difference a helping of chromium plating and silver paint made. The vertical twin was dropped, and the sports 250, 350 and 500cc overhead-valve singles gained the new and catchy titles of Tiger 70, Tiger 80, and Tiger 90, the figures hinting at their exciting performance potential.

The revamping was an interim measure only: Edward was at work on a new Triumph vertical twin of his own, a 500cc model announced in July 1937, as the Speed Twin. It was a machine which caught the motor cycle world by storm, and indeed it was to set a fashion copied by other factories all over the globe. The Speed Twin was followed for 1939 by a more sporting version, the Tiger 100. In 1940 there would have been a new 350cc vertical twin, but World War II caused that one to be put into cold storage.

A military version of the 350cc twin was put in hand, nevertheless, and it was sheer ill-luck that the first batch of fifty machines for the British Army was on the assembly line the night that the heart of Coventry – including the Triumph factory – was flattened in the first concentrated German Air Force bomb attack on the highly industrialised town.

Slowly, the shattered Triumph company came back to life, at first in temporary premises in Warwick where a restart was made on Army contracts – not with the little twin, but with the easier-to-make 350cc Model 3HW single. Meanwhile, planning permission had been granted for a completely new factory, alongside the old Coventry to Birmingham road at Meriden (a village reputed to be the exact geographical centre of Britain). The Meriden Works came into operation in mid 1942, producing not only the 3HW, but also two versions of the 500cc vertical twin engine, for use in portable generator plants. One of these was the AAPP (Airborne Auxiliary Power Plant), designed to charge the batteries of RAF bombers in flight, and in the interests of saving weight it was equipped with a cylinder barrel and head of silicon-aluminium alloy.

That cylinder barrel and head was to play an unexpected role when peace returned, because a Dublin farmer named Ernie Lyons won the 1946 Manx Grand Prix, the first race to be held over the Isle of Man circuit since the cessation of hostilities, on a Tiger 100 model with an AAPP top end. Furthermore Ernie's model had an unusual rear springing system in which the springs were within the oversize hub of the wheel itself. This was another Edward Turner invention, intended to avoid the necessity of re-designing the Triumph rear frame, and the Sprung Hub was soon available to all those enthusiasts who fancied it.

The long delayed 3T, a 350cc twin, was added to the Speed Twin and Tiger 100 for the peacetime range. The Grand Prix, developed from the Manx Grand Prix winner, was marketed as an over-the-counter racing model; it was no world beater, but a very useful workhorse for racing men of average ability.

From the AAPP engine was also evolved one of the best loved Triumphs of the post-war period, namely the TR5 Trophy, a competitions all-rounder which was to make its mark in scrambling, trials and ISDT type events.

By 1949, an important market for British machines was developing in the

USA, and to meet demand from that part of the world a 650cc twin, the Thunderbird, came to life. In time it was to become a favourite police patrol mount all over the world, by then sports editions of the 650cc machine – at first the Tiger 110, followed by the illustrious Bonneville – had appeared on the scene.

Neither was it all big stuff: at the other end of the capacity scale a 150cc single (the Terrier) had been reintroduced in 1953, to grow a few years later into the 199cc Tiger Cub. In 1951 Triumph (and Ariel) had been acquired by the BSA group, but there was no apparent integration between Triumph and BSA designs until 1968, with the arrival of the three-cylinder 741cc Triumph Trident; even here, there was a distinction between the Trident and its BSA cousin, the Rocket Three, in that the BSA had an inclined motor, the Triumph a vertical.

From 1968 on, however, there was a gradual coming together. With the setting up of a joint research establishment at Umberslade Hall a new frame, with a large diameter top tube serving also as an oil reservoir, was adopted for both 650cc BSA and Triumph twins. Meriden took over responsibility for developing the USA-style racing models, aimed at the prestigious Daytona 200 event. At the same time a BSA 250cc single cylinder model was marketed as a Triumph.

By this time the sands of time were fast running out for the BSA group, and by 1973 the whole operation was bankrupt. With governmental persuasion, a shotgun wedding with Dennis Poore's Norton-Villiers group was rushed through, but one of the first declarations of the new Norton-Villiers-Triumph combine was that in the interests of operating economy the Meriden plant would be closed, and work concentrated at the roomier (but far more antiquated) BSA works at Small Heath. There was more than a hint that the Triumph name would be allowed to die – or, even worse, would be used only on a cheaper version of the Norton motor cycle.

Rundown of the Meriden works was to begin in February 1974, and would eventually have led to over 1500 redundancies – and that the Meriden shop stewards would not permit at any price. Instead, they declared a 'sit-in', locked the gates to senior members of the staff and refused to allow completed machines to be despatched. One result of this was that Trident production came to a halt because, although the engines had been built at Small Heath, the frames had been built, and final assembly undertaken, at Meriden.

With a large stock of Trident engines on hand, NVT had perforce to make arrangements for building the complete machine at Small Heath. This implied manufacturing duplicate frame jigs, etc, and the delay meant that it was April 1974 before the first Birmingham Tridents came off the line. Back at Meriden, the stalemate continued, with around 2500 finished Triumphs gathering dust, and no spares emerging to keep existing models on the road. The picketing workers, however, were now seriously considering the formation of a co-operative to take over and run the factory themselves.

The election of a Labour government in February 1974, gave hope that this might indeed come to pass, and a meeting was arranged between the union leaders, and Secretary of State for Industry Anthony Wedgwood Benn and Eric Heffer, his Minister of State. At last, on July 10, came a Government announcement that the men would get official backing. In due course the blockade was lifted and the impounded machines began to flow once more. Even so, it was not until the following March that the

Meriden Motor Cycle Co-operative was formally created, with the aid of a £5 million grant.

Manufacture of 750cc Bonneville and Tiger 750 twins was resumed, by now with a left-side gear pedal to conform with US legislation introduced while the machines had been off the market. The co-operative, however, was a manufacturing unit only, and sales were still in the hands of Norton-Villiers-Triumph, who were the legal owners of the name and manufacturing rights. It was an irksome situation for the Meriden men, who were not allowed to bring in any modifications or improvements, and determination grew to buy the complete rights from NVT and handle their own destiny and development.

Above right: one of Triumph's most popular models was the Thunderbird This particular example is of 1958 vintage and has a 650cc engine

Right: a Triumph Speed Twin model of 1961.

Below right: perhaps the most famous Triumph model of them all was the Bonneville. This is a 1964 version.

Below: a Speed Twin of 1948 with non-standard paintwork and Siamese exhaust

It was not going to be easy, and yet it did happen, largely through the intervention of the giant General Electric Company, which agreed to purchase 2000 complete Bonneville twins from the co-operative and hold them in stock, so providing £1 million to aid the cash flow situation. Moreover, GEC provided technical assistance, and advice in setting up a marketing organisation.

In 1977 ambition was finally realised, and the Meriden Co-operative was fully in business on its own account, owning, building, and selling the 750cc twins. The fact that the year marked the Queen's Silver Jubilee as well was coincidental, but it gave Meriden the opportunity of building 2000 Bonnevilles (1000 for the British market, and 1000 more for export) in a special 'limited edition' finish of silver with blue tank panels and red and white striping. Production crept up to 300, and then to 350 machines a week; new colour schemes were adopted, and Triumph were able to greet 1978 with full order books.

Obviously, the Bonneville, based as it was on a 1937 design, could not live on indefinitely; by 1978 there was a new-generation vertical twin in prototype form, with contra-rotating balance weights to give the smooth running demanded for radio-equipped police work.

Unfortunately, the changes were not sufficient to boost sales again and, although the Co-operative struggled on, liquidation finally came in 1983.

Below: the late 1960s saw the dawning of the 'superbike' era and although many people believe the 750cc Honda Four to be the first of the superbikes it wasn't. This was the first superbike – the three-cylinder, four-stroke Triumph Trident, introduced in 1968. The model pictured is of mid 1970s, vintage.

Bottom left: Triumph's Formula 750 racer of the early 1970s was developed from the Trident threes. This is Paul Smart on a works Triumph in 1971

Bottom right: the classic Bonneville in one of its last incarnations. The 750cc ohv vertical twin was still very much the same as the 500cc unit of the 1937 Speed Twin

Velocette

It seems incredible that any motor cycle manufacturer could have commenced operations in the pharmaceutical world, yet that was the nature of the very first business venture embarked upon by Johannes Gutgemann, the founder of Veloce Limited, soon after he married during 1884 and settled in Birmingham. Johannes was the son of a merchant from Oberwinter, on the Rhine. When his father died, he decided to leave for England rather than complete the compulsory military training programme that was in operation in Germany at that time. He adopted the name of John Taylor and it was under the banner of Isaac Taylor and Company that his pill making venture was established. Profits from this business encouraged him to diversify into cycle manufacture, and during the early 1890s he opened a small workshop off Birmingham's Great Hampton Street. The business grew and,

as a result of a meeting between Taylor and another cycle manufacturer, William Gue, Taylor, Gue and Company was formed, to manufacture cycles under the trade name 'Hampton'. In 1896 the business became a limited company and in 1900 the name was changed to Taylor Gue Limited. By now, the company's activities had expanded beyond the manufacture of cycles. They were also making rickshaws for export to the Far East and had built a prototype forecar, the company's first connection with motor cycles.

Towards the end of 1904, Kelecom Motors Limited encountered financial difficulties and was purchased by Taylor Gue, who took over the firm's London premises. Kelecom had been manufacturing a single-cylinder 3hp motor cycle, sold under the trade name 'Ormonde', the engine of which had been designed by Paul Kelecom. Taylor had been making the frames for the 'Ormonde'

models and it seemed a logical step to take over the entire business when it collapsed. A year later, John Taylor decided to use the name 'Veloce' for the motor cycles that were now manufactured by his company, a significant development coming with the introduction of a new 2hp engine. Although the new model made its debut at the 1905 Stanley Show, it proved to be a failure and, on 19 October 1905, Taylor Gue went into voluntary liquidation.

Fortunately, John Taylor still had faith in the bicycle and earlier that year he had formed Veloce Limited, after acquiring premises off Spring Hill, Birmingham. He had received substantial financial backing from Edward Williams, a chainwheel manufacturer. It is interesting to note that soon after he had disposed of the pill making business so that he could devote all his time to this latest venture, John Taylor was approached by someone who had perfected a formula for making custard powder. He declined the offer, which was eventually taken up by Birds, who went on to become one of Europe's largest food manufacturers. Instead, Veloce Limited commenced the manufacture of bicycles. Neither of John's two sons, Percy and Eugene, showed much interest in the business at this time. Percy, the elder son, was apprenticed to a pattern maker and ultimately went out to India for a short period with a bicycle customer. Eugene also had a mechanical bent, and served his apprenticeship in the tool room of the famous New Hudson works in Birmingham.

While in India, Percy had become involved with the growing motor car trade and, on his return, he decided to build his own car. Joined by his brother, the two of them formed New Veloce Motors, to operate from the same premises as Veloce Limited. A 20hp car was eventually completed during 1908, using a number of bought in parts, such as the engine and radiator. Orders failed to materialise, however, and New Veloce diversified into other areas which included making roller skates. Gradually the business ran downhill, until it was absorbed completely by Veloce Limited, in August 1916.

Above left: following World War I, Veloce Ltd, which had been formed in 1905 as a bicycle manufacturer, produced this little 220cc two-stroke machine. It had a single cylinder

Left: a 1920 Ladies model DL2 Velocette. It had a two-speed gearbox, but no clutch or kickstart was fitted

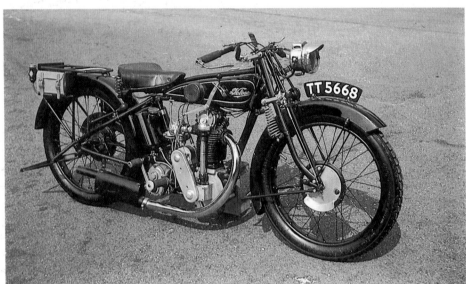

Meanwhile, the bicycle business had gone so well that John Taylor was marketing his products through subsidiary companies, each with its own brand name. Now that the motor cycle market had opened up, too, he decided to re-enter it, in spite of his earlier set-back. Percy and Eugene agreed to produce the engines at the Spring Hill premises, while John made the frames and cycle parts at Fleet Street. Percy was responsible for the engine design and the outcome was something that was quite remarkable for that era. He designed a unit-construction engine of 276cc capacity, having an integral oil pump with an oil-in-sump arrangement and a neat two-speed gear system that used cone clutches. Initially, the engine had an automatic inlet valve, but the layout was later changed to mechanically operated inlet over exhaust. The most interesting feature was an over-hung crankshaft, a feature that was to become the hallmark of some of the later models for many years.

Like those of many new and advanced designs, sales did not match up to

Above left: a racing model Velocette two-stroke of 1922. It had a capacity of 249cc and raced in that year's TT, taking third place

Left: a 350cc, overhead-camshaft Velocette Model K of 1925. A sports model, the KSS, was introduced later that year. It was capable of 80mph

Below: a 1928 Model KSS, which was an overhead-camshaft four-stroke. Note the 'water bottle' silencer, characteristic of the period and the rubber knee grips

expectations, mainly because the public seem reluctant to accept radical change. In consequence, it was necessary to market a second, more conventional model, not too unlike the 500cc Triumph of that time. This was a 499cc model, with direct belt drive to the rear wheel. Although the unit-construction model had been marketed under the trade name 'Veloce', the 500 was designated the VMC, for Veloce Motor Company. In offering a choice of two completely different models, the company secured a much better footing in the ever-growing motor cycle market and could now produce a catalogue giving different options in specification.

During 1911, John Taylor applied to the Home Office for naturalisation, and in 1917 he changed his name once again, by Deed Poll, this time to Goodman. When the cyclecar boom of 1912 and 1913 got under way, Veloce Limited announced their intention of manufacturing a vee-twin engine. Before this in 1913, they brought out a 206cc two-stroke, which, for the first time, carried the trade name 'Velocette'. There had been growing interest in the lightweight economy machine, especially now that motor cycling had become 'respectable' as far as lady riders were concerned, and John Taylor was perceptive enough to see

Right: a sight to gladden the heart of any old time British bike enthusiast – the famous Velocette trademark

Below: in 1929, Veloce Ltd were marketing the production racer 350cc KTT model. The following year saw KTT models taking the first eight places in the Manx Grand Prix

that there would be a vast market if only an 'everyman' type of machine, requiring the minimum of maintenance, could be developed. This theme persisted throughout the entire history of the company, as subsequent events will show. The two-stroke had at least two outstanding features: an overhung crankshaft arrangement used in conjunction with a *desaxé* cylinder and head, and a patent lubrication system in which oil was contained in a separate crankcase compartment and delivered to the various parts of the engine by exhaust pressure. Three models were available, a 'cheap' direct belt drive, a two-speed all chain drive and a ladies version of the latter, with a special 'dropped' frame.

World War I put paid to the vee-twin engine, and for that matter to the 296cc unit-construction model and the 499cc Triumph-like single. Instead, the factory switched over to munitions work, which included orders from Rolls-Royce.

After the war, production was concentrated on the two-strokes, only two of the three original models being available, the belt-driver having been dropped. Added refinements were an increase in capacity from 206 to 220cc, involving some crankcase redesign, and the use of an internal expanding rear hub brake. These were now listed as the D1 and DL1 models, the latter being the ladies model.

By the end of 1919, two new models had been announced, these being the D2 and the DL2. Similar in general specification to the earlier models, they employed a larger crankcase casting, giving better access to the overhung big-end assembly via a screwed 'door' on the offside. A reciprocating oil pump provided an improved lubrication system that could be regulated more positively, while the frame now had twin down-tubes and was fitted with a better shaped tank. Brampton forks completed the improved specification, which was complemented by the use of a gear control lever, not unlike a bath tap in appearance, mounted on the tank. Needless to say, these new models soon gained a very good reputation and would record up to 200mpg petrol consumption as well as provide a maximum speed of over 50mph. No wonder a works model won a gold medal in the 1919 ACU Six Days' Trial.

Over the next few years, the two-strokes underwent continuous refinement, a three-speed model being introduced in 1921, and fitted with an internal expanding front hub brake designed by Percy Goodman. A year later, a clutch was added to the gearbox for the first time, as was a kickstarter. Brampton Biflex forks aided the front suspension, to give freedom of horizontal movement. Two Sports models appeared during 1922, having an increased capacity of 249cc. They were intended for racing.

By 1923, the capacity of all models had been increased to 249cc. A Colonial model was added to the range, for overseas use, and even a lightweight sidecar outfit was offered.

With the everyman concept still in mind, a 'Light Two-Fifty' model was announced during 1924, having a curious reversion to belt secondary drive. Lightweight Brampton forks and the exhaust controlled lubrication system, both reminiscent of the 1913/14 period, helped keep the cost down to £38, but there were few takers. This end of the market has always been noted for being very fickle. The range continued to the H models of 1926, when the production of two-strokes stopped so that the factory could concentrate on something very different. Even then, this was not the end.

For some time the Veloce Board had been giving thought to the need for a new, high class production model that would add to the company's already very good reputation. The current trend towards high performance overhead valve models had not passed unnoticed and although Veloce had experimented with valve controlled two-stroke engines the overall results had proved disappointing. It was Percy Goodman who came up with the answer, a prototype overhead camshaft engine of 348cc capacity. Initial testing of the new engine, slotted into a new frame and cycle parts, showed up some minor defects and, as a result, the engine layout was changed in certain respects. Towards the middle of 1925, the first production models became available, with a 'Veloce' transfer on the tank. This had hurriedly to be changed, as the public did not associate this name with the splendid little two-strokes produced by the same company. So the new overhead cam model became a Velocette.

Three of the new models were entered for the 1925 Junior TT, but all three had to retire. 1926 was a quite different story, however. In the Junior Race of that year, Alec Bennett came home first on a 348cc

Left: a close-up of one of the most famous engines ever. It is the 350cc, single-cylinder, overhead-camshaft KTT engine designed by Percy Goodman

Below: a Velocette brochure of the 1930s

Right: G. Newman poses on his 350cc Velo at the Junior Manx GP of 1937

MOTOR CYCLES
1930

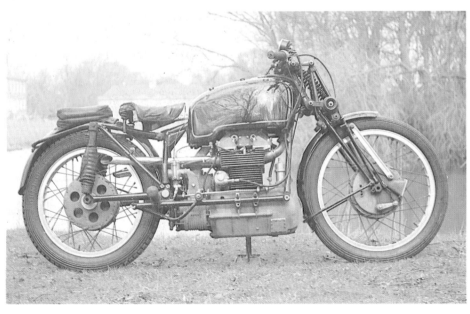

Velocette, to finish more than *ten minutes* ahead of the second place man. A second place followed in 1927, and two more outright wins were added in 1928 and 1929. It was due to the success of their two-stroke machines that the company had moved into larger premises at Six Ways, Aston, during February 1920. Now, due to the flood of orders resulting from the success of the overhead camshaft models, they had to move again. Soon after the 1926 TT win, they settled into the factory at York Road, Hall Green, previously occupied by Humphries and Dawes, makers of the OK marque. This was to be their final home, linking together the names Hall Green and Velocette.

The new overhead cam engine was of the dry sump lubrication type, employing bevel drive for the overhead camshaft, connected via a vertical shaft and Oldham couplings. By using what is known as a hunting tooth arrangement, it was possible to ensure the heaviest loading did not occur consecutively on the same set of mating teeth. Oil circulated at between 8 and 10lb per sq in pressure, which represents a flow of roughly one quarter pint each ten minutes at low engine speeds. Mechanically, the engine was quiet compared to its contemporaries and it was reasonably oil tight, too, despite the ends of the rocker arms extending through slots in the cambox to operate the valves.

The drive was transmitted via a three-speed gearbox of Veloce design, the earliest models having a face cam operated clutch, similar to that used on the two-strokes. Later, the more familiar Veloce method of clutch operation was employed, a quite unconventional method that separated the clutch by a form of servo-action. This gave rise to an unusual chain line, in which the secondary drive was on the outside of the primary drive – another Veloce hallmark. It enabled the width of the crankcase to be kept small and made gear ratio changes very much easier.

The first few models were fitted with Brampton forks, but, in the interests of improved road holding, these were subsequently changed in favour of Webbs. The bikes were known initially as the model K. A sports version was developed during late 1925, with a maximum speed of 80mph. This was the famous KSS

Top left: this lightweight Velocette of 1937 was powered by a single-cylinder, two-stroke engine of 249cc

Centre left: Velocette's highly unusual Model O was designed by the famed Phil Irving. It had a 600cc engine and final drive was by shaft

Left: the legendary 500cc, supercharged Velocette Roarer of 1939

model, which was continued in production until 1948, albeit with many modifications. Other models were added in the late 'twenties, such as the KE, KS and KES, all of which were variants of the overhead cam design, with specification changes to meet differing price ranges. The most outstanding development occurred during late 1928, when Harold Willis, who had joined Veloce Limited as Development Engineer, invented the first positive stop, foot-controlled gear change. Used on the 1929 Junior TT entries, it was applied to the production models soon afterwards.

In 1929, Veloce Limited broke fresh ground by marketing an 'over-the-counter' production racer, a replica of the TT winning KTT models. Such was the impact of the KTT that the bikes took the first eight places in the 1930 Manx Grand Prix. That same year, the company also ventured tentatively into dirt track racing, with an overbored 415cc model specially produced for riding on cinders. It was not a success, however, and only 22 were made.

By this time, the two-strokes were back in production again, to meet a continuing demand from those who required a smaller capacity and somewhat cheaper model. The model U appeared during 1928, an updated version of the overhung crank design, having a saddle tank and wired-on tyres. A Super Sports model, the USS, followed a year later, and this was very popular with clubmen. Somehow, the magic of the Velocette two-stroke had been lost with the advent of the even more popular overhead cam machines. The USS was to be the last of the overhung crank models and what remained of the U models were sold off for £32 each, redesignated as model 32. For some reason that is no longer apparent, they had a blue coloured petrol tank, a departure that hardly endeared them to the Velocette enthusiast.

Another bold move was made in 1930, when an entirely new two-stroke was introduced, the coil ignition 249cc GTP model. Pandering to public taste, a twin-port, coil ignition, overhead cam model was introduced at the same time, this being the iniquitous KTP. Although it had the advantage of being cheaper than its stablemate, it had its faults and by the end of 1931 it had disappeared from the

Top right: Peter Goodman races a 495cc Velocette model at Cadwell Park in 1946

Centre right: the Model MSS Velocette had a 500cc, pushrod-operated overhead-valve engine. This is a 1947 example

Right: the ultimate Velocette KTT model – the Mark VIII. This beautifully restored model is of 1947 vintage

catalogue, with no one to mourn its passing. Meanwhile, the overhead cam models continued in production, slowly losing the edge of their performance as the overall weight gradually increased. This was the electric lighting era and nearly everyone wanted a full electric lighting set included in the specification of their new bike. Some minor engine redesign was carried out during 1931, in order to give back the engine a little of its former zest. The four-speed gearbox was now coming into fashion and, by 1933, a new type of gearbox having four speeds was included in the specification of all the K models. A year later, a much deeper petrol tank, of increased capacity, helped make the general appearance much more attractive. The KTT racing models kept pace with the times, too, as race speeds rose. Hairpin valve springs were used during the 1932 season, and then an aluminium bronze cylinder head, giving rise to the much revered MKIV model. TT wins proved elusive during this period, but Velocettes were never out of the hunt and scored all manner of wins elsewhere. The GTP model was not neglected either, having firstly an aluminium alloy cylinder head, then a four-speed, foot-change gearbox. It was during this period that Veloce Limited adopted the practice of linking the carburettor to the oil pump, to give better control over the lubrication system – a ploy that was 'reinvented' by the Japanese some thirty years later.

With a 250cc two-stroke and a 350cc overhead camshaft model, it may appear that Velocette Limited had things just right. However, there was still one need to be met, for a machine that was cheaper than the overhead camshaft models, yet had better performance than the GTP two-stroke. Work to rectify this omission

was soon put in hand. The first prototype comprised a GTP frame and cycle parts, carrying a 350cc side-valve engine. Mediocre performance and lack of mechanical quietness led to a rethink, and Eugene Goodman came up with a high camshaft 250cc engine, with redesigned cycle parts to match. First announced during 1933 as the MOV model, this newcomer tipped the scales at 275lb fully equipped, and retailed at £47.10s. It was an instant success, being the forerunner of the famous 'M' series of pushrod singles, and with their characteristic 'map of India' timing cover. By lengthening the stroke of the engine it was quite easy to manufacture a 349cc version, catalogued as the MAC model, and this latter variant appeared only a matter of months later. In due course, a 495cc engine appeared, too, adding the MSS model to the range during 1935. This model used different cycle parts, however, especially with regard to the frame and forks, as the machine's use for sidecar work had to be considered.

Below: the LE Velocette was a new concept in motor cycling when it was introduced in 1948. Unusually styled, it featured a horizontally opposed, twin-cylinder, water-cooled, side-valve engine of 150cc. Final drive was by shaft

The advent of the 349cc MAC model necessitated further attention to the overhead cam models, as a situation had been reached where the cheaper model had virtually the same performance. Production of the overhead cam models came to a halt at the end of the 1935 season, so that attention could be concentrated on redesign. Although not generally appreciated, there was a break in the continuity of the overhead cam model line until the first production versions of the Mark II model became available during 1936. The new design used the same frame and cycle parts as the 495cc MSS pushrod single, but had an entirely new engine with an aluminium alloy cylinder head in which all the valve gear was fully enclosed. It was an impressive looking engine that gave the overhead cam models an entirely new image. Two models were available, the more sporting KSS version and the KTS, which had heavier and more efficient mudguards, wider section tyres and was better suited to normal touring work. Both models continued virtually unchanged until 1948, apart from during the war years.

This continuity also applied to the MOV, MAC and MSS models, only the GTP two-stroke and the KTT racers undergoing further development. In the former case, a ported piston was fitted during 1934, with port modifications to suit, in an attempt to improve performance. An oil bath chaincase and, later still, a much deeper and larger capacity fuel tank, followed. The racers passed through the Mark V and VI stages, none of these versions passing into the hands of the public. This was true too of the double overhead camshaft model used during the 1936 Junior TT, sadly without success. Even rotary valve engines were built and tested, again without success. All this led to the very beautiful Mk VII model and ultimately the Mk VIII version, which was virtually identical apart from the use of a swinging arm frame, fitted with air damped rear suspension units. It was a Mk VIII model that carried Stanley Woods to victory in the 1939 Junior TT, an occasion that was tinged with sadness when Harold Willis passed away, from meningitis, on the eve of this victory. A brilliant engineer and a real character in his own right, Harold was sorely missed on the racing scene. Some of his witticisms live on today.

The highlights of the 1939 TT was the appearance, during practice only, of the unique 500cc supercharged twin, known as the 'Roarer'. Piloted by Stanley Woods on its first outing, it was anticipated that this latest Velocette offering would offer a serious challenge to the foreign multis that were now beginning to dominate racing. Sadly, the chance never came. The war intervened and, after the war, the FIM banned super-chargers in road racing. A road-going twin, having some similarities with the 'Roarer', was also stillborn as a result of the war. Only one example was made, and this, fortunately, has survived. It was designated the model O.

During World War II the factory once again become involved with contract work of all kinds for the armed forces. Some machines were made, however, mainly for use by the fire service and for similar civilian duties. A special version of the MAC model, known as the MAF, was produced for the French Army, and later for use by British servicemen, some of these bikes seeing service in the western desert. There was no question of volume production, however, as was the case with Norton, BSA and Matchless.

When production was resumed after the war, only the MOV, MAC, MSS and KSS models were listed. The last named had the benefit of a slightly larger inlet valve and a year later, in 1948, all were supplied with Dowty telescopic front forks. The Webb girder fork, used with such success in the past, was no longer in production. 1948 proved to be the swan-song of the MOV, MSS and KSS models and, from 1949 onwards, only the MAC model remained in production. The reason was only too apparent: it was a newcomer to the Velocette range that brought the company closer than ever to their dream of the 'everyman' model.

The LE model made its debut during October 1948, and took the motor cycling world by surprise. Unlike anything that had previously originated from Veloce Limited, it took the form of a 149cc, water-cooled, flat twin, with shaft drive to the rear wheel. The engine was mounted transversely in a pressed-steel frame and was built in unit with the gearbox, the drive shaft being taken through the centre of the nearside swinging arm tube. Starting was by means of a long handle that also retracted the centre stand, and the gearchange was by hand, too, with a car-type gate. The specification included footboards, built-in leg shields, panniers and a glove box. Every consideration had been made so that the newcomer was attractive to those who would not normally own a motor cycle, and its attractions included its exceptional quietness. Charles Udall took credit for the design, Eugene Goodman carrying out all the production planning and the installation of new equipment for all the steel pressings needed. Such were the expectations for the LE (so named after the contraction of the words little engine) that it was anticipated that even the MAC would be phased out when the orders came rushing in.

Alas, the public were as fickle as ever and, although the LE came nearer than any other design to captivate their attention, the bike never quite made the grade. In November 1950, it was found necessary to increase the engine capacity to 192cc, the maximum possible, and it was in this form that the LE continued until the end of its days. Other changes were made as time progressed, including a reversion to a kickstarter and a four-speed, foot-change gearbox. Even if sales to the public were not exceptional, innumerable police forces used the LE for a variety of local duties. This necessitated fitting a special high output

Below: R. Boughey's 500cc Velocette at the Manx Grand Prix of 1955

Bottom: this is the 500cc Velocette which in 1961 established a world record for 24 hours continuous running at the Montlhéry circuit in France

generator when extra electrical equipment was fitted.

Velocette racing activities had now terminated completely, despite Freddie Frith and Bob Foster taking 350cc World Championships in 1949 and 1950 respectively with the now ageing KTT model. The Race Shop closed soon after the death of Percy Goodman in 1951, at the very time when he had commenced work on a liquid-cooled in-line four, so that Veloce Limited could retain a stake in the world of motor cycle racing. Yet this was by no means the end of the company's interest in competition events. The advent of the spring frame MAC model during 1953, and the completely redesigned MSS model a year later, led to the development of a scrambles model and an endurance version for export to the USA. Although the scrambles model,

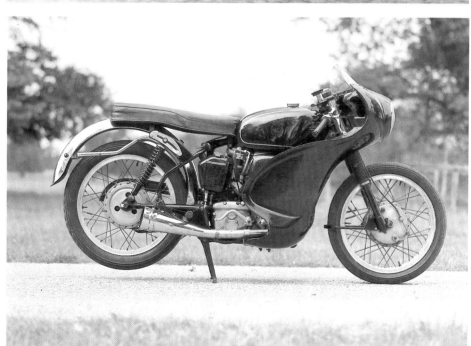

later available in both 350 and 500cc sizes, never proved highly successful, it led to a further and more interesting development. During 1956, the company announced two new super sports models for general road use, the 350cc 'Viper' and the 500cc 'Venom'. Clubman's racing versions of both were also made available, much to the delight of those who mourned the phasing out of the KTT during the 1951 season.

Towards the end of October 1956, an overhead-valve version of the LE was announced, named the Valiant. It remained in production until late 1963, when it was quietly phased out. The Mk 3 LE bottom end was not really up to the high standard of performance obtainable from the overhead valve modification. It was during this latter year that another version of the LE appeared, known as the Vogue. It differed in having a glassfibre body, finished in a two-tone colour scheme, and twin headlamps. Less than five hundred were made.

activities were now at a standstill. Although a Mk VIII KTT Velocette had won the 1948 and 1949 Junior TT races and secured the 350cc Championship for Veloce Limited, it was becoming apparent that the KTT was losing its competitiveness. Production of KTT models

Below: the unusual Velocette Vogue had a four-stroke, horizontally opposed, twin-cylinder engine of 200cc

Reverting to the MAC model, it was found necessary to keep this model in production when the anticipated level of LE orders failed to materialise. By now, this model was getting a little out of date and it needed a certain amount of redesign to bring it back into line. The new all-alloy engine appeared during 1951, and the model was fitted with telescopic forks of Veloce manufacture. The frame was still rigid, however and, in 1953, a new design of spring frame had to be fitted, in order to keep up with current trends. There was a growing demand for a 500cc single, too, and in 1954 an entirely new MSS model was announced, this time having an engine that differed internally in many respects from that of the MAC. It was the development of the MSS engine that led the company to take an interest in scrambling, for their racing

ceased at the end of 1950, when work had already commenced on the design of the liquid-cooled four.

Although outclassed, the Velocette scrambler showed promise, and it was this development that led to the introduction of the 'Venom' and 'Viper' models in 1956. The 349cc 'Viper' owed no allegiance to the MAC model. Indeed, the engine was devised by reducing the stroke and not the bore, a complete reversal of the way in which the original MAC model stemmed from its smaller brother, the MOV. The introduction of the 'Venom' and 'Viper' models permitted the company to re-enter the sports machine market and, by varying the specifications of both models, a high performance 'Clubmans' model in either capacity could be purchased. Two 'over the counter' Scrambles models were also

available and an Americanised version of the MSS, known as the 'Endurance' model was also in the range. A continuous process of refinement ensured the 'Venom' and 'Viper' models kept pace with their competitors and, for a spell, it was possible to obtain either model with the engine unit enclosed in a glassfibre moulding. A special fairing could also be obtained, giving rise to the 'Veeline' models that even included the 'Valiant'.

The company's greatest feat was performed during March 1961, when a team of riders took a 'Venom' Veeline Clubmans model to Montlhéry, in France, and established a world record for 24 hours continuous running, at an average speed of 100.05mph. This was all the more fitting as it was a 350cc Velocette

Left: a magnificent Velocette Venom Clubman model of 1966. The machine was fitted with a single-cylinder, pushrod-valve, four-stroke, 500cc motor. Alongside is a close-up of the powerful drum brake fitted to the Clubman model

Below left: another classic 'Velo' model was the Thruxton. It represented the ultimate development of the M Series models. In many ways it could be likened to a latter day KTT Mk VIII model, because its performance, for a pushrod single, was little short of staggering. The model pictured, together with a close-up of its engine, is of 1967 vintage. This was basically the last of the really classic Velocette models, because a few years later, in 1971, the company went into voluntary liquidation. Indeed, many people felt that it was remarkable that Velocette had lasted so long in the face of the growing Japanese opposition

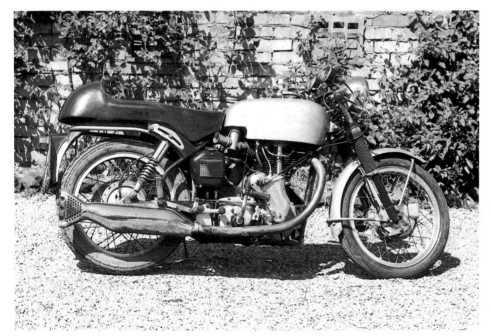

which had claimed the hour record at 100.39mph in 1928.

One more great machine was to emerge from Hall Green during 1964, the 'Thruxton' model that represented the ultimate in the development of the 'M' series of singles. In many respects it could be likened to a latter day version of the Mk VIII KTT model, for its performance was comparable – little short of remarkable for a pushrod engined machine, and even impressive by today's standards.

Veloce Limited was now finding itself in increasing financial difficulties. A rash venture into the production of a scooter, the 'Viceroy', had not helped matters. It occurred during 1960 and represented yet another attempt to get into the 'every-man' market. Although the scooter was of a very clever design, featuring a horizontally opposed, twin-cylinder two-stroke engine, the Italian manufacturers

had too firm a hold of the scooter market and the project was doomed to failure. The venture cost the company money it could ill afford and this marked the beginning of the rundown. During the early part of 1971 the company went into voluntary liquidation, there being no other way out.

Viewed in retrospect, it seems surprising that this small family company managed to hold out for so long, when so many of its larger competitors went under much earlier in the face of keen competition from Japan. Even during the more successful years, Veloce Limited had always to work to a tight budget and to exercise care with all their committments, producing a quality product in limited numbers for the dedicated enthusiast. Perhaps the most remarkable factor is that such an abundance of talent could be found under one roof and that it

was Veloce Limited who led the way with so many innovations which others were glad to follow. Certainly there was a quite unique atmosphere within the works which, until later years, gave visitors the impression of one very happy family. This, however, was hardly surprising for, right from the very beginning, Johannes Gutgemann and his family had seen things this way. Those they employed were regarded as an extension of their own family and the respect with which they were regarded bore testimony to this sensible policy.

Sadly, the forgotten man seems to be Percy Goodman, the quiet genius who was the driving force behind the scenes after his father had passed on. He was the originator of the very advanced unit-construction single of 1909 and later the overhead camshaft models that did so much for British prestige.

Vincent

or a manufacturer intent on building the best motor cycles possible, if only customers could be found to buy them, times were hard in 1954 and 1955. For the firm which above all others epitomised that idealistic approach to business – Vincent Engineers Ltd of Stevenage, Hertfordshire – it was no less than humiliating that they should have to resort for diversification to the marketing under their own name in Britain of the little mopeds and lightweight utility motor cycles then being built in Germany by NSU. The humiliation can scarcely have been less than the resultant frustration: in spite of some restriction in supplies, Vincent sold and delivered about 20,000 of these tiddlers in six months, making such a success of the introduction that the concessionaries promptly formed their own company to handle the business instead.

The motor cycle that earned Vincent's stupendous reputation was as different from the Neckarsulm tiddlers as it could be. The Vincent Series B Black Shadow, when it went into production in 1948, was nothing less than the world's fastest standard production motor cycle, and it remained the fastest long after the firm had despairingly given up production. Well into the 1960s and even today, when it is wrapped in a mystique carefully cultivated by thousands of fanatically enthusiastic owners, the big Vincent retained that commanding air about it when you met one on the road, and many a rider of avowedly super-sporting machinery would be humiliated by having some much older Black Shadow come pass at the canter, its rider rigged in that peculiar and distinctive riding position – feet wide apart, hands close together, the body leaning forward against the wind with the arms straight but the trunk as slack as a sack of potatoes, comfortable yet poised ready for anything. The Vincent was a machine about which legends might be spun, but about which the truth would serve well enough.

The Black Shadow proved to be without peer, on paper or on the road. When the magazine *Motor Cycling* reported on it in July 1948, they said that it was impossible to define an open-road cruising speed, the limit being set only by road conditions and the rider's abilities. The point did not need to be laboured, for they found the top-gear maximum speed to be 122mph (a French magazine managed 128) with acceleration requiring less than fifteen seconds to reach 92mph in a quarter of a mile. There was

nothing on two wheels to compare with this; even on four wheels there was little to rival such performance.

Quite apart from its performance, which was achieved in production tune on the dreadful contemporary petrol with a research octane number of less than eighty, the truth about the big Vincent was quite simply that it was a masterpiece. By contemporary standards, it cost a lot of money, but even an examination of the detail work evident on its exterior showed that it was money well spent. For example, there was a full range of adjustment for the gear lever, the brake pedal, the footrests, the handlebars and anything else that could conceivably require adjustment; tommy bars allowed really rapid wheel removal with no tools necessary but a pair of pliers for undoing the spring clip on a chain link if removing the rear wheel; the brakes and the chain tension could be adjusted by finger and, when for the Series C

version, which emerged in the winter of 1948–9, the Brampton front forks were replaced by Vincent's own Girdraulic, the trail and spring rate could be altered simultaneously for solo or sidecar work in a minute or two.

Such details might fascinate, but even they tell much less than the full truth about the splendour of the Vincent's design. It was the progeny of a marriage between two fascinating minds, the creatively imaginative and idealistic English-

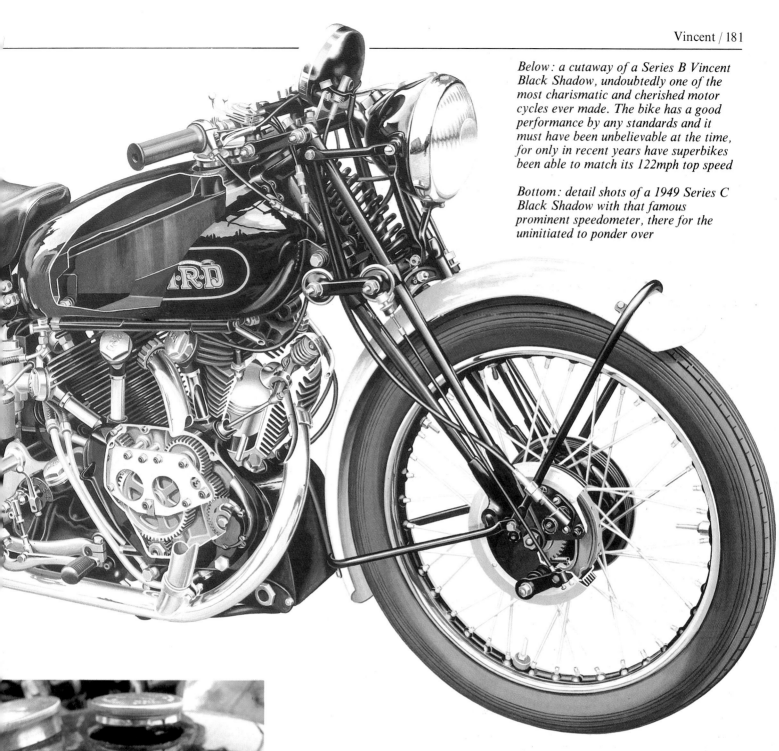

Below: a cutaway of a Series B Vincent Black Shadow, undoubtedly one of the most charismatic and cherished motor cycles ever made. The bike has a good performance by any standards and it must have been unbelievable at the time, for only in recent years have superbikes been able to match its 122mph top speed

Bottom: detail shots of a 1949 Series C Black Shadow with that famous prominent speedometer, there for the uninitiated to ponder over

man Philip Vincent, and the ingenious and practical Australian Phil Irving. These two great luminaries of motor cycle engineering were perhaps complementary in the sense that they interacted to moderate each other's excesses or inadequacies, so that the designs they produced represented less than the sum of their abilities. On the other hand, the motor cycle that they created was greater than the sum of its parts; yet any one of those parts might bear witness to the mutually contributory interaction of those antipodean brains. Those Girdraulic forks revealed their joint philosophy: their geometry was similar to that of the traditional girder forks, their springing and damping media and characteristics were such as were generally associated with the then increasingly popular telescopic forks, while their mechanical strength and (which was much more important) stiffness were superior to either. Each fork blade was a high-duty alloy forging, and the whole sub-assembly was completely free from the flexibility, slippiness, binding and trochaic distortion that afflicted most other kinds of front suspensions.

Structural integrity was really what most distinguished the Vincent, although the majority of people, bemused by that seemingly effortless but evidently incomparable performance, might be excused for failing to appreciate it duly. If it be a prerequisite of good steering and handling in a motor cycle that its wheels be retained relative to each other and to the steering head in those planes that they were intended by the designer to occupy, then it must be admitted that chassis stiffness, all the way from wheel spindle to wheel spindle, is of extreme importance, and in the matter of frame stiffness the Vincent had few if any rivals. Paradoxically, it had little or no frame – just a sheet-steel box concealed by the fuel tank, extending from the steering head to the rear spring and damper unit and having the engine slung beneath it by the two cylinder heads. The rear fork or sub-frame was pivoted on tapered roller bearings in an anchorage on the rear of the particularly massive crankcase and transmission casting, and the rigidity of the engine structure was so immense as to impart to the machine as a whole a beam and (more particularly) a torsional stiffness such as only the space frame of the racing Guzzi of the mid 1950s might rival. Only the rear fork sub-frame betrayed the design by being visibly imperfect in its stressing: it was only partially triangulated, and it seems that even Vincent could not avoid the contagion of curved tubes. Even so, his rear forks were much less susceptible to distortion than almost any others of that period of time.

The engine that held everything together repaid intimate study. Little might be learned of the massive vee-twin from its exterior, save that it was clearly intended to generate and dissipate some considerable heat, being enamelled black all over. It was also clear from the disposition of the pushrod tunnels that the camshafts were located deliberately high in order to minimise the valvegear's

reciprocating mass, and the knowledgeable might deduce from the wide angle at which those tunnels were splayed that the rods were set parallel to the valve stems. Probing within would disclose much more ingenuity in the valve design. The rockers engaged the valves halfway down their stems, engaging a shoulder, while the valve springs were up at the thin end as remote as possible from the sources of heat. This strategem shortened the pushrods and thus reduced the reciprocating mass still more, and it also reduced the discrepancies in length due to thermal expansion between the valve stem and the rest, so that rocker clearances could be minimised for mechanical quietness and durability, being set at zero when the engine was cold. Moreover, the valve stem was supported by guides on both sides of the rocker, relieving the stems from cantilevering loads and maintaining concentricity to such good effect that valve seat maintenance might be almost forgotten by the owner.

Even so, it was the bottom half of the 55° vee-twin engine that was most meritorious. The engine and gearbox were conceived as parts of the same structure, the massive light-alloy castings being stiffened by substantial internal walls to produce a construction in which all bearings were positively located, all loads were properly distributed and all components were constrained to remain precisely where they were put. Every exposed face joint was free from the imposition of such loads as might cause distortion and oil leaks. Materials were as

Above: the awe-inspiring power unit of the 1947 Series B Vincent Rapide

Below: a 1931 Rudge-engined Vincent

good as could be obtained at the time, and where performance could be improved by surface polishing this was done, as in the case of connecting rods, rockers and parts.

Vincent's passion for the proper distribution of mechanical loads was indulged not only in the engine and transmission but even in the brakes. Each wheel carried two of these, one on each side, so as to balance the stresses to which the wheel and forks were subjected. The brakes were rather small, amassing between them only 36 square inches of lining area, which admittedly was more than most machines of the day

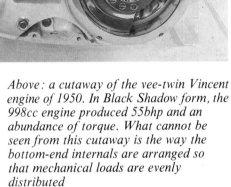

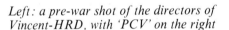

Above: a cutaway of the vee-twin Vincent engine of 1950. In Black Shadow form, the 998cc engine produced 55bhp and an abundance of torque. What cannot be seen from this cutaway is the way the bottom-end internals are arranged so that mechanical loads are evenly distributed

Left: a pre-war shot of the directors of Vincent-HRD, with 'PCV' on the right

Above: around 3000 examples of the 50cc Miller-engined Firefly were built after production commenced in late 1952. The moped was a world apart from the bikes that made Vincent's name

but less than a few could boast. Nevertheless, they were shown to work very well and on many occasions the Vincent was proved capable of stopping at rates of deceleration considerably exceeding g: *Motor Cycling* recorded a halt from 30mph in $22\frac{1}{2}$ feet, which was better than 1.3 g. Apparently, the ribbed cast-iron brake drums of the Black Shadow, replacing the plain steel drums of the earlier Rapide tourer upon which the machine was based, ensured reasonable retention of this braking ability, for the Shadow did quite well in contemporary racing despite its then considerable weight.

It was twenty years earlier that the first production models to bear the Vincent name appeared, and only twenty years before that when Philip Conrad Vincent was born in London of parents whose home was normally their cattle ranch in Argentina. Vincent's father had been born in England and set him back there for his preparatory and public schooling, and it was an early measure of the boy's innate abilities that he came top in the Harrow entrance examination. While he was at Harrow, he acquired and developed his passion for motor cycles: his first was a little BSA 350, the next a 398 ABC which, for all its irritating faults, impressed him with its comfort and good handling, much of which he ascribed – in defiance of currently popular dogma – to the spring frame. A sixteen-year-old schoolboy withal, young Vincent was already astute enough not to confuse ends and means and, while approving of sprung rear wheels in principle, he recognised that the ABC practice left a good deal to be desired. The design that he produced to overcome the worst of the trailing fork's shortcomings involved triangulating it in the plane of its swing, and it very closely resembled the later Bentley and Draper frame that was adopted for manufacture by, amongst others, Brough Superior – probably the only other manufacturer of fast twins to display perhaps the same ethos, and certainly the same glamour, but nothing like the engineering ability, of a Vincent. In the two years that were to pass before the schoolboy could progress, as a Cambridge undergraduate, to building his own prototype motor

coming, subject to the monitoring of Vincent's project by an agricultural engineer named Frank Walker, also a keen motor cyclist, whom Philip's father chose to be managing director of the new firm. Together, they found some suitable premises at Stevenage (a century earlier they had been occupied by Offords, the distinguished carriage-builders who were by this time established in London), and

cycle, Vincent revised the design considerably until it eventually crystallised in a form that was to remain unchanged, except for the addition of hydraulic damping and some detail refinement, until the last Vincent motor cycle had been built.

By the time he went up to Cambridge in 1926 to read Mechanical Sciences at King's College, Philip had already made up his mind to be a motor cycle manufacturer, and he persuaded his father to put up the money for building one of the prototypes that he had designed. The first of these, completed in 1927, was perhaps rather heavy by the standards of its time, but it had unusually large brakes and robust front forks to fit it for the eighty or more mph of which it was capable with its overhead-valve MAG 350 engine. This machine gave him some 10,000 miles of faultless service, and encouraged him to solicit further financial aid from his father. This was forth-

in that same year, 1928, they learned that the name HRD Motors Ltd was for sale. The initials were those of the brilliant racing rider Howard Davies who had himself embarked on the commercial production of motor cycles as recently as 1925. He too had aimed at the quality market, and his products were respected as having achieved that aim, but Davies found himself more distinction by winning the Senior TT at record speed. That performance may have mattered at the time, but hindsight suggests that the HRD's most important contribution to motor cycling was that it started the saddle-tank fashion which was to be adopted by virtually all manufacturers in three years, and brought to an end the era of the long, low, lean-tanked vintage motor cycle. Certainly, Vincent had been favourably impressed by that tank, as he had been even as a schoolboy by all Davies's bikes and by the man himself and, now that the HRD company had

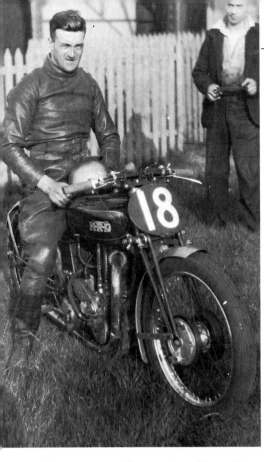

ceased trading, he hoped that the famous monogram would carry the market's goodwill with it and overcome customers' natural reluctance to buy an untried new model from the drawing board of a youth of whom they had never heard.

This judgment of his customers was probably right. Indeed, most of Vincent's judgments of his customers, and of others, was tantamount to condemnation of them, and in this he was probably right, too, although he needs no telling: confident of his own intellectual abilities, he is not one to suffer fools gladly. At least he was intelligent enough not to prolong the beating of his head against any wall: having first built his prototype in a pin-jointed triangulated frame, and then a JAP-engined 250 in a spine frame, he recognised that the ultra-conservative public would have enough to face in reconciling themselves to the rear suspension to which he was passionately committed, and that they could not also stomach an unconventionally superior structure amidships, so he reverted to the commonplace bicycle type of

diamond frame for the majority of his production models.

'Production' is a word that must be interpreted generously. Only four of the two dozen different models that he built up to 1934 ever reached a production run reaching into two figures in any given year. Perhaps it is unfair to categorise all those two dozen as different models, however, for in many cases the differences were between one proprietary engine and another of different make or merely of different size or degree of tune (almost forgotten, perhaps deservedly, was a run of about thirty little three-wheeled delivery vans, known as Bantams, begun in about 1932). Vincent used Villiers, MAG, Blackburne, JAP and Rudge engines, and built one bike in 1934 with a 250cc Cross rotary valve engine. He was a great admirer of the Rudge, but commercial considerations prompted a fairly extensive use of JAP engines, and his general dissatisfaction with most of these was sorely aggravated by troubles with a batch of allegedly superb special new ones that were foisted on him for his 1934 Senior TT machines. His reaction

Above: C. J. Williams aboard his JAP-engined 1934 TT bike.

Left: a Series C Comet 500 of 1949; similarities between this power unit and its 'doubled-up' stablemates are obvious

Right: top-speed testing a '48 Black Shadow

Below left: the cover of the 1929 Vincent-HRD catalogue

Below: a supercharged 500cc bike, which was built for the TT of 1936. It was withdrawn before the event

to this experience is best summarised in his own words, culled from his published autobiography, for if read carefully they reveal a great deal more than was perhaps originally intended:

'After these experiences, we never wanted to see another JAP engine as long as we lived, and decided that we should design and manufacture our own. Fortunately, I had available Phil Irving, who in my opinion is one of the best conventional motor cycle engineers in the world, with an amazing knowledge of all the good things that other people were doing currently, down to fine design details.

'I myself have ever been an inventive type of designer, always seeking to incorporate details which would represent a worthwhile and big advance over previous designs.

'In the subsequent design which evolved during the next three months, I had to keep my own instincts fairly in check because we could not spare the time to prove satisfactorily many unconventional features, so we tended to lean heavily on Phil's remarkable working knowledge of our competitors' efforts.'

What emerged from all this was an upright single-cylinder ohv 500 incorporating for the first time Vincent's clever double valve guides and high camshaft location. Very little alteration was needed to the prototype, the only snag being heavy oil consumption and viscous drag which was cured by modifying the scavenging. The machine was made in standard form as the Meteor, in sports trim as the Comet and in racing guise as the TT Replica. They performed well, the Comet easily exceeding 90mph, and their handling and outstanding braking made them so popular with hard riders that the demand arose for something of a similar quality but with really exceptional and exciting performance.

The way to achieve this was realised in 1936 by Irving as he idly toyed with a drawing and a tracing of the timing-side crankcase half of the current engine. Turning the tracing over and superimposing it, he discovered that if he lined up the centres of the crankshaft and the timing gear idler, he was virtually looking at the layout for a 1000cc 47° vee-twin. That included angle was simply twice the

Below: Stevenage rider George Brown, aboard Nero, checks with timekeeper Major General A. H. Loughborough after a practice run at Thurleigh Airfield, Bedford, in 1961. George was attempting British and World kilometre records

Bottom: a Comet; note the twin instruments and air horns

offset of the idler gear from the cylinder axis of the 500, and it was admittedly 43 degrees away from vee-twin perfection, but the majority of motor cycle vee-twins were 40 degrees from the right angle anyway. There was not much to be lost and a great deal to be gained, because the extra crankcase holes for the second cylinder could be produced simply by inverting the original drilling jig. That autumn, the prototype Rapide engine was started, run-in for three hours and then opened up to reach 108mph in a fully equipped motor cycle. Bearing in mind that this was in Meteor tune, the potential of a big twin tuned to the same level as the sporting Comet was extremely tempting. The dream had to be postponed. The proprietary gearbox, a four-speed Burman, could not cope with the unprecedented torque of the Rapide even in its basic form. The clutch had to be molly-coddled for a start but, if it survived, the cogs, the layshaft bearings and even the casing, would fail. Despite this, the Rapide was popular, 77 being bought before the outbreak of war in 1939, and one of them was timed at nearly 113mph for a kilometre at Brooklands, ridden by George Brown, then an experimental tester at the Stevenage factory.

During the war, Vincent and Irving worked on a marine engine design for the Air Ministry, and dreamed of the motor cycle that they would produce when such things might be resumed. Towards the end of the war, they had some time to start designing the post-war Rapide, the Series B, and in nightly brainstorming sessions they worked out how to overcome the Series A shortcomings. Once again, the bike was to be a quiet, flexible, easy-going but very fast tourer that would be capable with a little tuning of being very, very fast. The clutch problem was dealt with by Vincent's clever notion of a self-servo drum-type clutch engaged by a small and lightly loaded single-plate servo clutch. With this complete answer to the clutch problem, it was then feasible to have a cross-over drive in the gearbox and crankcase desirable, en- for reasons of alignment and clearance); this in turn made unit construction of gearbox and crankcase desirable, encouraging the concept of that massive assembly as a stressed structural member in place of a conventional frame. In thus doing away with such impediments as the front down-tubes, the two designers were able to open out the included angle between the cylinders to 50°, allowing normal production magnetos to be employed, and at the same time to shorten the wheelbase from the 58½ inches of the Series A Rapide to a rather handier 56. What was left in the end was an unusual vehicle, for here was a case where one did not take the engine out of the motor cycle to work on it: one positioned a suitable supporting block beneath the engine and then took the cycle away from it, something that could be done in a matter of minutes. There were all sorts of brilliant details, from the bilateral prop stands which could be combined as a front stand (for engine support) to the kick starter, the dynamo drive, the dual seat and just about every little item you

super-sporting Series B. The name was explained by the machine's appearance: the new Vincent was immediately recognisable by the all-black finish applied to the exterior of the engine, cylinder barrels and heads, crankcase, brakes and all. As well as being an interesting and indeed brave bit of styling, the black finish did a useful job in improving heat dissipation, and with this in mind it was done properly – as indeed most things were on these uncompromising twins. It was not just a matter of squirting black paint on to aluminium and letting it lift off later, as in such circumstances it undoubtedly would. Instead, the light alloy parts were all given a treatment known as the Pylumin process, an inhibited etch which guaranteed an excellent bond for subsequent paintwork. Beneath this radiant exterior lurked higher-compression pistons, highly polished ports, rockers and connecting rods, and modified valve gear allowing the engine to make the most of larger-bore carburettors. The ribbed cast-iron brake drums were introduced to combat distortion and fade, and there were some differences in instrumentation and electrics, the most emphatic of which was the huge 150mph speedometer.

In standard tune and on commercially available petrol (which was pretty rough stuff, remember), the Black Shadow generated 55bhp; 100bhp was available from the alcohol-fuelled engine of the racing model, the Black Lightning, which was added to the range when the Series C was begun a year later. All over the world, national and world records for sprints and top speed fell to these machines, sometimes in factory standard specification and sometimes modified to suit the venue (with no front brake for the Bonneville salt flats, for example, where a

Above: a Black Prince of 1955. The public were caught somewhat offguard by such a radical bike and it did not achieve the success of its predecessors, so it was hastily 'unfaired'

Right: Ted Davis, Vincent tester, aboard the Black Knight prototype in 1954

cared to examine. All that was left of the Series A was the bore and stroke, the rear suspension and four brakes. The Series B was far more refined, far more practical, far cleaner, far more impressive in every way and was certainly no slower: 110mph came easily on 45bhp, and at tick-tock rpm that was an absolute revelation when it appeared in 1946. People went racing and record-breaking on it, either in standard trim or modified in all manner of ways. Yet, had they waited, much of the work could have been done for them, as it was when the Black Shadow appeared in 1948 as a

Lightning pushed the American record beyond 150mph). Apart from the long and brilliant series of sprint records established by George Brown, who left the factory in 1951 but carried on modifying and campaigning three prodigious Vincents known as *Gunga Din, Nero* and *Super Nero* (the last of these being supercharged), perhaps the most meritorious was the achievement of Russell Wright and Robert Burns in 1955 when they set new world solo and sidecar records of 185.15 and 163.06mph, respectively, all on a narrow and bumpy road in New Zealand. These runs were made with an unsupercharged Lightning, and were the last such records to be set by what could fairly be described as a standard conventional motor cycle. Meanwhile, other splendid things were being done in the half-litre category, for when the Series C was introduced it brought with it some very pleasant single cylinder 500s, the Comet, the Meteor and the racing Grey Flash, upon the last of which some very impressive results were secured not only by George Brown but also by a racing tyro with a brilliant future ahead of him, young John Surtees.

Alas, the times were not conducive to the sale of big high-performance motor cycles that were built up to a standard

Below: a Vincent Series B Rapide, owned by Mike Berry. One can see that the rear mudguard of this bike is hinged in the middle to give easy access to the wheel

rather than down to a price. Moreover, Vincent's rivals had been improving their designs quite considerably over the years since the Shadow made its appearance, while Vincent's designs had almost stood still. This was because the little firm's small design and development staff had been engaged upon another of those frustrating Government jobs that so seldom realise their initial promise, this time for a high-performance version of their vee-twin engine called the Picador, to power a small target drone aircraft. It was not until 1954 that Vincent could start thinking about a successor to the Series C, but at least his experience with the Picador taught him something useful, which was to substitute coil ignition for the previous magneto. It also gave him experience with 100 octane petrol, which was now freely available, and no less significantly it had given him time to appreciate the enthusiasm (and to a limited degree the judgment) of the members of the flourishing Vincent Owners' Club. Accordingly, he asked them what improvements they would like to see, and took due note in devising the Series D. One of the most important requirements was for easier cleaning and better rider protection, since to pilot a big Vincent all day at the speeds of which it was untiringly capable was very fatiguing for the rider. What emerged from all this was a new kind of black bike, encased in glass reinforced plastic fairings – the Black Knight which was equivalent to the

Rapide, the Black Prince, which was successor to the Black Shadow, and the 500cc Victor. There were some significant mechanical changes, too: a lever-operated roll-on centre stand, like that of some pre-war Rudges, made the bilateral props superfluous, some overdue calculations of longitudinal weight transfer persuaded the designers that one of the two rear brakes was superfluous.

Most of the public were horrified, thinking that motor cycles ought to parade themselves naked at whatever cost to the rider. Poor Vincent had to re-introduce the D Series in unfaired form, which must have made him despair of the commonsense of such customers as remained capable of paying for one of his machines, while only a few of the more intelligent real long-distance runners acclaimed the superiority of their enclosed models. Whatever the cry or the outcry, the business was not there: insurance rates were rising, national bans were falling (an originally marvellous marketing outlet in South America was lost through no fault of the factory, for example), and many other equally famous and more popular motor cycle manufacturers were going to the wall. Selling NSU tiddlers did not help: Vincent motor cycle production finished in 1955, although the man himself remained active, inventive and ingenious. It was hoped that enthusiasts might yet see a Series E, but this hope proved to be forlorn.

Index

Numbers in italics refer to captions